KING OF THE SEVEN CLIMES

A History of the Ancient Iranian World (3000 BCE - 651 CE)

Ancient Iran Series | Vol. IV

UCI Jordan Center for
Persian Studies

King of the Seven Climes: A History of the Ancient Iranian World (3000 BCE - 651 CE)
Edited by Touraj Daryaee

© Touraj Daryaee 2017

Touraj Daryaee is hereby identified as author of this work in accordance with
Section 77 of the Copyright, Design and Patents Act 1988

Cover and Layout: Kourosh Beigpour | ISBN: 978-0-692-86440-1

KING OF THE SEVEN CLIMES

A History of the Ancient Iranian World (3000 BCE - 651 CE)

Edited by
Touraj Daryaee

UCI Jordan Center for
Persian Studies

— 2017 —

The publication of this book was made possible through a generous gift by the
Razi Family Foundation

Table of Contents

INTRODUCTION

In a Middle Persian text known as "Khusro and the Page," one of the most famous kings of the ancient Iranian world, Khusro I Anusheruwan, is called *haft kišwar xwadāy* "the King of the Seven Climes." This title harkens back to at least the Achaemenid period when it was in fact used, and even further back to a Zoroastrian/Avestan world view. From the earliest Iranian hymns, those of the Gāthās of Zarathushtra, through the Younger Avesta and later Pahlavi writings, it is known that the ancient Iranians divided the world into seven climes or regions. Indeed, at some point there was even an aspiration that this world should be ruled by a single king. Consequently, the title of the King of the Seven Climes, used by Khusro I in the sixth century CE, suggests the most ambitious imperial vision that one would find in the literary tradition of the ancient Iranian world. Taking this as a point of departure, the present book aims to be a survey of the dynasties and rulers who thought of going beyond their own surroundings to forge larger polities within the Iranian realm.

Thus far, in similar discussions of ancient Iranian history, it has been the convention to set the beginnings of a specifically Iranian world at the rise of Cyrus the Great and the establishment of the Achaemenid Empire. But in fact, this notion is only a recent paradigm, which became popular in Iran in the late 1960s owing to traditions of Classical and European historiography. At the same time, there are other narratives that can be given for the history of the Iranian World, including those that take us to 5000 BCE to sites such as Sialk, near Kashan, or other similar archaeological localities. As attractive as an archaeologically based narrative of local powers can be, however, the aim of the present work is to focus on political entities who aimed at the control of a larger domain beyond their own local contexts. As a result, this book starts its narrative with Elam, the influential civilization and kingdom that existed long before the Achaemenids came to power. Elam boasted a writing system and a complex culture and political organization contemporaneous with that of Mesopotamia, and was made up of cities such as Susa and Anshan. As Kamyar Abdi shows in his chapter, the Iranian civilization owes much to the Elamites and their worldview and conception of rulership. Thus, we do not start the present narrative with 550 BCE and Cyrus, but with 3000 BCE, in the proto-Elamite Period, when signs of a long lasting civilization on the Iranian Plateau first appeared.

The chapter on Elam is written by Kamyar Abdi, who has excavated Elamite sites and has studied its history extensively. His long survey details the history of Old, Middle and New Elamite periods with their intricate dynastic divisions and lines that survive in historical records, from the lowland Susa to highlands of Anshan and Shimashki. There are inscriptions and records left by Elamite rulers that attest to their visions and ideas of kingship, royalty and statecraft. By the Middle Elamite period, monumental religious buildings such as Chogha Zanbil were built to rival that of Mesopotamia. The Neo-Elamites had an important impact on the Achaemenids and also on Cyrus the Great, who in fact hailed from the Elamite city of Anshan. In order to understand Cyrus's policies and world-view, we must understand Elam and Anshan beside that of the history and culture of the Persians. Abdi's essay provides a comprehensive narrative of Elam and establishes its importance for the history of the Ancient Near and the the Iranian World.

Hilary Gopnik has excavated Median sites and is well familiar with sites like Godin Tape and has already published wonderful research, placing the Medes in the context of Iranian and Ancient Near Eastern history. As her chapter posits, the Medes have had no voice of their own, as it was their enemies and foreign sources that observed and recorded them. Hilary Gopnik surveys all the varied and at times contradictory sources on the Medes and provides a unique narrative of their history. Additionally, her examination of such Median sites as Tepe Nushi Jan, Godin Tepe, and other sites provides a better picture of this confederacy. As she concludes, the Medes built new forms of government based on consensus and negotiation, and they also left the legacy of an empire for us.

Lloyd Llewellyn-Jones, an expert in Achaemenid history, provides a detailed summary of the Persian Empire from Cyrus of Anshan to Darius III. Here, Cyrus the Great, Darius I and other royals are individually presented. But beyond kings, the idea of kingship, administration, and the methods with which a world empire was held together are also given full treatment. If anything is to be remembered about the Achaemenid Empire, it is its capability to bring peace (Pax Persica) and the ability to rule a large part of the Afro-Eurasian world. This feat, as Llewellyn-Jones demonstrates, is achieved through ceremonial and ideological traditions that were both Iranian and Ancient Near Eastern. The afterglow of this empire is also treated, for better or worse, in light of the Eurocentric view of the past, as well as Iran's own encounter with the Achaemenids.

Omar Coloru presents a much-needed discussion of Seleucid history in the context of Iranian history, where with the conquest of Babylon in 312 BCE, the Greco-Macedonians began their career in the Iranian World. Here we are presented with a detailed political history of the Seleucids, which shows signs of co-existence with the Iranian populations in some parts of the domain, while it is in conflict with other kingdoms, for example, that of the Elymais in Southwestern Iran. This is followed by the Seleucid interaction with the Fratarakas of Persis whose loyalty to the Achaemenids is shown through their artistic and numismatic remains. The constant warfare between the Seleucids and their enemies weakened and terminated their rule, at least in their Iranian context, and provided the opportunity for the Arsacids to become masters of the Iranian realm.

Leonardo Gregoratti provides a history of the Arsacids who had moved from Central Asia in the third century BCE to the Caspian Sea region. In time, they came to dislodge the Seleucids, eventually confronting Rome in the west. Gregoratti discusses the structure of the

Arascid Empire, where the Great King was able to harness the loyalty of the local kings and members of the Parni tribe. The strength and structure of the Arsacid Empire is a subject that is discussed here and receives detailed treatment. Their social, economic and political history is made clear based on the Classical sources, but also from the Nisa documents, which Gregoratti successfully uses for his essay.

Touraj Daryaee and Khodadad Rezakhani present a brief history of Sasanian studies and their political history. While the Roman Empire is important for the political history of the Sasanians, Daryaee and Rezakhani also look to the East and the center of the Sasanian realm and provide a balance in the world-view and horizon of the empire. They also discuss the ideological underpinnings through which the Sasanian Empire was able to sustain itself for some four centuries, from the time of Ardashir I to the downfall of Yazdgerd III. The economy, religion, language and literature of the Sasanian Empire are given a brief treatment to provide a general picture of this great late antique empire.

Finally, Khodadad Rezakhani discusses the Kushan Empire, the so-called "Iranian Huns," and the Western Turk Empire. As he argues, the discussion of the Khushans and their successors is important in understanding the history of ancient Iran. The Kushans present an important context for the actions and political and ideological beliefs of both the Arsacids and the Sasanians, whose fate and tradition is intermingled with that of the Kushans and other political powers of East Iran. With the wealth of new Bactrian sources, beside that of inscriptions and coins, we can now better understand the social, economic, and political history of East Iran vis-à-vis its "West" Iranian and Central Asian neighbors. This was a world that was rapidly changing through the influx of new people and tribes moving from the borders of China to the Eurasian steppe zone. By looking at the material culture and the literary sources, Khodadad Rezakhani demonstrates the interaction between various powers of Eastern and Western Iran and its effect in forming both the late antique and the mediaeval world.

The essays in this collection, covering a large temporal span, from the proto-Elamite period to late antiquity, present a picture of ancient Iranian history that goes beyond the normal boundaries set by many other historical surveys. By discussing the history of the Elamite civilization, the Seleucids, the Kushans, and other polities often considered peripheral in Iranian history, the book aims to provide a new way of looking at this history. Through the prism of an ideological concept, the kingship of the seven climes, which is as influenced by the ideals of Iranian-speaking tribes as it is by traditions of Mesopotamia and Elam, the essays are put in a particular framework of study. This is the framework that unites these varied temporal and geographical entities within a concept that emerges recognizably as the Iranian World in the Middle Ages and beyond.

Finally, I would like to thank Mr. Ramin Yashmi for creating a map for the book, representing important cities and centers on the Iranian Plateau.

Touraj Daryaee
Maseeh Chair in Persian Studies & Culture
University of California, Irvine

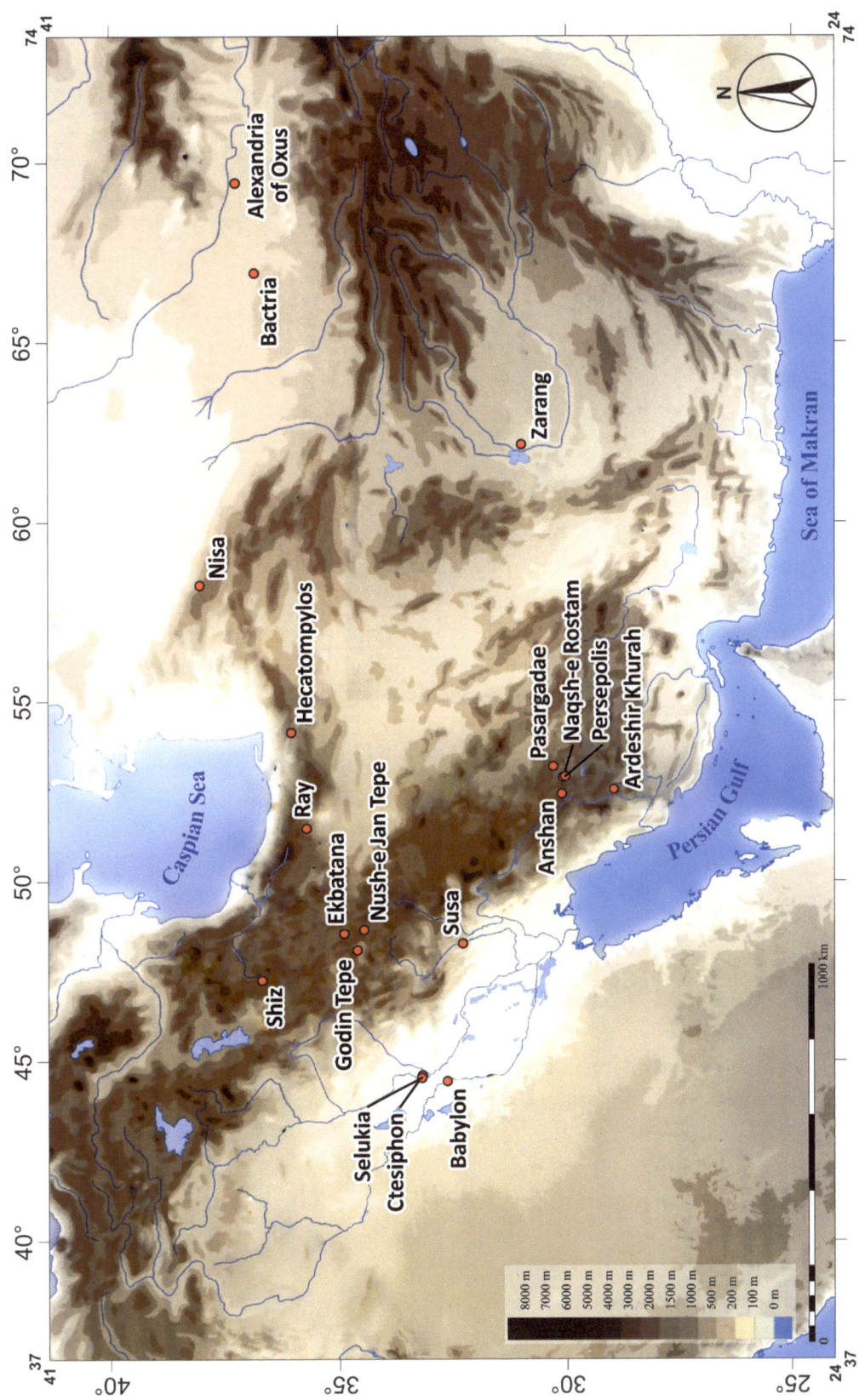

Iranian Plateau and the Near East

Alexandria
of Oxus

Bactria

Zarang

Nisa

Sea of Makran

Hecatompylos

Pasargadae
Naqsh-e Rostam
Persepolis
Ardeshir Khurah

Ray

Anshan

Ekbatana

Nush-e Jan Tepe

Shiz

Godin Tepe

Susa

Persian Gulf

Caspian Sea

Selukia
Ctesiphon

Babylon

N

8000 m
7000 m
6000 m
5000 m
4000 m
3000 m
2000 m
1500 m
1000 m
500 m
200 m
100 m
0 m

1000 km
0

THE KINGDOM OF ELĀM
Kamyar Abdi

Introduction

The civilization of Elām (ca. 3000 BCE to 200 CE) was one of the longest-lasting and, at the same time, least-known civilizations of the ancient Near East. The large geographical extent of this civilization – located entirely within political borders of modern Irān, and the limited number of archaeological excavations at Elāmite sites and a general lack of interest among Iranian and international archaeological community towards Elām are some of the key factors in our rudimentary and disjointed knowledge about this ancient civilization (but see Cameron 1936; Amiet 1966; Hinz 1972; Carter and Stolper 1984; Potts 2016).

In professional circles , however, thanks to over a century and half of archaeological and philological research, a general picture of Elām's history, predominantly political, has been put together by a small, and diminishing, cohort of 'Elāmitologists'. This is a hard to pronounce and rarely heard title scholars who study various aspects of Elāmite civilization have given themselves, *a la* their colleagues in much better-established fields such as Assyriology, Sumerology, and Hittitology, among others.

Our knowledge of Elām's political history, along with even more nascent of Elām's social and political organization and its economic, cultural, ideological, religious, ethnographic and demographic milieus, is quite piecemeal. we know that not always, but at least during brief eras in its long history, Elām was an important political and sometimes a formidable military force on the turbulent landscape of the ancient Near East. This often prompted prompting more powerful and influential political and cultural entities, particularly Babylonia and Assyria in Mesopotamia proper, to deal with Elām in one way or another. Here rests another thorny problem, that if not most, but a substantial portion of our knowledge about ancient Elām comes from more comprehensive Mesopotamian sources whose authors were accustomed – rightfully or not – to vilify the Elāmites as their archetypical nemesis.

Thanks to the discoveries made in the 1970s, we now know that Elām was geographically vast (Vallat 1980, 1993; Amiet 1986), perhaps larger than its contemporary civilizations in Šumer, Babylonia, and Assyria. In fact, Elām seems to have been much larger than both its western neighbors in Mesopotamia than the early generations of Elāmitologists perceived. We now know that Elām proper included a lowland component, i.e., the alluvial plain in southwestern foothills of the Zageos mountains – called the 'Susiana' plain by us and Šušan by the ancients, and a highland component, i.e., the Kur River Basin, some 600 km to the southeast in the heart of the southern Zagros mountains, called Marvdasht by us and Anšān by the ancients. The mostly highland hinterlands surrounding these two core regions were apparently also part of Elām, or at least had strong cultural, social, political, and perhaps ethnic and linguistic ties with Elām.

The two core regions of Elām – Šušan in the lowland and Anšān in the highland – were respectively centered around two early urban centers of Šušan (modern Susa) (Amiet 1988; Harper et al. 1992) and Anšān (Modern Malyān) (Sumner 1988; Abdi 2005). In this paper, these ancient and modern toponyms will be used interchangeably.

Here is yet another problem with our lop-sided knowledge of Elām: Susa, Elām's gateway with points west, i.e., Mesopotamia, and for economic and probably political reasons, a city whose control was much desired by Mesopotamians has been subject to over a century of extensive excavations (Abdi 1994; Chevalier 1997), whereas Anšān (modern Malyān) – arguably the main political center and the repository of the Elāmite culture was only discovered as recently as 1968 and only 0.2.5% of its area of 200 hectare has been excavated so far . Therefore, our knowledge of Elām is heavily biased toward the lowlands, especially Susa, and to a much lesser degree, on a few other sites in Susiana, e.g., Kabnak (modern Haft Tepe), Al Untāš-Nāpirišā (modern Choghā Zanbil), and few other sites. The only exception in this lowland-highland dichotomy is Liyān or Tol-e Pāytol (ancient name unknown) on Bushehr peninsula on the Persian Gulf coast.

In the two core regions of Elām – Šušan in the lowland and Anšān in the highland – both with settlement histories going back to millennia earlier, were laid the foundations of two distinct societies with their own characteristic subsistence pursuits (intensive irrigation agriculture combined with small-scale village-based animal herding by the former and large-scale pastoralism combined with small-scale agriculture by the latter). This naturally gave rise to two distinct sociopolitical formations to manage these economies and maintain a delicate balance between the people engaged in them. Cultural and economic ties were soon established between the two lowland and highland components of Elām, These ties were further augmented through ethnic and cultural affiliation between the two regions. Ostensibly, a combination of internal socioeconomic factors and external stimuli, probably from western neighbors, initiated the decisive process of state formation in Šušan and Anšān. From combination of these two political formations emerged the civilization of Elām.

HISTORY OF ELĀM

Following the outline devised and generally used by Elāmitologists, for the purpose of this paper, Elām's long history has been divided into Proto-Elāmite period (ca. 3200-2700 BCE), Old Elāmite period (ca. 2700- 1600 BCE), Middle Elāmite period (ca. 1450-1000 BCE), Neo-Elāmite period (ca. 1000-647 BCE), and Perso-Elāmite period (ca. 647-520 BCE). Needless to say, these divisions as well as the purported 'dynasties' are *post facto* schemes devised by Elāmitologists with no particular meaning for ancient Elāmites who were accustomed to, like people in most other ancient civilizations, using the regnal years of their rulers for reckoning and recording written documents.

For all intends and purposes, the Proto-Elamite period should be considered the first and formative stage in the history of the civilizations of Elam. The wide distribution of Proto-Elāmite material culture, especially administrative devices, e.g., tablets, seals and seal impressions, across the Irānian Plateau suggests that we are dealing with a mercantile system that had established outposts in distant corners of the Irānian Plateau or perhaps exported its administrative and accounting systems to these outposts who were engaged in economic and commercial activities. However, we know next to nothing about the political system behind these activities or the agents who ran these outposts (Alden 1982). A few pieces of archaeological evidence, such as the monumental building excavated in Area ABC at Malyān (ancient Anšān), decorated with polychrome frescos, and a considerable amount of luxury goods, as well as Proto-Elāmite tablets can be interpreted as evidence for an emerging political system, and perhaps the earliest physical manifestation of the Elāmite civilization. Our knowledge of the Political organization of the Proto-Elamite period is next to nothing, but we can guess that Proto-Elamite economic activities on the Iranian Plateau were essential in establishing the sociocultural networks that later served as the life blood of Elām (T. F. Potts 1994).

Two major issues pertaining to Proto-Elāmite writing system vis-à-vis our reconstruction of Elāmite history continue to trouble us: first, that the historical information to be extrapolated from Proto-Elamite texts are negligible (Dahl 2009), and two, whether Proto-Elāmite was a direct precursor to the Elāmite language or even the physical manifestation of a language to begin with or simply an accounting system? This is an important question far from resolved. Second, an important and controversial question remains, since the earlier generation of scholars believed that based on morphological similarities, a case can be made that Proto-Elāmite writing system was the precursor to a much simplified and abridged writing system called 'Linear Elāmite' that appeared after a little-known hiatus of some six hundred years.With Linear Elamite we seem to be in a comparatively much better condition. Whatever the origins and background of Linear Elāmite and the relation (or lack thereof) between Proto-Elamite and Linear Elamite, this peculiar writing system is closely associated with one of the first figures in Elāmite history: Puzur-Inšušināk, evidently the last king of the 'dynasty' of Awān of the Old Elāmite period. The corpus of inscriptions in Linear Elāmite from Susa, in particular, has been a major source of information on the life and career of Puzur-Inšušināk (Steinkeller 2013).

The Old Elāmite period (ca. 2700-1600 BCE)

The Old Elāmite period, when the administrative, political and ideological foundations of the civilization of Elām were being laid down, is unfortunately also one of the least explored and least-known eras in the history of Elām. Apart from archaic deposits at Susa excavated in early stages of the development of archaeology in Irān, especially at Susa, when excavation methods were crude and recording imprecise (Mousavi 1996), no other site with Old Elāmite deposits has yet been excavated, thus leaving us with equivocal knowledge and understanding of this crucial period in the history of Elām. Based on epigraphic and historical sources, however, Elāmitologists have been able to discern three 'dynaties' in Old Elāmite period: Awān, Šimāški, and Sukkalmaḫ.

The 'dynasty' of Awān (ca. 2700-2100 BCE)

Below will be presented a rather unorthodox study of the 'dynasty' of Awān, starting from the end and making our way back through time, for a number of key issues in this period are anchored to Puzur-Inšušinak, the last king of Awān.

There has been much debate on the origins and chronology of Puzur-Inšušinak. He seems to have started out as ensi (governor) of Susa, but gradually became GÌR.NÍTA (ruler?) of Elām and eventually lu-gal (king) of Awān. Puzur-Inšušinak's rise in Elām's political hierarchy may be attributed to his military campaigns and expanding of his territory in both western Irān and central Mesopotamia during the turbulent era between the collapse of the dynasty of Agade/Akkad (ca. 2150 BCE) and the rise of the Third Dynasty of Ur (ca.2110 BCE), but it seems that despite his title 'king of Awān' and inclusion of his name among the kings of Awān in the 'Susa king-list' (See below) Puzur-Inšušinak was in fact not an Awānite but a Susian (Glassner 1998), first because he is named after Inšušinak, the patron deity of Susa (Šušan) and the fact that his first documented official post was governor (ensi) of Susa, presumably still under Akkadian administration. This takes us to another question regarding Puzur-Inšušinak: his date. The earlier generation of scholars (cf. Cameron 1936; Hinz 1972) believed that Puzur-Inšušinak reigned sometime after Narām-Sin of the dynasty of Agade (2254-2218 BCE), but using art historical analyses, Pierre Amiet perceptively argued for a date closer to the Third dynasty of Ur, an acute observation that was confirmed in 1987 by the discovery in Isin and translation of an Old Babylonian copy of an inscription by Ur-Namma (previously pronounced 'Ur-Nammu'), the founder of the Third Dynasty of Ur, dating Puzur-Inšušinak to *ca.* 2100 BCE.

This new dating creates some problems with the chronology of the 'dynasty' of Awān. Puzur-Inšušinak (now securely dated to around 2100 BCE), names his father as Šimpi-išhuk in his Susa inscriptions, but this individual is not mentioned in the 'Susa king-list' (see below), whereas Puzur-Inšušinak's predecessor in the 'Susa king-list' is an individual by the name of 'Hita' who is obviously not Puzur-Inšušinak's father, but is generally believed to be the Elāmite ruler who signed a treaty with Narām-Sin of Agade (Hinz 1967). This interesting text in Old Elāmite cuneiform can rightfully be described as the first historical document in the history of Irān (Hinz 1967).

Narām-Sin has securely been dated to 2254 to 2218 BCE, so Hita (the presumed author of the treaty with Narām-Sin) must also have lived sometime in the twenty-third century BCE. We are therefore faced with a perplexing question: how can we bridge the century-and-half interval between Hita and Puzur-Inšušinak (or Narām-Sin and Ur-Nammu in Mesopotamian chronology)? Of course, there is a reference that Hita was contemporary with several Akkadian emperors, from Sargon to Šar-kāli-šarri, but at this point 150 years for Hita's reign seems impossible to reconcile.

The Susa 'King List'

We shall now turn to perhaps the most important document pertaining to the earliest part of Elām's history. This is a small tablet the size of the palm of a hand (8.2 x 6.4 x 2.7 cm), discovered in 1930 in de Mecquenem's excavations at Susa. Vincent Scheil, realizing the significance to the text on this tablet quickly published it). The text, in Akkadian, dating to around 1800-1600 BCE (Sukkalmaḫ period), most probably a *post facto* political declaration rather than an actual historical document (Glassner 1996) gives the names of twelve kings of Awān, followed by twelve kings of Šimāški.

This is a peculiar list, for it neither gives genealogical relationship between listed individuals, nor their regnal years. However, these peculiarities did not discourage Père Scheil from describing these two dozen individuals as members of "dynasties élamite d'Awān et de Simaš.". The first seven names (Peli, Tārip, Ukutāhiš, Hišur, Šušuntārānā, Nāpilihuš and Kikutānteimti) although Elāmite on onomastic grounds (Zadok 1984), have not been found in any other text, whether Elāmite or Mesopotamian. The eighth individual, Luhiššān is most probably Luh-Išān, son of Hišep-Rātep, the 'lugal (king) of Elām' mentioned in C7 and C13 inscriptions of Sargon of Agade. Hišep-Rātep, the ninth person's name, is perhaps Elāmite rendering or an orthographic variant of Hišep-Rāšini, described by Sargon also as 'lugal (king) of Elām'. Whether the father-son names were reversed in the Susa king-list or this is a case of homonyms unrelated with two individuals nonetheless contemporary with Sargon we are not in a position to determine at the moment.

Putting these pieces of information together, we can speculate that as early as the Late Uruk-Jemdet Nasr period in Mesopotamian Chronology and Proto-Elāmite or Susa III-Late Banesh periods in Irānian Chronology, there was cultural/economic/political entity in southwestern Irān known to Mesopotamians as Elām. Evidently, from Early Dynastic period (ca. 2700 BCE onwards) Elām emerged as a political force that engaged Mesopotamian polities, sometimes successfully, but obviously inferior in military power to the mighty Akkadian Empire (2334-2154 BCE) with which it had to take on a more conciliatory approach, best represented in "Elām's Treaty with Narām Sin" . However, as soon as the Akkadian Empire collapsed, the Elāmites – under their ambitious ruler Puzur-Inšušināk – found an opportunity to assert their political identity. This was a short-lived opportunity though, for an equally powerful Mesopotamian empire rising at the city of Ur soon brought Elām under control, yet the seed of upheaval were already sown, and the next Elāmite dynasty, that of Šimāški was rising.

The dynasty of Šimāški (ca. 2200-1900 BCE)

The 'king-list' from Susa gives the names of another group of twelve individuals under the heading of "Twelve Kings of Shimaski", again with no genealogical or regnal information. In one of his inscriptions, Puzur-Inšušināk refers to a king of Šimāški who, during one of his campaigns (presumably in western Irān) came to him and paid him homage. The king of Šimāški in Puzur-Inšušināk inscription is not named, but this reference indicates that while Puzur-Inšušināk was active at Susa, there was already an institution of kingship at works in Šimāški, so there is an overlap of unknown length between the 'dynasty' of Awān and the 'dynasty' of Šimāški. However, based on a double synchronism with Ur III texts and Puzur-Inšušināk's aforementioned inscription, Steinkeller (2013) has recently argued that the unnamed king of Šimāški can only be Kirnāme, the first king (and the presumed founder) of the dynasty of Šimāški.

Seemingly friendly relations and policies of interdynastic marriage seem to have maintained the fragile peace between the Empire of Ur and the state of Šimāški for a number of generations, but the deteriorating condition of the Empire of Ur that seems to have begun during the reign of Ibbi-Sin (from 2028 BCE onward), plus instigations by Išbi-Errā, the treacherous governor of Isin unleashed the Elāmite wrath upon the Empire of Ur. In 2004 BCE, an Elāmite- Šimaškian joint force under Kindattu – the sixth King of Šimaški on the 'Susa king-list' – descended upon Mesopotamia "like a roaring storm", sacked and destroyed several cities, overthrew the Third Dynasty of Ur and as a clear act of humiliation "carried Ibbi-Sin to the land of Elām in fetters".

With destruction of Elām's main opponent and liberation of Susa, the victorious Elāmites could now properly call themselves "Kings of Šimaški and Elām." However, the Mesopotamian threat was always present. An ephemeral incursion by Gungunum, King of Lārsā lead to temporary loss of Susa and ousting of a later king of Šimaški, Idaddu II (probably in 1927 BCE). In the meantime, maintaining control over such a vast territory (from Susiana to the Central Plateau of Iran and perhaps east of Fārs towards Kerman) proved to be difficult, prompting the Elāmites to think of a more structured organization of their territory. The process of reorganizing Elām began with Ebārat (or Epārti) II, one of the last kings of Šimaški, but the change was so drastic that his successor Šilḫaḫā seemed appropriate to begin a new political system ('dynasty') called the 'Sukkalmaḫ' ('Grand Regents').

The Dynasty of Sukkalmaḫs (ca. 2000-1500 BCE)

The title 'Sukkalmaḫ' denoted an early Meseopotamian post that can be found in texts as early as the Early Dynastic period. It became a rather common position – roughly equivalent to 'prime-minister'— in the time of the Empire of Ur, especially in the city-state of Lāgaš that was responsible for administration of the eastern provinces of the Empire of Ur including Susa and Susiana. It is therefore not surprising that Kuk-Kirmaš of Susa was the first Elāmite ruler we know of who began to call himself 'Sukkalmaḫ of Susa', but it was his predecessor Šilḫaḫā who named himself 'Sukkalmaḫ of Elām' and was generally perceived as the traditional founder of the dynasty of Sukkalmaḫs and a semi-legendary ancestor not only to later Sukkalmaḫ, but also himself revered for the rest of the Sukkalmaḫ period and even later (see below). While Šilḫaḫā was apparently the founder of the Sukkalmaḫ dynasty, the architect of the Sukkalmaḫ system of government was presumably Ebārat (or Epārti), almost certainly Ebārat II, the ninth king of Šimaški in the Susa king-list after whom at least one more Šimaškian by the name of Idaddu II also ruled before the dynasty of Šimaški came to a close. In much later sources of Šutrukids (ca. 1100 BCE) Šilḫaḫā has even been called "the beloved son of Ebārt [Ebārat II]", but whether this was a genealogical fact or a dynastic legend (formulated much later) we do not know.

These developments, however, seem to suggest that there was perhaps several generations of overlap between the dynasty of Šimaški and the dynasty of Sukkalmaḫ, and the transition from the former to the latter was a smooth handover of power from one lineage in the royal house of Šimaški to another lineage headed by Ebārat II and the introduction of a new system of government that was to rule Elām for some five centuries (longer than any dynasty in Irānian history) and usher in an era of unsurpassed political, military and economic prowess in the history of Elām.

Three important points regarding the Sukkalmaḫ dynasty need to be addresses first: the peculiar Sukkalmaḫ system of governance. Their order of succession, and the even more peculiar system through which the rulership acquired legitimacy in the Sukkalmaḫ dynasty.

In one of the earliest modern studies of the history of Elām, George Cameron (1936) proposed a system for Sukkalmaḫ dynastythat despite several decades of further research and debate, seems to have achieved general approval among Elāmitologists. According to Cameron, during the Sukkalmaḫ period the political power was vested in the hands of a triumvirate, i.e., three members of two generations of the royal family: the triumvirate consisted of a senior ruler, often titled Sukkalmaḫ (grand regent), a medium co-regent – usually Sukkalmaḫ's brother - entitled sukkal (regent) of Elām and Šimāški and a junior co-regent entitled sukkal of Susa, usually the Sukkalmaḫ's son or sister's son.

While being of royal blood through female line was evidently an important factor in succession, in practice it seems that when the Sukkalmaḫ died, the throne passed to the sukkal of Elām and Šimāški and eventually to sukkal of Susa. Despite a variety of alternatives and a number of other titles used in these five-hundred years, the standard norm seems to have been basically the one outlined by Cameron (above). In reality this is a time-proven system of co-regency also practiced in Mesopotamia (and even Egypt and other early and even later states) to familiarize the junior and relatively inexperienced members of the royal family with intricacies of running a heterogeneous and complex-- for lack of a better term – 'confederacy' that Elām had become at the time of Sukkalmaḫ dynasty. Yet, we should bear in mind the problem of lop-sided nature of sources from Elām I mentioned earlier in this paper, i.e., that the majority of texts dating to Sukkalmaḫ period, that are by no means limited, are discovered in Susa, so our view of the working of a system as complex as that of the Sukkalmaḫ dynasty comes primarily from Susa. Where, evidently only the most junior member of the triumvlrānte resided, whereas the more powerful and senior members of the triumvlrānte presumably resided and ruled from Anšan. For example, one of the most prominent Sukkalmaḫs, Siwe-pālar-huhpak has only left behind inscribed bricks at Malyān = ancient Anšan, whereas no inscribed bricks with his name has been discovered at Susa. This evidence, obviously with reservations, may suggest that Siwe-pālar-huhpak was engaged in construction work at Anšan (where he lived), but never built anything at Susa (where he may have visited, but never resided in).

Over twenty individuals associated with the Sukkalmaḫ dynasty have been recorded. Only eight individuals, however, bear the haughty title of THE Sukkalmaḫ. The last relatively well-documented and securely dated Sukkalmaḫ was Kuk-Nāšur II, who based on contemporaneity with Ammisaduqa of Babylon can be dated to around 1620 BCE. After Kuk-Nāšur II there were apparently four more Sukkalmaḫs about which we know next to nothing due to scarcity of textual sources, but it appears that the Sukkalmaḫ dynasty have lasted well into the early fifteenth century BCE. The circumstances surrounding the end of this long-lasting and influential dynasty is shrouded in mystery.

The Middle Elāmite period (ca. 1500-1000 BCE)

The end of the Sukkalmaḫ dynasty marks the closure of the Old Elāmite period. There is no evidence that the Sukkalmaḫs fell before a foreign adversary or as a result of an internal insurrection. Just as ambiguous as the end of the Sukkalmaḫs, is the origins of the next dynasty (the Kidinuids), followed by two other dynasties of 'Ige-hālkids' and 'Šutrukids', named after their respective founders. These three dynasties ushered in a new period in Elām's history that Elāmitologists lump together as the Middle Elāmite period. This is the second so-called 'golden age' in Elām's history, but not for reasons described for the Sukkalmaḫs, but for new large-scale constructions at Haft Tappeh and Chogha Zanbil, and major military campaigns in Mesopotamia that ultimately lead to a Babylonian backlash and collapse of the Elāmite state at the end of the Šutrukid dynasty. This is so-called 'dark age' in early first millennium BCE from which Elām took some two hundred years to recover.

The Kidinuid dynasty (ca. 1500-1400 BCE)

In excavations at Level XII of Chantier A at Ville Royale at Susa, there was discovered a tablet impressed with the seal of a certain 'Kidinu' who calls himself 'King of Susa and Anshan'. In the same stratigraphic layer and the one immediately above it were discovered tablets with names or seal impression of several late Sukkalmaḫ rulers, including Tān-Uli, Temti-Hālki, Kuk-Nāšur II, III, or even IV, and Kuduzuluš (perhaps II) . The stratigraphic correlation of these documents (discussed in detail in Steve *et al.* 1980) suggests that as the dynasty of Sukkalmaḫ was approaching its end (For reasons unknown), several polities and at least one dynasty was emerging in lowland Elām to take its place. Nothing, however, is known about the circumstances surrounding the rise of the new dynasty or its origin, but it is likely that Kidinu and his successor, about whose genealogical filiation we know nothing, were from Susa or at least Susiana, not the highlands. The title 'king of Susa and Anšān (or Anzān) – as opposed to titles used by the Sukkalmaḫs – is the archetypal title of Middle Elāmite rulers and may point to a change in political ideology about which we are not in a position to enunciate. As for variants of this title, it has been argued that the rulers titled 'King of Susa and Anšān' ruled only in Susa, whereas those titled 'King of Anšān and Susa' ruled at Anšān. But rejecting this hypothesis, others have argued that the title 'King of Susa and Anšān' is just attested in Akkadian texts, whereas the title 'King of Anšān and Susa' exclusively appear in texts in Elāmite, presumably as a way to appeal to Akkadian and Elāmite speakers of the Elāmite confederacy.

Despite reservations about the genealogical integrity of the Kidinuid 'dynasty', Kidinu is generally considered by Elāmitologists to be the 'founder' of a 'dynasty' and the first ruler of the Middle Elāmite period.

Kidinu was apparently followed by a certain Tān-Ruhurāter, who is only known from a cylinder seal in a private collection that resembles that of kidinu in describing Tān-Ruhurāter as 'King of Anzān and Susa (Steve *et al.* 1980: 93). Nothing else, especially his filiation with Kidinu, is known, but his use of the name of a king of Šimāški, some five hundred years earlier (ca. 1970 BCE), is yet another indication of the new dynasty of kings of Susa and Anzān purposefully attempting to invoke old Elāmite memories. Then there is a mysterious individual by the name of Šāllā who is simply called 'King of Susa' in a handful of texts from Susa (Steve *et al.* 1980: 96), but whose filiation with kings preceding him in not known.

With the next ruler, Inšušinak-sunkir-nāppipir we are in a slightly better situation. An important event marks the reign of Inšušinak-sunkir-nāppipir in particular and Middle

Elāmite period in general. For the first time that we know of, the royal Elāmite court is neither based at Susa nor at Anšan. But, evidently during the reign of Inšušinak-sunkir-nāppipir, the royal court began relocating to Haft-Tappeh (ancient Kabnak) some 15 km E-SE of Susa. While it was evidently Inšušinak-sunkir-nāppipir who began relocation to Haft-Tappeh, it was his successor (again with no information on filiation) Tepti-Āhār who is responsible for major construction work at this site.

Kassites of Babylon may have even been responsible for the fall of the Kidinuid 'dynasty', for the Babylonian Chronicle P, describes that Kurigālzu II (1332-1308 BCE) defeated a certain 'Hurpātilā' on his way to attack Elām. Hurpātilā was presumably Tepti-Āhār's successor and the last of the KIdinuids.

The Ige-Hālkid dynasty (1400-1200 BCE)

It seems that, after the fall of the kidinuids, another powerful house was prepared to take up the mantle of Elāmite kingship. This new dynasty, with fairly well-documented genealogical relations, in this author's opinion, originated from Deh-e No (ancient Hupšan) where three copies of an inscribed brick with the name of 'Ige-Hālki' (founder of the new 'Ige-Hālkid' dynasty) have been discovered (Vallat 1980: 12, no. 50). Here he, following earlier Middle Elāmite rulers, calls himself 'King of Susa and Anšan'.

Ige-Hālki, the founder of the dynasty, evidently had two sons: the elder son was Pāhir-Iššān who has left behind no inscription, but according to the 'Berlin Letter' Pāhir-Iššān married the sister of "the powerful king Kurigalzu." This cannot be Kurigalzu I as he ruled in mid-14th century BCE during the Kidinuid dynasty, but must be (contra D.T.Potts 2016: 202), based on the Babylonian Chronicle P, Kurigālzu II (1332-1308 BCE) who defeated a certain 'Hurpātilā', presumably Tepti-Āhār's successor and the last of the Kidinuids. This would suggest that there was a certain chronological overlap between early Ige-hālkids and very late Kidinuids.

It appears that when Pāhir-Iššān passed away, his younger brother Attar-Kittāh (Ige-hālki's other son) became king. Attar-Kittāh is attested on two maceheads from Choghā Zanbil (obviously family heirlooms) that bear him name and the name of his father Ige-Hālki. Attar-Kittāh seems to have quickly established himself at Susa and began restoration of the temple of Inšušinak. Whether Attar-Kittāh also married a Kassite princess we do not know, but his son, Humbān-Numenā married Kurigalzu II's daughter who, presumably, gave birth to the most famous and industrious of the Ige-Hālkids, Untaš-Nāpiriša, the builder of the most magnificent monument from ancient Elām, the complex at Choghā Zanbil.

Untaš-Nāpiriša is the Elāmite ruler *par excellance*. Born to an Elāmite king and a Kassite princess and himself married to another Kassite princess (daughter of Burnāburaš II, 1359-1333 BCE), Untaš-Nāpiriša could claim royalty from both sides. Apart from an abundance of texts from Susa, including inscribed bricks commemorating restoration and renovation work at the temple of Inšušinak, inscribed bricks with his name are discovered in places sacred to various deities all over Susiana, including several sites in Susiana as well as on Rām Hormoz plain.

Untaš-Nāpiriša's masterwork is, however, the Choghā Zanbil complex that he built on a previously unoccupied ground on the banks of the river Dez some 40 km SE of Susa and less than 10 km to the SW of Deh-e No (ancient Hupšan), the presumed home of the house of Ige-Hālki. Apart from being an architectural marvel, Choghā Zanbil (ancient 'Al Untāš-Nāpiriša' = the city of Untāš-Nāpiriša), built in a peculiar 'Elāmite' technique using millions of bricks, thousands of which are inscribed by hand, is a political statement in the form of federal religious complex which, apparently, also served a funerary function.

Even a brief survey of the Choghā Zanbil complex, its various monuments and structures or the artifacts discovered in it during nine seasons of excavations (1951-62) and more recent explorations is beyond the scope of this paper. It would be enough to say that by building shrines in honor of twenty-five deities from all over Elām, the main lower courtyard (First stage of construction) dedicated to Inšušinak - the main deity of Susa and the lowland Elām – and the central ziggurat (second stage of construction), with its *kukunnum* or high temple dedicated to Nāpiriša - the main deity of the highland Elām - Untāš-Nāpiriša gave a new, symbolic meaning to his royal title of 'King of Anzān and Susa.' While Untāš-Nāpiriša's extensive restoration work throughout Susiana may at least be taken as an indication of his piety, the building of Choghā Zanbil can be interpreted as a sign of his political aspirations through religious means.

Like every earnest king, Untāš-Nāpiriša also had to fulfill his duty as the 'expander of the realm.' In an undertaking unheard of in Elām since the time of Sukkalmaḫs several centuries earlier, Elāmites went on the offensive and marched into the Zagros to the north of Der. Here, from a place called Tupliaš, Untāš-Nāpiriša looted a statue of the Amorite god Immeriya and took it back to Susa, added a dedicatory inscription to his father-in-law Burnaburiāš and placed it in the temple of Inšušinak.

Kidin-Hutrān II, Untāš-Nāpiriša's son with his Kassite queen, himself married to a Kassite princess, took on a more confrontational attitude towards Babylonia and attacked Mesopotamia at least twice, overthrowing two Kassite kings (Enlil-Nadin-Šumi in 1224 BCE and Adad-Šumma-Iddina in 1217 BCE) and sacked and destroyed several Mesopotamian cities in the process.

It can be argued that the reasons for Elāmite change of attitude towards the Kassites is to be found in the 'Berlin Letter'. With the rising power of Assyria in the Middle Assyrian period, Assyrians began encroaching upon Babylonian territory and interfering in Babylonian politics. The Assyrian disregard for Babylonian sovereignty reached unprecedented levels when Tukulti-Ninurta I (1243-1207 BCE), king of Assyria, overthrew the Kassite king Kaštiliašu IV (1232-1225 BCE) and placed a puppet king by the name of Enlil-Nadin-Šumi on the Babylonian throne. For Elāmites of the Ige-Hālkid dynasty who were related to the royal of house of the Kassites through several generations of interdynastic marriage and considered themselves more legitimate heirs to the Babylonian throne, the Assyrian action was unacceptable. Kidin-Hutrān II therefore quickly marched against Babylonia and removed the Assyrian puppet Enlil-Nadin-Šumi before the first anniversary of his reign was up (1224 BCE). Later in the same year, Tukulti-Ninurta I was assassinated in a palace coup, keeping the Assyrian court too preoccupied to launch a counterattack against Elām. Adad-Šumma-Iddina, another Assyrian puppet in Babylon also met with the same fate in 1217 BCE, until Adad-Šumā-Usur, came to the throne as the legitimate Kassite king, halting Elāmite attacks. Yet, as the Berlin Letter explains, Elāmites continued to demand the Babylonian throne due to their relations with great Kassite kings of the olden times. This was an Elāmite *ideé fixe* that lead to a much more pugnacious Elāmite attitude toward Babylonia during successors to the Ige-Hālkids, the warmonger kings of the Šutrukid dynasty.

An important question to be asked is that who wrote the Berlin Letter? A number of Elāmitologists believe that the author was Šutruk-Nāhunte, the founder of the Šutrukid dynasty or his equally quarrelsome son Kutir-Nāhunte to justify the aggressive Elāmite policy towards Babylon. More recently, however, it has been argued that the author of the 'Berlin Letter' cannot be anyone but Kidin-Hutrān II, for the planning and execution of his campaign closely matches what is recorded in the Babylonian Chronicle P.

What happened later is unclear. Construction at Choghā Zanbil seems to have come to a halt right after Untāš-Nāpiriša passed away, but some people may have lived at the site without necessarily partaking in religious activities (Pons 1994). Kidin-Hutrān II too may have passed away shortly after returning from his Babylonian campaign. There is reference to at least two (perhaps three) more kings of the Ige-Hālkid dynasty, but we neither know much about them, nor about how the Ige-Hālkid dynasty came to a close.

The Šutrukid dynasty (ca. 1200-1000 BCE)

How the Ige-Hālkid dynasty came to a close and the Šutrukid dynasty came to power is a matter of debate. The fact that Šutruk-Nāhunte continued to use the title of 'King of Anzān and Susa' and the practice of interdynastic union with Kassites by marrying the eldest daughter of Meli-Šipak (1186-1172 BCE), the Kassite king of Babylon, suggests that he may have been related to the Ige-Hālkids. But Šutruk-Nāhunte gives his father's name as 'Hāllutuš-Inšušinak,' an otherwise unknown individual. So, at this point establishing a genealogical link between Šutrukids and Ige-hālkids is a matter of conjecture. Goldberg (2004), however, argues that Hāllutuš-Inšušinak may have been son-in-law of Nāpiriša-Untāš, one of the last of the Ige-Hālkids, and therefore related to the royal house of Ige-Hālki not by blood, but by marriage. As for Hāllutuš-Inšušinak himself, whether he was a king is a question that has divided Elāmitologists for decades: there are those who believe that he was in fact a king and those who do not think he ever reigned. Meanwhile, we have at our disposal another line of evidence, though not very convincing, in support of some sort of connection between the Ige-Hālkids and the Šutrukids: The goddess Manzat continued to be an important deity in the Elāmite pantheon during the time of both dynasties. Šutruk-Nāhunte not only restored her temple at Hupšan (Deh-e No), but also built her a new temple 3 km to the north of Choghā Zanbil, Whatever the circumstances surrounding the transition from the Ige-Hālkids to the Šutrukids, the fact remains that the Šutrukids took the aggressive Babylonian policy of the late Ige-Hālkids to an unprecedented and devastating level, that ultimately consumed both the Kassites and the Elāmites.

To Elāmites, Šutruk-Nāhunte and his two sons and successors may have seemed archetypal kings of Anšān and Susa, doing what is expected from them: restoring and renovating temples and shrines of various deities at Susa and elsewhere in Elām as indicated by many fragments of inscribed bricks of all three of them. They also expanded the realm by launching multiple invasions in various directions, especially into Mesopotamia; to Mesopotamians Šutruk-Nāhunte and his two sons where the incarnation of Elāmite wickedness who wreaked havoc in Mesopotamia and committed heinous crimes. Despite a long tradition of interdynastic marriages with the royal house of Kassite for nearly two centuries, the Elāmite approach towards Mesopotamia in general and Kassites in particular grew increasingly aggressive with Kidin-Hutrān II in the fourteenth century and continued in the next two centuries BCE under Šutruk-Nāhunte and his successors.

Šutruk-Nāhunte (ca. 1190-1155 BCE) invaded Babylonia in 1158 BCE, overthrew the Kassite king Zābābā-Šummā-Iddina (1158 BCE) and pillaged many Mesopotamian monuments, carried them back to Susa, inscribed them with his grandiose titles and dedicated them to temple of Inšušināk at Susa. Šutruk-Nāhunte's eldest son and successor, Kutir-Nāhunte (ca. 1155-1150), who was appointed the military governor of Babylonia by his father, launched his own invasion of Mesopotamia upon ascending the throne and overthrew the last Kassite king Enlil-Nadin-Ahhe (1157-1155 BCE), effectively bringing the Kassites –the longest-ruling dynasty in Babylonian history – to a close. Šutruk-Nāhunte's second son and successor, Šilhāk-Inšušināk (ca. 1150-1120), who realized that there is nothing much left to pillage and plunder in Babylonia, turned his attention to the north and launched a massive and extensive campaign that took him to the central Zagros and borders of Assyria. This was perhaps the largest expansion of Elāmite imperial militarism during which Šilhāk-Inšušināk claims to have invaded and captured tens of domains and hundreds of town and cities, presumably the many tappehs that dot the landscape of western Irān and northern Irāq.

The Elāmite carnage in Mesopotamia obviously had economic and political reasons. Elāmite invasion of Mesopotamia was a typical capture and plunder operation without any intention of Babylonian annexation to an Elāmite 'empire.' Šutruk-Nāhunte's appointment of Kutir-Nāhunte as the military governor of Babylonia while the Kassites were still around and quite capable of putting another legitimate king (Zābābā-Šummā-Iddina) on the Babylonian throne can be taken as an indication that Elāmites did not have a strategic plan the occupation of of Babylonia. Not even this level of administrative interference in Babylonian politics can be seen on the part of Kutir-Nāhunte and Šilhāk-Inšušināk while they finally achieved one of their main objectives, i.e., the overthrow of the last Kassite king Enlil-Nadin-Ahhe and destruction of the Kassite dynasty. This was an apt and timely power vacuum that Elāmites failed to exploit and let Nebuchadnezzar I (1125-1104 BC) of the Second Dynasty of Isin take advantage of, with detrimental consequences for Elām.

Military activities did not discourage the Šutrukids from fulfilling their other important responsibilities as upstanding kings, i.e., engaging in numerous building activities at Susa and elsewhere, as far as the temple of the great goddess Kiririšā at Liyān on the Persian Gulf coast where Humbān-Numenā had built a temple earlier and Šilhāk-Inšušināk, as a dutiful king, restored.

Šilhāk-Inšušinak›s successor, Hutelutuš-Inšušināk he failed to keep the Šutrukid dynasty and the Elāmite state afloat for long. With Elāmite failure to install a more permanent occupying administration in their conquered territories in Babylonia, a strong Mesopotamian backlash was inevitable. Nabuchadnezzar I (1125-1104 BCE), the fourth king of the second dynasty of Isin launched an unexpected attack on Elām in the middle of the summer, when Khuzestan is unbearably hot, thus surprising an unprepared Hutelutuš-Inšušināk and engaged him on the bank of the river Karkheh, where he was defeated and then "disappeared." Nebuchadnezzer then took the statue of Marduk and the goddess Il-āliya back to Babylon. Nebuchadnezzer's triumph brought him considerable fame and popularity during his life time and among future generations.

Yet, Hutelutuš-Inšušinak did not simply "disappear" as the Babylonian inscription wants us to think, but he fled to Anšān (modern Malyān, 40 km north of Shirāz) and built a temple and dedicated it to Nāpirišā, Kiririšā, Inšušinak, and Šimut (M. Lambert 1972: 66). Fragments of inscribed bricks from this yet-undiscovered temple, found on the surface of Malyān by the late William Sumner in 1968 and their translation by the late Erica Reiner corroborated with similar inscribed bricks already in the Louvre lead to one of the most important discoveries in the study of ancient Elām, i.e., the location of Anšān, substantially changing our perspective on the historical and political geography of Elām.

It seems that after Hutelutuš-Inšušinak, his younger brother Šilhinā-Hāmru-Lāgāmār succeeded the Elāmite throne. No inscription belonging to Šilhinā-Hāmru-Lāgāmār has yet been discovered, but in texts from Susa there is a reference to a certain Humbān-Numenā who may have belonged to the extended Šutrukid royal house, for he is not mentioned in inscriptions of Šilhāk-Inšušinak as a member of the royal Šutrukid family, but ruled at Susa for a while as a Šutrukid. In the meantime, texts from Malyān refer to three individuals whose names are broken and incomplete (Akšir-?, Hu-?, and Šutruk-?) as Sugir (another Elāmite word for king) of Anšān. But who these three individuals were and what was their relationship to the Šutrukid royal house was, if any, we do not know. By all accounts and purposes the Šutrukid dynasty, and with it the Middle Elāmite period, was over. This was around 1000 BCE or slightly later.

The Neo-Elāmite period (ca. 1000-520 BCE)

The Neo-Elāmite period is arguably the most cumbersome and complex period in the history of Elām (Watters 2002). Our reconstruction of Neo-Elāmite history is predominantly based on the sources left behind by their former nemesis, the Babylonians, and current archenemy, the Assyrians. Meanwhile, indigenous Elāmite sources at our disposal are rather limited and disjointed. The archaeological evidence for the Neo-Elāmite period consists of bits and pieces from Susa, as well as a number of rock reliefs in eastern Khuzestan and two elite tombs from Arjān, Bebāhān and Jubaji, Rām-Hormoz in southeast corner of Khuzestān, that despite their rich grave goods provide us with little information on the main trajectory of the Neo-Elāmite history.

Furthermore, various group of Elāmitologists engaged in research on Neo-Elāmite period, each working with mutually incompatible sets of data have devised their own chronological schemes and periodizations of the Neo-Elāmite period that are sometime hard to corroborate. I have used the most popular periodization with some minor modifications of my own towards the tail end: NEI (ca. 1000-744 BCE), the so called Elāmite 'dark age', i.e., from the end of the Šutrukid dynasty to the appearance of the first attested Neo-Elāmite ruler, NEII (743-647 BCE), the period of intense conflict between Elām and Assyria , culminating in the sack of Susa by Aššurbānipāl, and NEIII=Elāmo-Persian period (647-520 BCE), from the sack of Susa to suppression of the last political vestiges of Elām by Darius I (the Great) and incorporation of Elām into the Achaemenid Empire. In most of Neo-Elāmite period we do not know of a coherent dynasty to speak of, just sporadic kings whose genealogical filiation do not exceed one or two generations at most. Towards the end of the Neo-Elāmite period, however, we have information on a handful of 'dynasties', but their cultural and political affiliation with to the mainstream Elāmite state is debatable at best.

The Neo-Elamite I period (ca. 1000-744 BCE)

The NEI is possibly the least known period in the history of Elām. According to archaeological research, Malyān=Anšan seems to have shrunk from a city of 20-30 thousand people in the Kaftari period (ca. 2500-1500 BCE) to a town of 4-8 thousand people during the following Qale- Middle Elāmite period . The decline seems to have continued as Malyān may be abandoned by NE I period or seasonally occupied by non-sedentary people. Population may have shifted to the foothills of the Zagros, e.g., Rām-Hormoz and Behbahān plains. Settlement at Susa, however, seems to have continued on a much smaller scale. References to the so-called Elāmite dynasty in Babylon of a single king named Mār-bitti-apla-usur (984-979 BCE) or the introduction of the so-called 'Ekamite bow' to Assyria are of no consequence. While total absence of NEI texts, either royal or private is obviously perplexing (considering that "the absence of evidence is not evidence of absence"), the fact that towards the end of the reign of Adad-Nirāri III (810-783) there was an Elāmite ambassador at the Assyrian court in Kalhu (Nimrud) suggests that there was a functioning state apparatus somewhere in Elām. Assuming that this 'state' was based at Susa, why it has left us no written testimonies is a question that can only be answered with future excavations.

The Neo-Elamite II period (ca. 743-647 BCE)

Thanks to the Babylonian Chronicle, we know that in 743 BCE, a king named Hubān-Nikāš, son of Hubān-Tāhrā ascended the Elāmite throne and ruled until 717 BCE. The Babylonian Chronicle does not call Hubān-Nikāš I the founder of a particular Elāmite dynasty, but a group of Elāmitologists have come up with a 'dynasty' called the 'Humbānids' that ruled at Susa from ca. 770 to 585 BCE. More than historical reality or genealogical filiation, the 'humbanid dynasty' is perhaps devised to give some order to the convoluted Neo-Elāmite history and multitude of kings whose familial background and relationship to one another has occupied Elāmitologists for decades. However, the fact that four kings in this dynasty may have been brothers has prompted some scholars to describe this as a revival of the old Sukkalmaḫ tradition regarding legitimacy of kingship after over a millennium.

Going over every Neo-Elāmite king and controversies surrounding discrepancies in how their names are recorded in Babylonian or Assyrian and Elāmite sources, their dates, and relationship to one another is way beyond the scope of this paper and I refer the interested readers to more comprehensive sources. However there are four major and interrelated developments in the Neo-Elāmite period that are crucial to our understanding of the course of the Elāmite history and Elām's connection with the next phase in the history of Iran. These four developments are Elām's relationship with Assyria, fragmentation of Elām in NEII=III periods, arrival and settlement of Irānnian people in both highland and lowland Elām, and the rise of several, polities one of which played a crucial role in the formation of the Achaemenid Empire.

The roots of animosity between Elām and Assyria can be traced back to the reign of Hubān-Nikaš in Elām and Tiglāt-Pilesser III in Assyria. Since the foundation of the Neo-Assyrian empire by Aššurnāsiripāl II in 883 BCE, Assyria emerged as a militarized and expansionist polity for the next two and a half centuries that eventually brought the entire Near East and even Egypt under Assyrian yoke. But for long, Assyria's imperial ambitions were aimed toward the west into Syria and the east into Media. In a southward turn, Tiglāt-Pilesser III (744-727 BCE) twice launched campaigns against the Aramean tribes of southern Babylonia, once pursuing them as far as the 'Uqnu' River, i.e., the eastern arm of the Tigris in southern parts of the Central Zagros. Elāmites seem to have considered this act an encroachment by Assyria upon their sphere of influence, but refrained from military response. Perhaps reconciliation or passive resistance before Assyria was a wiser course of action for Elām, but the Elāmites underestimated the power of the Assyrian juggernaut and went on the offensive, perhaps misguided by an ineffectual response in their first encounter with Assyria. Some twenty year after the first Elāmite-Assyrian encounter, when the Chaldean Marduk-apal-iddina II (the Biblical Merodach Bālādān) of the Bit-Yākin 'house' put together a coalition against Assyria under Sargon II (721-705 BCE), the Elāmites, still under Hubān-Nikaš, decided to march against the Assyrians. March they did and they also defeated the Assyrians at Der in 720 BCE. While by every indication, the Elāmite won the battle, in the long run they seem to have lost the war, for this time Assyrians held fast, and apparently took this as a pre-emptive strike from an enemy that they did not consider a threat up to that point.

Meanwhile, one should bear in mind that the Babylonian-Elāmite coalition was an oxymoron, for these two nations shared a long and painful history, and now, though Merodach Bālādān acting as the leader of the anti-Assyrian coalition, the costly burden and consequences of engaging the mighty Assyrian Empire fell upon the Elāmites. Apart from supporting the nuisance that was Merodach Bālādān, Assyrians and Elāmites had to quarell over the petty kingdom of Ellipi, somewhere in Luristān, that brought the Assyrian wrath upon the Elāmites. The Ellipi affair and Elām's blind support of Merodach Bālādān – now the ultimate *persona non-gratta* in the eyes of Assyria – seems to have brought about a *coup d'etat* against the next Elāmite king Šutruk-Nahunte II (717-699 BCE) by his brother Hāllušu (699-693 BCE), who himself was apparently toppled by the people of Elām in a revolution, an extremely rare and unusual event in the history of the Near East. After a short reign, Hāllušu too was captured, imprisoned and slain by his own people. Hāllušu was succeeded by a certain Kutir-Nahunte II, from whose reign the deterioration of the Elāmite state seems to have commenced. Sennacherib, clearly sensing instability in Elām, marched against Susiana, but Kutir-Nahunte II chose not to put up a fight and instead to abandon Susa and flee to Madaktu and then to Hidālu (whose locations have been much debated without a consensus). The revolutionary mood that Elām was experiencing was also going to topple Kutir-Nahunte II's successor, a certain Kudur, who after just ten months on the throne, abandoned Susa and escaped to Madaktu and Hidālu. That seemed a wise course of action at the time, although in the long run, it damaged the prestige of Kutir-Nahunte II in particular and Elāmite kingship in general, and commenced a process of fragmentation that one authority has described as the rise of "Factionalism and Warlordism" in Elām.

As we all know, revolutions usually create more problems than they solve, and in conjunction with constant struggle with Assyria over mostly Babylonian affairs, Elām entered a period of anarchy that continued throughout the rest of the so-called 'Humbanid dynasty.' Internal and external problems, triggered the destabilization of the Elāmite kingship that had begun from the time of Sennacherib, reaching a turning point with the battle of Til-Tubā (653 BCE) between Tepti-Humbān-Inšušinak (Assyrian 'Te'ummān') and Aššurbānipāl.

The battle of Til-Tubā, the Elāmite defeat and beheading of the King of Elām Tepti-Humbān-Inšušinak and his nephew and presumed heir apparent Temti-tiri (Assyrian Tāmmāritu) on the battlefield was a major blow to Elām. Aššurbānipāl seems to have been pleased with the results of the battle of Til-Tubā, for the reliefs showing scenes from this fateful battle were prominently displayed at his palace in Nineveh.

Aššurbānipāl, clearly frustrated and agitated, decided to find a final solution to his Elāmite problem by following up on the battle of Til-Tubā and his crushing victory over Elāmites. He therefore launched three campigns against Elām under Hubān-Hāltāš III (ca. 648-645 BCE) who chose guerilla warfare and evasive maneuvers before the Assyrian army. With no king on the Elāmite throne, a group of citizens called the Elders of Elām, apparently the *de facto* rulers of lowland Elām in the absence of a king, opened negotiations with Aššurbānipāl whose reponse to them is preserved in one of the most interesting documents pertaining to the history of Elām.

But Aššurbānipāl's modest demand for the surrender of the Chaldean rebel Nabû-bel-šumāti and his cohort, who, for many years had received shelter and assistance from Elāmites in his conflict with Assyria, was not met, presumably due to the confusion in Elām. So in a final campaign in 647 BCE reported in detail in a number of different inscriptions and illustrated on Aššurbānipāl's palace reliefs in Nineveh (Nadali 2007), he marched on Elām and sacked and destroyed Susa and many other towns and cities in lowland Elām to the borders of Hidālu in the foothills of Zagros and Bāsime on the Persian Gulf coast.

The Neo-Elāmite III = The Elāmo-Persian period (647-520 BCE)

For the earlier generation of scholars, the Assyrian invasion of Elām and the 647 BCE sack and destruction of Susa and the lowland Elām by Aššurbānipāl, marked the end of Elām as a state and a civilization, but we know that neither the Assyrain devastation was as total as they wanted us to think, nor the Elāmites were as feeble as the Assyrians thought. In fact, the Elāmite endurance and resilience in the aftermath of Aššurbānipāl's sack of Susa lead to what some scholars have described as a revival of Elām, especially at Susa. Business was apparently soon resumed as usual, as demonstrated by over 300 economic tablets discovered at different parts of Susa, a shrine for Inšušinak built and decorated with glazed bricks by Šutur-Nāhunte II (ca. 625-600 BCE). At this period, a number of kings surface in tablets and inscribed bricks, most interestingly an Āttā-Hāmitti-Inšušinak (ca. 530-520 BCE) who erected a stele and was bold (or oblivious) enough to call himself 'King of Anšan and Susa,' though both Susa and Anšan were already absorbed into the Persian Empire (see below).

In the meantime, a recently discovered tomb of this period at Jubaji in the southeast vicinity of Rām-Hormoz of two young women, presumably related to Šutur-Nāhunte II (ca.

625-600 BCE) indicates that the Elāmite royalty were still economically well enough to bury their family members with rich personal ornaments and grave goods.

However, as a result of the debilitated authority of the centralized Elāmite state based at Susa after the Assyrian onslaught, Elām was gradually breaking down into a number of polities scattered from Susa to Anšan and north into Luristān. The first separate polity to emerge was probably at Hidālu. Hidālu's autonomous tendencies date back to the time of Aššurbānipāl where despite warnings that Tāmmāritu (Elāmite Temti-tiri) has treacherous intentions, Aššurbānipāl installed him as a client king at Hidālu. Tāmmāritu soon revealed his intentions and was beheaded, along with his uncle Tepti-Humbān-Inšušināk at the fateful battle of Til-Tubā, but Hidālu broke away from Elām under Tāmmāritu's unknown successors. Hubān-Nikāš II, also installed by Aššurbānipāl as a client king at Madaktu, was the other polity to break away from the now emasculated Elāmite state. Meanwhile, Acropole texts refer to a certain Āppālāyā, king of Zar; there is also a reference to a kingdom of 'Zamin' mentioned in Elāmite letters from Nineveh, and a Kingdom of 'Samati', presumably in Luristan, and a certain Hubān-Šutruk, the ruler of 'Gisāt' mentioned in the enigmatic – and yet-unpublished (!) – bronze plaque found in the Persepolis Treasury. There is also the cryptic tomb of Kidin-Hutrān, son of Kurluš at Arjān (Álvarez-Mon 2010), who is not mentioned as a king, but given the wealth displayed in his grave goods, including presumed royal insignia, especially the now famous Arjān gold ring, could very well have been a member of the royal house of Huhnur.

Another important development in this period is the appearance of a considerable number of names described as Irānian (Tavernier 2007) in the textual evidence from Susa, especially those of non-royal nature. This suggests that, when things were beginning to get back to normal at Susa in the aftermath of the Assyrian attack and retreat, a new group of people were arriving at Susa (see various papers in Álvarez-Mon and Garrison 2011) .

A considerable number of individuals from or associated with the 'Elamite' polities mentioned above also bear Irānian names, suggesting that there was an influx of Irānian people into formerly Elāmite territories. A similar migration of Irānian people was apparently also going on in the Central and Northern Zagros.

Perhaps the most important polity to emerge in Neo- Elāmite II-III periods, to play a pivotal role in the next chapter in the history of Iran, was the one formed at Anšan. Although 'king of Anšan and Susa' was an ancient and time-honored title used in Elām since the time the Sukkalmahs, and the official title of the rulers of the Middle Elāmite period that some of Neo-Elāmite rulers also continued to use, it seems that with the fall of the Šutrukids at the end of the Middle Elāmite period, the Elāmite state ceased to have an effective control over highland Elām, including the city and land of Anšan. Irānian people were apparently arriving in Anšan from points north for a few centuries and adapting to Elāmite culture and its established traditions, especially the institution of kingship that had deep roots at Anšan. Thus began a process of 'acculturation' between Elāmites and 'Persians' (Henkelman 2008) that ushered in the last chapter in the history of Elām and the first chapter in the history of the Achaemenid Empire, a critical era that I choose to call Neo-Elāmite III=the Elāmo-Persian period (ca. 647-520 BCE).

Of course, individuals with Irānian names, presumably the early Persians, have been surfacing in written sources as early as the late Neo-Assyrian period. But these individuals were primarily associated with a land called 'Pārsuā' or 'Pārsumāš' not Anšan, giving rise to a long debate among scholars called the 'Pārsuā vs. Anšan debate' that is beyond the scope of this paper. Suffice to say that a clan took advantage of lowland Elām's internal chaos and external conflict to fill the power vacuum that had left an important center as Anšan vacant and established a new dynasty that can be considered a prelude to the Achaemenid Persian Empire. Other researchers have called this dynasty 'Teispids' (after Greek Teíspēs) or 'Čišpids' (after Old Persian 'Čišpiš'), the name of its presumed founder, a certain Čišpiš about whom we no almost nothing besides the fact that he had an Irānian name and, according to Cyrus II (the Great) was his eponymous ancestor and a king of Anšan. However, according to Darius I (the Great) this Čišpiš was the son of Achaemenes, another enigmatic individual with an Irānian name who was the alleged founder of the Achaemenid lineage. Again, the controversies surrounding the lineages of Cyrus and Darius are beyond this paper.

For the purpose of this paper, however, I choose to call this dynasty 'Anšanites' after their place of origin. We have some basic information on genealogy and homeland of this dynasty based on a quintessential document in Irānian history by a late member of this dynasty: the Cylinder of Cyrus II (the Great). In this key document, Cyrus provides us with the following straightforward and incontrovertible testimony about his lineage:

> I am Cyrus, king of the universe, the great king, the powerful king, king of Babylon, king of Sumer and Akkad, king of the four quarters of the world, son of Cambyses, the great king,, king of the city of Anšan, grandson of Cyrus, the great king, ki[ng of the ci]ty of Anšan, descendant of Teispes, the great king, king of Anšan, the perpetual seed of kingship (translation after Finkel 2013: 20-22).

Furthermore, in the Sippar cylinder of Nabunaid (last king of Babylon), Cyrus is referred to as the 'king of Anšan' with determinative KUR (for land), while in the Cyrus cylinder, both determinatives of KUR (land) and URU (city) are used, indicating that he had claim both over the land and the city of Anšan. Also, on an inscribed brick from Ur, Cyrus calls himself and his father Cambyses I, as 'king of Anšan'. It seems that the emphasis by Cyrus on Anšan, not Elām or Persia is purposeful and meaningful. Unfortunately, despite much speculation, we still don't know what exactly what Cyrus was trying to invoke this reference to Anšan and his family's association with it.

These hints have, however, led to a long discussion among scholars on the ethnic origin and sociocultural background of Cyrus the Great and his Anšanite predecessors. Cyrus can both be viewed as an Elāmite with strong Persian tendencies or a Persian with a solid knowledge of Elāmite culture and traditions. What is important is that lowland Elāmites' viewed him as a legitimate ruler marching from Anšan to Susa to restore the ancient and traditional institution of Elāmite kingship after a long disruption, whereas to the Persians, Cyrus was one of them for his primary wife was the daughter of a prominent member of the Persian nobility. To the Medes, he was the grandson of their king and the only heir to the Median throne, and, last but not least, to Babylonians, he was a savior sent by their supreme god Bel-Marduk. To make a long story short, everybody loved Cyrus, even the

Greeks, i.e., the future archenemy of the Achaemenids, as well as the Hebrews, who must primarily be given the credit for transforming 'Cyrus, king of Anšan to Cyrus Maior' and turning him into perhaps the most celebrated monarch of antiquity. In a region accustomed to multilingualism, Cyrus may have conversed with his family and retinue in Old Persian, spoke to his subjects in Median, Elāmite, or even Babylonian. But, the *lingua franca* or at least the administrative language of the empire he was building had to be Elāmite, a logical trajectory in centralized administration and keeping written records that Cyrus inherited from Elāmites and passed on to Darius I (the Great) (522-486 BCE), his veritable successor and the architect of the empire Cyrus had begun to build. It is therefore not at all surprising that the earliest written testimonies of the empire, most notably the Bisotun inscription, Darius' foundation inscription on the south side of the Persepolis platform and, most importantly, the Achaemenid administrative archive at Persepolis are in Elāmite, a language that continued to be used (at least in royal inscriptions) well to the end of the Achaemenid period.

But drawing a line between language and ethnicity, especially in ancient times in a fluid environment such as southwestern Irān is a tricky business. Darius may have replaced the 'Anšānite' dynasty of Cyrus with an 'Achaemenid' dynasty of his own, but there was no fundamental change in the Irānian character of the empire which was always and continued to be an eclectic entity in many respects, combining not just Elāmite and Persian elements, but also Babylonian, Assyrian, Median, Urartian, Anatolian and even Egyptian features.

However, some individuals – namely Haššinā, Martiya, and Atamaitta who felt particularly committed to the presumed Elāmite identity and ethnicity of Cyrus and his line were first to rebel, not once or twice, but thrice, against the 'Persian usurper' out to overthrow the last vestiges of the Elāmite state (for controversies surrounding Darius' rise to power see Dandamayev 1976 and Wiesehöfer 1978).

While Elām as a political entity may have ceased to exist when it was absorbed into its heir and successor, the Persian Empire, Elām continued to exist as a cultural entity for many more centuries for which I refer the interested readers to more comprehensive studies.

Acknowledgements

Writing a paper while residing in Irān is not an easy task. While many resources have become available on-line in recent years, a large number of journals and books, especially older publications should be obtained the old fashion way through friends and colleagues (thanks Gods for PDF). I'm much indebted, first and foremost, To Dan Potts for not only providing me with a copy of the second edition of his most recent book on Elām (D.T. Potts 2016), but also for sending me a fairly large number of references via e-mail, not to mention for promptly answering my many questions on matters Elāmite. I also thank Wouter Henkelman for sending me a number of his recent publications and answering my questions, as well as Matt Stolper, who frustrated with this old student of his who hasn't done his homework, nonetheless went to him for quick answers to his many questions. I also thank Liz Carter for answering several questions of mine. These are extremely busy people, so they were unable to read and comment on this paper on such a short notice due to my delay in putting the paper together on time, so I take full responsibility for any factual or interpretive errors. Last, but not least, I thank Touraj Daryaee for entrusting this Elām afficiando with writing the chapter on Elām. Map 1-3 are made is made by Ramin Yashmi to whom I'm grateful.

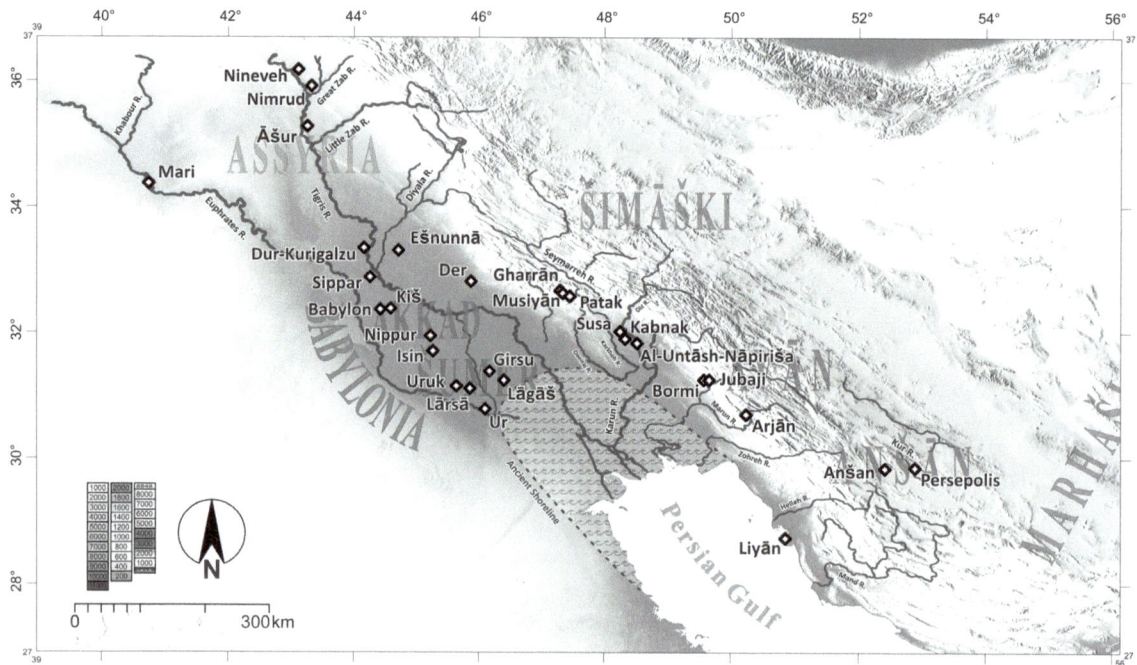

Map. 1. General map of the Near East with the location of lands and archaeological sites mentioned in the text.

Map. 2. Map of Susa with major excavated areas marked in red.

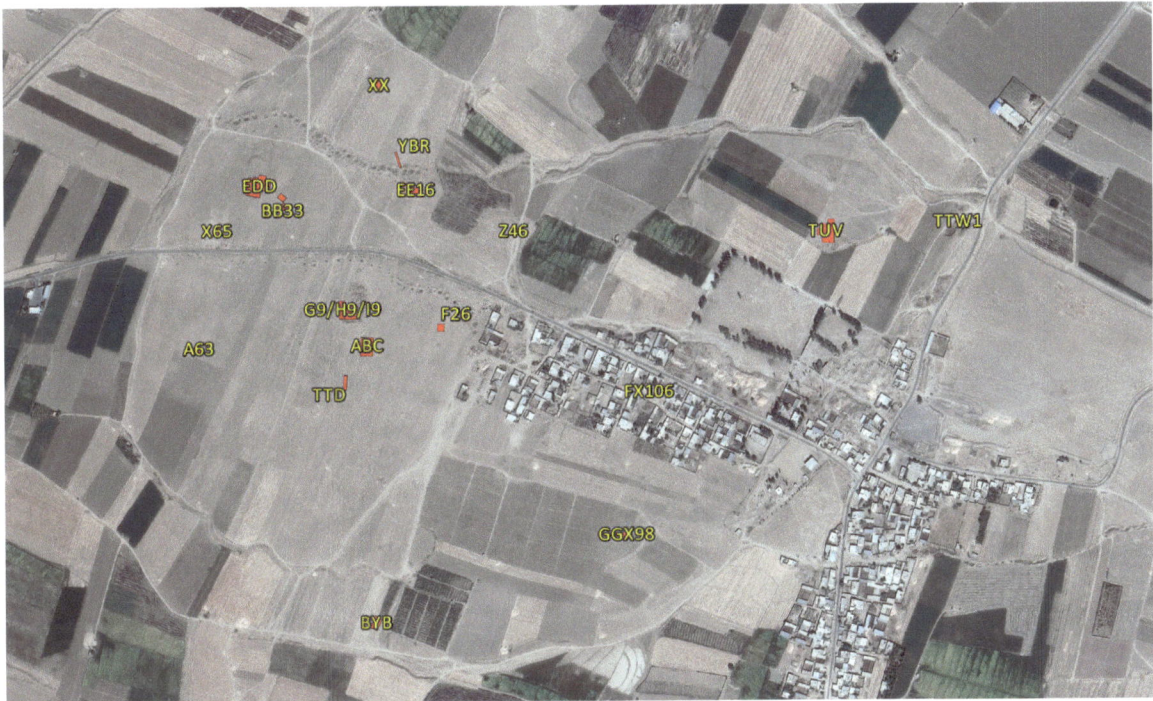

Map. 3. Map of Malyān with major excavated areas marked in red.

Figure. 1. Two views of the broken seated statue of Puzur-Inšušināk with an Akkadian inscription, discovered in early excavations at Susa, about 2100 BCE, The Louvre (seze Scheil 1913).

Figure. 2. Large clay tablet with the so-called "Elamite Treaty with Narām-Sin" in Old Elamite cuneiform, discovered in early excavations at Susa, about 2200 BCE, The Louvre.

Figure. 3. The so-called "Susa King-list", discovered at Susa in 1930, about 1800-1700 BCE, The Louvre.

Figure. 4. Modern impression of the chalcedony cylinder seal, about 3 cm high, bearing the name of Ebarat [II] of the Šimāški- Sukkalmaḫ transitional period (ca. 1920 BCE), provenience unknown, Gulbenkian Museum of Oriental Art, Durham University.

Figure. 5. The impression of the seal of Kidinnu, the presumed founder of the Kidinuid 'dynasty.'

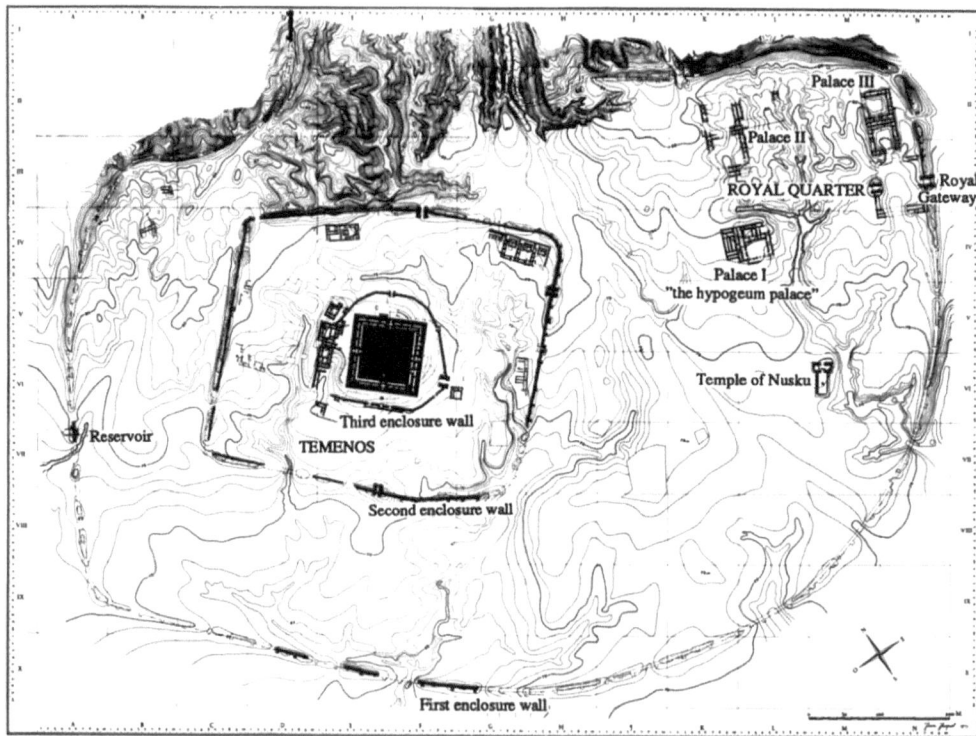

Figure. 6. Aerial photograph of the Choghā Zanbil complex (al-Untāš-Nāpirišā).

Figure. 7. Fragment of the Hutelutuš-Inšušināk inscribed brick, found in 1968 by William Sumner on the surface of Malyān, a find that led to the discovery of Anšān, University of Pennsylvania Museum.

Figure. 8. The relief from the battle of Til-Tubā (653 BCE) depicting the beheading of the King of Elām Tepti-Humbān-Inšušināk and his nephew Temti-tiri (Assyrian Tāmmāritu), excavated in the Palace of Aššurbānipāl at Nineveh, The British Museum.

Figure. 9. The relief from the Palace of Aššurbānipāl at Nineveh depicting the sack and destruction of Susa by Assyrian troops in 647 BCE, The British Museum.

Figure. 10. Restored stele of Āttā-Hāmitti-Inšušināk (ca. 530-520 BCE, 93.5 x 65.6 cm, Susa, The Louvre.

Figure. 11. General view of the tomb of the two young women presumably related to Šutur-Nāhunte II (ca. 625-600 BCE) after excavations whence only the tomb structure and remnants of the bronze bath tub caskets are still in situ, Jubaji , Rām-Hormoz.

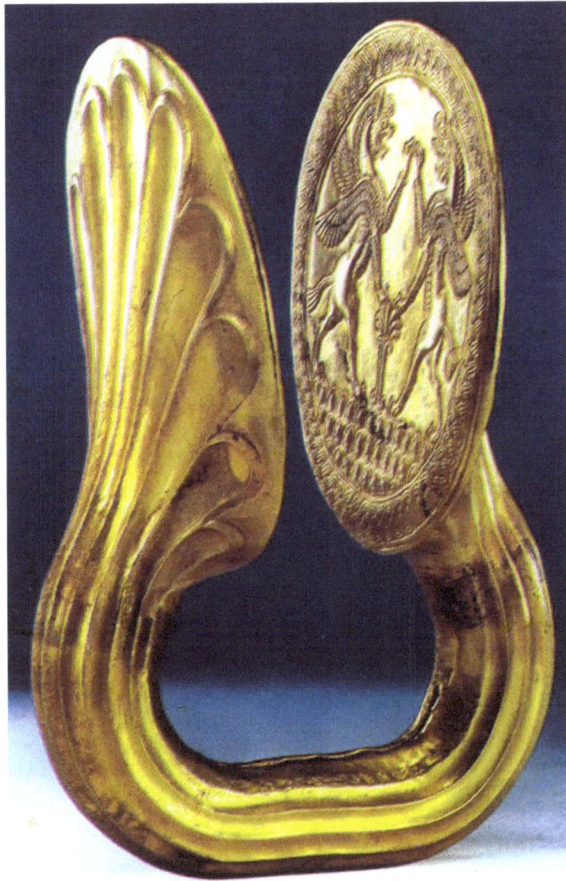

Figure. 12. The gold ring with the inscription of Kidin-Hutrān, son of Kurluš from the Arjān tomb , Iran National Museum.

Figure. 13. The Cyrus Cylinder commemorating his conquest of Babylon, excavated in Babylon, The British Museum.

Bibliography

Abdi, K. 2005. "Maliān," *Encyclopedia Iranica* (available online only).

Álvarez-Mon, J. 2010, *The Arjān Tomb: At the Crossroad of the Elamite and the Persian Empires*, Acta Iranica 49. Leuven: Peeters.

Álvarez-Mon, J. and Garrison, M.B. eds., 2011, Elam and Persia. Winona Lake IN: Eisenbrauns.

Amiet, P. 1966, *Elam*, Auvers-sur-Oise: Archée.

Amiet, P. 1986, *L'âge des échanges inter-iraniens, 3500–1700 avant J.-C.*, Notes et Documents des Musées Nationaux 11, Paris: Éditions de la réunion fed musées nationaux.

Amiet, P. 1988, *Suse, 6000 ans d'histoire*, Paris: Monographies des Musées de France.

Ascalone, E. 2006, *Archeologia della'Iran Antico: Interazioni, integrazioni e discontinuità nell'Iran dell III millennio a.C.*, Nisaba 14, Messina: Di. Sc. AM.

Cameron, G.G. 1936, *History of Early Iran*, Chicago: University of Chicago Press.

Carter E. and M. W. Stolpr, 1984, *Elam: Surveys of Political History and Archaeology*, Berkeley and Los Angeles: University of California Publications.

Dahl, J. 2009, "Early writing in Iran, A Reappraisal," Iran 47: pp. 23–31.

Dandamayev, M. A. 1976, *Persien unter den ersten Achämeniden (6. Jahrhundert v. Chr.)*, Wiesbaden: Ludwig Reichert.

Harper, P. O. and Aruz, J. and Tallon, F., eds. 1992. *The Royal City of Susa: Ancient Near Eastern Treasures in the Louvre*, New York: Metropolitan Museum of Art.

Henkelman, W.F.M. 2008, *The Other Gods Who Are: Studies in Elamite-Iranian Acculturation based on the Persepolis Fortification Texts*, Achaemenid History 14, Leiden: Nederlands Instituut voor het Nabije Osten.

Hinz, W. 1967, "Elams Vertrag mit Narâm-Sîn von Akkade," *Zeitschrift für Assyriologie* 24: pp. 66-96.

Hinz, W. 1972, *The Lost World of Elam*, London: Sidgwick & Jackson.

Potts, D. T. 2016, *The Archaeology of Elam: Formation and Transformation of an Ancient Iranian State*. Second edition, Cambridge: Cambridge University Press.

Potts, T.F. 1994, *Mesopotamia and the East: An Archaeological and Historical Study of Foreign Relations ca. 3400-2000 BC*. Oxbow Publications: Oxford University Committee for Archaeology.

Sumner, W. M. 1988, "Maljan, Tall-e (Anšan)," Reallexikon der Assyriologie 7, pp.306–320.

Sumner, W. M. 2003, *Early Urban Life in the Land of Anshan: Excavations at Tal-e Malyan in the Highlands of Iran*, Monograph 117, Philadelphia: University Museum.

Steinkeller, P. 2013 "Puzur-Inšušinak at Susa: A Pivotal Episode of Early Elamite History reconsidered," pp. 293–318. In De Graef, K. and Tavernier, J., eds., *Susa and Elam: Archaeological, Philological, Historical and Geographical Perspectives. Proceedings of the International Congress held at Ghent University, December 14–17, 2009.* MDP 58. Leiden: Brill.

Steinkeller, P. 2014, "On the dynasty of Šimaški: Twenty years (or so) after," pp. 287–96. In Kozuh, M. et al. eds. Extraction & Control: *Studies in Honor of Matthew W. Stolper,* Studies in Ancient Oriental Civilizations 68. Chicago: The Oriental Institute.

Vallat, F. 1980, *Suse et l'Elam,* Paris: Recherche sur les grandes civilisations.

Vallat, F. 1993. *Les noms géographiques des sources suso-élamites,* Répertoire Géographique des Textes Cunéiformes 11, Wiesbaden: Reichert.

Watters, M. W. 2000, *A Survey of Neo-Elamite History,* State Archives of Assyria Studies 12, Helsinki: The Neo-Assyrian Texts Corpus Project.

Wiesehöfer, J. 1978, *Der Aufstand Gaumātas und die Anfänge Dareios' I.,* Habelts Dissertationsdrucke, Reihe Alte Geschichte 13, Bonn: Habelt.

THE MEDIAN CONFEDERACY
Hilary Gopnik

The Medes

Unlike the other dynasties discussed in this book, the pre-Persian Medes have no voice of their own to tell their story. We know the Medes only through the accounts of their enemies, the Assyrians and Greeks, or through the politicized histories composed by later imperial powers. If the Medes used writing at all, it must have been with a script like Aramaic that was written on perishable materials because no historical accounts, literary texts, bureaucratic records, or even merchants' receipts survive to give us clues as to how they led their lives. Fortunately the archaeological record is a little more forthcoming, so that at least we can reconstruct how the Medes interacted with the material world, and we can then hypothesize about what that indicates about their society, politics, and beliefs.

The major gaps in knowledge about the Medes have created a confused and sometimes contradictory picture of their early history. Historians have alternately treated early Median communities as petty kingdoms, unruly tribes, religious innovators, robber-baron fiefdoms, and the basis for an Iranian empire. Their sustained presence in the history of ancient Iran has meant that scholars often try to impose later incarnations of Media onto the past without accounting for the marked shifts in the socio-political and geographic realities that occurred over the one thousand years of history in which a group called the Medes participated. This chapter will outline the existing evidence for the early Medes—before they became part of the Achaemenid Persian Empire—and will argue that these Median communities do not fit easily into any of the conventional historical models that have been used to explain them.

There are two main historical sources for the growth and expansion of Media: the contemporary accounts of the Assyrian Empire, which was attempting to control its neighbors to the east, and the stories of Greek historian Herodotus, who was writing for a Greek audience some 200 years after the height of Median power.

Who were the Medes?

Like many groups in the ancient world, it is difficult to place the Medes in a modern framework of group identity. They were alternately described as the people living in a given region (the central Zagros Mountains), people speaking a single language (Indo-Iranian Median), people belonging to a specific "Median" ethnic group, and people organized in a shared socio-political system (regional chiefs and later a king). In the absence of written records, the language spoken by the Medes is lost to us, but some small elements of it have been reconstructed from place names, personal names, and some suggested Median linguistic remnants in Old Persian (Rossi 2010, Zadok 2002). There have been many attempts both through archaeology and linguistics to pinpoint when exactly the Medes arrived in Iran and where exactly they settled, but there is very little evidence and no clear scholarly consensus (Witzel 2013). We can say for certain that the neighboring Assyrians recognized a group of people that they identified as coming from the "land of the Medes" (*māt madayya*) as early as the reign of Shalmaneser III (858–824 BCE), and it is almost certain that Indo-Iranian-speaking peoples had settled in Western Iran at least some 500 years—if not 1,000 years—earlier than this. Attempts at correlating changes in pottery types with the arrival of the Medes (for example, Young 1967) have proved fruitless, as it has become evident that pottery styles only rarely correlate with ethnic or language groups. Most scholars now believe that the arrival of Indo-Iranian speaking populations into Western Iran was not the result of one mass migration, but instead small groups of nomadic pastoralists infiltrated the area from the northeast over a long period of time, perhaps dating back to the early second millennium BCE. These pastoralists gave rise to a variety of cultural and linguistic groups, one of which eventually coalesced into the people that the Assyrians called the Medes (Rossi 2010).

The geographic extent of Media is also the subject of debate. Our only good source of information are the texts from the neighboring Assyrian Empire, which set out to conquer the region, but the Assyrians didn't really know the area well, particularly as they ventured eastwards. It is clear that the heart of Media lay in the central Western Zagros Mountains near Hamadan, but the eastern border of Median territory is still unknown. Much depends on the identification of the mountain the Assyrians called Mount Bikni, which Assyrian King Tiglath-Pileser III (744-727 BCE) claims to have reached in his campaign against the "mighty Medes of the rising sun" in 737 BCE (Tadmor and Yamada 2011, 47- 38b). Bikni has been identified as either Mount Alvand just south of Hamadan in the eastern range of the Zagros (Levine 1973), or Mount Damavand some 350 kilometers further east near the southern shore of the Caspian Sea (Radner 2003). Bikni is described by the Assyrian king Esarhaddon (680-669 BCE) as "the mountain of lapis lazuli" (Leichty 2011, Esarhaddon 1, iv 46) but since neither of these mountains has lapis deposits and both are on the trade routes through which the mineral must have come from the east, this does not help clarify the geographic extent of the Median presence. We have very little archaeological evidence to support either identification since many Median sites are deeply buried below later occupations, but the easternmost site with potentially Median pottery is Tepe Ozbaki, which lies 75 km west of Tehran (Majizadeh 2000, 2001), and it is probable that at its maximum expansion, Media extended at least that far east. Whatever its reach at any given time, it is clear that the geographic definition of Media was always flexible and variable. The land was defined not by borders but by its people. It was the *māt madayya* in Assyrian terms—the land of the Medes—and not the country of "Media."

If we cannot draw borders around a Median territory, we do know that the Medes were defined by their life in the Zagros Mountains. They sowed grain in the broad valleys and pastured their animals on the hillsides, moving from summer to winter pastures as the weather demanded (Gopnik 2010). And the weather in winter was harsh. One Assyrian governor wrote home explaining his delay in getting back to the capital from Media in early spring: "Concerning what the king, my lord, wrote to me: 'Be at Calah on the 1st of Nisan [March]' – we are clearing the roads, but it is snowing and snow is filling them up. There is very much snow...The year before last, (when) there was as much snow, rivers were frozen and the men and horses who were with me died in the snow. I shall be in the king my lord's presence on the 6th or 7th of Nisan." (Lukko 2013, 190)

The Medes raised sheep, goat, and cattle for meat, milk, and wool, but it was the Median horses that were considered their most treasured resource. The horses were allowed to graze along with the cattle until they were two years old, and then they were captured and trained. The Medes were known for their horsemanship, and when the Assyrians demanded tribute from them it was almost always in the form of horses trained for riding. The mountains could be a difficult terrain to negotiate for the uninitiated, and the Medes were able to take advantage of their home turf to escape the Assyrian military. They are often described as "fleeing into the mountains," and it is clear that the Assyrians did not, or could not, follow them.

The Medes according to Herodotus

The most complete narrative of the early history of the Median state comes to us from the Greek historian Herodotus. In the mid-fifth century BCE, Herodotus set out to write the history of the conflict between the Greeks and their eastern rivals. His immediate concern was the Persian Empire, which had staged an ultimately unsuccessful invasion of Greece some 50 years earlier, but Herodotus painted his history with a broad brush that included everything from the source of the Nile to gold-digging ants in India. The Medes—regarded by the Greeks not only as the precursors to the Persians but as an abiding component of Persian military power—take a central place in his narrative, and we are treated to detailed, if fanciful, accounts of their rise to power.

According to Herodotus, the Medes were living in small villages with independent rulers, when a certain Deioces embarked on an elaborate scheme to make himself king. First, he set himself up as a talented and supremely fair judge, adjudicating all cases according to "the truth of the facts" (Herodotus, History I:97, trans. Greene, 1987). Then—when he had made the people dependent on his system of justice—he abruptly withdrew his services, throwing the Median communities into disarray and lawlessness. In response, the Median people held a mass meeting in which they decided (and here Herodotus specifies that the meeting was probably stacked by the friends of Deioces) that they must have a single king to ensure fair dealing. "Deioces was so much in everyone's mouth," they asked him to be their leader. He agreed but laid down increasingly stringent conditions until he had set himself up as an exclusive and dictatorial king who could be seen only by his closest advisors, and who had a network of spies crisscrossing the country. After Deioces's death, his son Phraortes inherited the throne, but—Herodotus tells us—Phraortes was not content to rule only Media and extended his kingdom by assuming control over Persia, which at that point was probably a fairly small state to the south of Media. It would be up to Phraortes's son, Cyaxeres, to muster enough forces to finally defeat the state that had dominated most of the Near East for some 250 years with the destruction of the Assyrian capital at Nineveh in 612 BCE, proving the Medes to be "right good men" (Herodotus History I:95, trans. Greene, 1987) and allowing Cyaxeres to establish an empire of his own stretching from the Halys river in Anatolia to the eastern border of Media. According to Herodotus, the establishment of this border was hard fought; Cyaxeres's army battled with the King of Lydia, Alyattes, for five-years for the control of Eastern Anatolia with the conflict ending only after an eclipse of the sun (which is conventionally dated to 585 BCE) scared both parties into reaching a truce, sealed by the marriage of Alyattes's daughter Aryene with Cyaxeres's son Astyages. Under Astyages, the Medes would maintain sway over this territory until it was wrested from them by Astyages's grandson the Persian king Cyrus the Great.

Herodotus's critics have been harsh about his historiography from the beginning. Greek historian Thucydides accuses him (albeit indirectly) of treating subjects that are "beyond the reach of evidence …time having robbed most of them of historical value by enthroning them in the region of legend" (Thucydides, History of the Peloponnesian War, Book 1: 21, trans. R. Crawley, 1934). Although Herodotus takes great pains to indicate that he has considered his sources, it is abundantly clear that (like all historians) his understanding of history is the product of his own construct about how power changes hands and historical events unfold. His overall model is of a succession of empires (Assyrian to Median to Persian), but he also looks to the decisions of individual actors as the catalyst for change. It is likely that Herodotus's story of Deioces's rise to power from wise judge to dictatorial monarch has much more to do with his own vision of how kingship might develop in a non-state society than it does with any actual sequence of events. But, although the details may well belong to the "region of legend," the tale indicates that the Persian informants, who must have been the source for Herodotus's story, believed that during the eighth to seventh centuries BCE the Medes were organized as a series of independent chiefdoms rather than a state, and that it was still possible for the Median people as a whole to control decision making; the contemporaneous Assyrian historical accounts as well as archaeology seem to match this view of the past.

The growth of the Median Empire in the sixth century BCE has most recently become the focus of criticism of Herodotus's version of Median history. Although it was long assumed that the Median Empire was the immediate precursor to the Persian Empire as Herodotus claimed, in the past fifteen years scholars have seriously questioned the very existence of such an empire. This skepticism crystalized in a 2001 symposium in Italy in which scholars came together to discuss the continuity of empires from Assyria, through Media to Persia (Lanfranchi, Roaf, & Rollinger, 2003). It soon became clear that the consensus of researchers was that there was no historical or archaeological evidence other than Herodotus and later classical historians to support the existence of a Median Empire, and that it was likely that Herodotus had simply invented the unified state of the Medes in order to fill the void between Assyria and Persia in the east. Renowned ancient historian Mario Liverani summarized this position in the introduction to the publication of the meeting: "It seems clear that the Babylonian information on Media can be read as a reference to a state (not to say an empire) only if we read it on the guidelines of the classical sources. But if we are able to forget for a moment such a pre-conceived opinion, the Babylonian sources can much better describe the image of a destructive and untamable force rather than a unifying leadership" (Liverani, 2003, p. 7). As I will discuss below, the reimagining of the Median Empire as an "untamable force" rather than an organized state, however, has itself now come under question as new archaeological evidence has found Median ceramic and architectural elements in Transcaucasia to the north of Media in the late seventh and early sixth century BCE, suggesting a new Median presence in surrounding regions after the fall of Assyria.

The Medes according to the Assyrians and Babylonians

Where Herodotus provides us with a narrative version of Median history written 150 years after the events, Assyrian and Babylonian records give us a contemporaneous, if highly selective, glimpse into Median society. Assyria was the dominant military, political, and cultural power in much of the Near East from the mid-ninth to late-seventh century BCE. For over 200 years, Assyrian kings, based in their capitals on the northern Tigris River, managed to wrest control of much of the surrounding territory from their neighbors until at their height in the seventh century they controlled the entire area from the eastern shore of the Mediterranean to the western reaches of the Zagros mountains. There are essentially three kinds of Assyrian documents that tell us about the Medes: the official royal annals of the Assyrian kings, the many letters to the capital from various officials stationed in the eastern reaches of the empire, and "omen texts" which seek advice from a god in response to a specific question. Each provides a very different view of the interaction between the Assyrians and the Medes they sought to control.

The first mention of the Medes comes from the famous Black Obelisk of Shalmaneser III (858-824 BCE):

> Moving on from the land Parsua I went down to the lands Mēsu, Media (the land of the Medes), Araziaš, (and) Harhār, (and) captured the cities Kuakinda, Hazzanabi, Esamul, (and) Kinablila, together with the cities in their environs. I massacred them, plundered them, (and) razed, destroyed, (and) burned (those) cities. I erected my royal statue in the city Harhār. (Grayson 1996, p. 68, AO 102.14, ll. 120-125)

The Medes then appear again as enemies in the inscriptions of Shalmaneser's son Shamshi-Adad V (823-811 BCE)

> I marched to the land of the Medes (KUR ma-ta-a-a). They took fright in the face of the angry weapons of Assur and of my strong warfare, which have no rival, and abandoned their cities. They ascended a rugged mountain (and) I pursued them. I massacred 2,300 soldiers of Hanasiruka the Mede. I took away from him 140 of his cavalry (and) carried away his property and possessions in countless quantities. I razed, destroyed, (and) burned Sagbita, (his) royal city, together with 1,200 of his cities. (Grayson, 1996, p. 185 AO 103.1, ll. 27-35)

These early royal inscriptions give the impression of raids into poorly known enemy territory rather than any concerted attempt at directly controlling the region. The figures are clearly greatly exaggerated since even if we read "cities" as towns or villages, it seems impossible that they numbered anywhere near 1,200 or that they could muster 2,300 soldiers. The royal annals were designed as propaganda, and the standard sequence of conquest, looting, and destruction was as much a rhetorical trope as it was a description of actual events. Shamshi-Adad seems to identify Hanasiruka as a king, although this will be the only time that the Assyrians call a Median leader "king." Still, some themes that will recur over the next hundred years first appear in these inscriptions: the Medes live in towns, they are horsemen, and they flee into the mountains to escape the Assyrian army.

It is only under the kings Tiglath-Pileser III (744-727 BCE) and his son Sargon II (721-705 BCE) that the Assyrians attempted to take direct control of Median territory by founding new Assyrian provinces in the western Zagros. They also converted some Median towns to Assyrian centers, renaming them with the prefix *kār*, which meant "harbor" or "trading station" (Chicago Assyrian Dictionary K p. 234 *kāru* A-3a). Again, the royal display inscriptions are colorful, sometimes grotesque, narratives of conquest that can only be understood as heavily filtered and distorted accounts of Assyrian "victory".

From the reign of Tiglath-Pileser III:

> I, Tiglath-pileser, king of Assyria, who personally conquered all of the lands from east to west (lit. "from sunrise to sunset"), appointed governors in places where the chariots of the kings, my ancestors, never crossed over. In my ninth palû, I ordered (my troops) to march against the Medes. I conquered the cities of city rulers who were unsubmissive. I defeated them and carried off their booty. I firmly placed my steles in the city Bīt-Ištar, the city Ṣibar (Ṣibur), Mount Ariarma and Mount Silḫazu, mighty mountains. I received payment from those who did submit: I received 130 horses from the city Bīt-Ištar and its district; 120 (horses) from the cities Ginizinanu, Sadbat, (and) Sisad...; 100 (horses) from Upaš of (the land Bīt)-Kapsi (lit. "son of Kapsi"); 100 (horses) from Ušrû of the land Nikisi; ...100 (horses) from Uitana of the city Mišita; (ii 40′) 100 (horses) from Ametana of the city Uizak. (Tadmor and Yamada 2011, Tiglath-Pileser III 35, 2.25)
>
> From the reign of Sargon II: The people of Ḫarḫar drove out Kibaba, their mayor, and sent word to Talta of Ellipi (that they wished) to be his vassals. That city I captured and I carried off its spoil. People of the lands my hand had conquered I settled therein. I set my official over them as governor. The upper canal of Bit-Ramatua, the lands of Urikatu, Sikris, Shaparda, Uriakku, six districts, I captured and added them thereto. The weapon of Aššur, my lord, I appointed as their deity. Kār-Šarrukīn, I called its name. From 28 mayors (bēl āli) of the land of the mighty Medes I received tribute, and I set up my image in Kār-Šarrukīn. (ARAB 2, I.11)

These passages from Tiglath-Pileser's and Sargon's annals may tell us much more than the kings' boasting intended. The extensive list of horse tribute in Tiglath-Pileser's inscription makes it clear that, where other conquered areas might deliver booty of gold, wooden furniture, oil, grain, wine, or men, horses are the tribute of choice from Media. From Sargon's annals we learn that, even in the idealized world of the royal inscriptions, the Medes are capable of shifting allegiance away from the Assyrians. The appointment of an Assyrian governor and the renaming of Ḥarḥar to Kār-Šarrukīn (roughly translated as Sargonmart) is part of a pattern of response that sought to more directly control these towns. At the same time we encounter the term "mighty Medes" (madayya dannu), which becomes the most frequent way to refer to the Medes during this period. The persistent use of this term is surprising; the Assyrians are usually concerned with denigrating their enemies rather than aggrandizing them: In Sargon's annals Manneans are called wicked, the people of Syria dogs, the ruler of Carchemish is said to have sinned, and the arch-villain of Sargon's narratives, Rusa the Urartian, is compared to a woman in labor, a fleeing bird, and a pig. It isn't clear if the Assyrians specify that the Medes are mighty because they feared them or because they wanted to rhetorically boast of them as allies, but the fact that the Medes are both visually and rhetorically distinguished from other enemies highlights their special status in the eyes of the Assyrians.

The scribes of both kings tell us that one very concrete way of establishing suzerainty over a town or region was to set up a stone stela with the image of the king and an inscription detailing the results of rebellion. Remarkably, one of these stelae was discovered by archaeologists in the 1960s in the heart of Media at the village of Najafabad[1] in the Assadabad Valley of the Zagros Mountains. It had an almost life-size image of Sargon II on one side (Figure 1) and on the other a long, detailed description of the king's campaign in Media that had been only summarily treated in the homeland version of the annals (Levine, 1972). Part of it reads:

> At that time, the people of the city of Harhār who are submissive to Aššur (and) perform corvée duty [. . .] They drove off [Kibab]a, their city ruler, and withheld the horses (which were) to be given yearly as their tribute. They strengthened their city wall and repeatedly requ[ested (military) aid . . . before] the day had progressed [x double-hours] I had brought about their defeat; I inflicted a major defeat on them. I impaled their fighting men on stakes.
> The land of Igali, the land of Sikris, (and) the land of Bit-Uargi, distant regions whose name(s) the kings who preceded me had never heard, [...] My [awe in]spiring splendour overwhelmed them and they abandoned their cities. They gathered their people (and) their property and [...] the land of Abra... for their support [...] I put to the sword and took the remainder of them as booty, (namely) people, horses, mules, oxen, sheep, (and) donkeys. ... to/for [...] I tore

---

[1] The site as a whole, formerly spelled Najafehabad, dated to much later Sassanian and Islamic period occupations. The stela had probably been brought there as a relic during the Sassanian period (contra Radner 2013).

down, demolished, (and) set on fire.[2]

This local inscription also features the Ḫarḫar rebellion, although tellingly the consequences of the revolt are painted even more severely in the account designed to be read by Median communities.

All these inscriptions use the unusual term "bēl-āli" for the Median leaders, a term that is occasionally applied also to other rulers of polities in the Zagros mountains, but otherwise unknown in the Assyrian records. Literally translated the term means "head of a city" but it has been variously translated as "mayor," "chieftain," "city leader," or "city lord." Each of these translations reveals the cultural and intellectual context of the translator, but none seems to capture the full texture of what it was to be a bēl-āli.[3] The term as used by the Assyrians is probably also a reflection of their own interpretation of a power structure that was unfamiliar to them and could only be rendered in terms that the Assyrians themselves understood.

A remarkable series of letters found in the Assyrian capital cities of Nimrud and Nineveh go a long way to further enlightening us about the Median communities that the Assyrians were trying to control. These letters were written by palace officials stationed in conquered regions to the king back home. Where the display inscriptions were pure propaganda, the letters reflect the confused and often conflicting realities of imperial administration. The Assyrian governors were torn between their own interests, the demands of the Assyrian palace, the complex machinations of local leaders, and the power of the surrounding populace to just say no by refusing to appear to deliver tribute or pay obeisance. The Assyrian officials were ostensibly backed by the Assyrian military, but it is clear in the letters that the palace wanted to avoid military responses to rebellion. The Medes themselves often seem to play a cat and mouse game with the Assyrians who nominally controlled them by retreating to their mountain centers when they didn't care to engage with the Assyrians. When a new governor was appointed in Kār Šarrukīn, his first set of orders from the palace was to placate and reassure the Median bēl-āli: "Concerning the city-lords [bēl āli] about whom the king my lord wrote to me (saying) 'Speak kindly with them! Your friend and enemy should not be treated differently' . . . The son of Asrukanu has come to visit. I dressed him in purple and put silver bracelets on his wrists" (Fuchs and Parpola 2001, SAA XV, 91). Where the populations of other regions were subjected to mass deportations and heavy demands for forced labor and tribute, the Assyrians seemed wary of antagonizing the Medes, and a tone of strained tolerance and negotiation dominates the letters home.

It is clear from these letters that the position of bēl-āli could be hereditary; a certain Karakku, the bēl-āli of the Median city of Uriakku, swore loyalty to Sargon II in 714 BCE, but a few years later the governor stationed in Kār Šarrukīn writes: "Concerning what the

---

[2] This translation was generously provided to me by Grant Frame. It will be published as part of the Royal Inscriptions of the Neo-Assyrian Period Project.

[3] The term is almost always written with the logogram EN-URU. In Akkadian the plural form is bēl-ālāni and I have used this plural form when required here.

king my lord wrote to me: 'arrest and imprison the son of Karakku of Uriakku, and appoint Rametî in his stead!' I had the son of Karakku arrested and imprisoned, as the King my lord wrote, and we sent Rametî in his stead"(Fuchs and Parpola 2001, SAA XV, 85). Apparently Karakku's son Uppite had succeeded him as *bēl-āli*, but had then committed an offence against the king, probably by withholding tribute. So the position of *bēl-āli* was dynastic, even though the Assyrian king could sometimes depose rulers who displeased him. A tantalizing broken line, however, follows this passage in the letter: "The Uriakkeans did not agree to be under him but said: 'The son of Irtukkanu [Rametî]. . . [broken line]." We know from subsequent letters that Rametî was eventually appointed but this single broken line suggests that the people of Uriakku had some say in the matter, or at least that their opinion mattered enough to write about it to the central administration. Clearly the threat of force wasn't always sufficient to keep the Medes in line. Even the palace favorite Rametî later seems to play a waiting game with the Assyrian officials as the governor writes a few months later: "the son of Irtukkanu, city lord [bēl āli] of Uriakku—after the magnates had moved on from his presence, he visited me, brought the rest of the tribute, and will take it to the magnates"(Fuchs and Parpola 2001, SAA XV, 101). An interesting postscript to this whole episode occurred in the following year when the governor was on leave back at the capital. On his return he found that Karakku's son, Uppite—who had presumably remained captive in Kār Šarrukīn—escaped to a neighboring town with his four sons. They were eventually recaptured and their subsequent fate is unknown, but the power of the family was not easily quashed by the Assyrian king's displeasure.

If during the reign of Sargon II, the mighty Medes appear to be contained by diplomacy and the strategic backing of competing factions, by the reign of his grandson Esarhaddon (680-669 BCE), the Assyrians have seemingly lost ground in Media. Although we don't have the diplomatic correspondence from Esarhaddon, another set of records reveals trouble in the Median provinces. These omen texts are phrased as inquiries to the god Shamash with the answer sought in extispicy—the examination of the innards of an animal, usually a ram. Again and again in these texts, the king inquires about the power of the Medes and their allies, the Cimmerians and Manneans. One Median *bēl-āli* in particular—Kaštaritu, *bēl-āli* of Karkaššî—becomes the focus of the king's concern: "Šamaš, great lord, give me a firm positive answer to what I am asking you! Kaštaritu, city lord of Karkaššî, who wrote to Mamitiaršu, a city lord of the Medes, as follows: 'Let us act together and break away from Assyria.' Will Mamitiaršu listen to him? Will he comply? Will he be pleased? Will he become hostile to Esarhaddon, king of Assyria this year? Does your great divinity know it?"(Starr 1990, SAA4-41)

Even the formerly routine collection of horse tribute from the Medes now seems to be fraught with difficulty. One inquiry asks about a contingent of officials marching to Media to obtain horses: "Will they (be able to) march about for as many days as they wish, will they, either going or returning, escape, be saved, or save themselves from the troops of the Medes, or from the troops of the Manneans, from the troops of the Cimmerians, and from any other enemy? Will they stay alive and well, and return alive with the tribute of horses, and set foot on Assyrian soil? Will Esarhaddon hear good news? Will he be delighted and happy?" (Starr 1990, SAA4-65)

Median *bēl-ālāni* also appear in another curious set of documents found on a floor in a temple annex to the palace at the capital of Nimrud. The clay tablets were deliberately smashed during the destruction of the site in 612 BCE, but they had been written some sixty years earlier during the reign of Esarhaddon. Known as the adê tablets, these texts record oaths made by eight Zagros-dwelling *bēl-ālāni* who swore loyalty to the Assyrian king and his crown prince Ashurbanipal (668-ca. 631 BC). Although the meaning of these oaths has been hotly debated since their discovery in 1955—suggestions have ranged from vassal treaties to the swearing in of a corps of Median bodyguards to the crown prince (Liverani 1995, Scurlock 2012)—a recent discovery of a very similar tablet from the Syrian site of Tell Tayinat points to an empire-wide attempt at making all allies swear allegiance to the crown-prince before Esarhaddon's death (Fales 2012). We are told in one of Esarhaddon's inscriptions that six years earlier one of these *bēl-ālāni*, Ramataya of Urakazabarna, a Mede, had himself come to the Assyrian court, bringing tribute of horses and lapis lazuli, to seek aid from Esarhaddon against rival *bēl-ālāni*. In the event, it would appear that the oaths and alliances fell apart, and the tablets that recorded them were taken from the storage room in the temple and crushed.

If by the mid-seventh century, the Median *bēl-ālāni* threatened to form alliances that would create a coalition of the willing against the Assyrians, there is no hint that the basic political organization of the Medes as independent *bēl-ālāni* was in flux as Herodotus's story of Deioces's rise would suggest. Yet by 614 BCE, a Babylonian chronicle records the arrival on the scene of Umakištar, a leader of the Median army, whom most historians identify with Herodotus's Cyaxeres. Umakištar sacked the traditional Assyrian religious center of Ashur and formed an alliance in front of its city gates with the Babylonian king Nabopolassar—who failed to show up for the actual battle in time. Two years later, the Medes, led by Umakištar joined Nabopolassar en route to Nineveh and the two forces laid siege to the Assyrian capital:"they carried off the vast booty of the city and the temple and turned the city into a ruin heap" (Grayson 2000, Chronicle 3, l. 45). Although one line in the chronicle (l. 38) refers to "the king of the Umman-manda" (an archaic name for powers from the east) seemingly in reference to Umakištar, Umakištar himself is never directly called the king of the Medes. Again, the traditional association of Umakištar with Cyaxeres the king depends in large part on accepting the Herodotean version of history. It remains possible, instead, that the chronicle presents Umakištar as a "king" in order to provide a suitable confederate to Nabopolassar instead of listing a more accurate but less dramatically effective coalition of the Median *bēl-ālāni* who may have actually provided the troops for the defeat of the Assyrians. Umakištar returned home after the defeat of Nineveh, and the Medes virtually disappear from the contemporaneous historical record of Babylon until the sixth year of Nabonidus's reign (550 BCE) when it is recorded that the Median king Ištumegu (Astyages), was seized in a military coup, allowing Cyrus, king of Anšan, to loot the Median royal city at Ecbatana, thus spelling the end of the Median dynasty and the beginning of the Persian Empire (Grayson 2000, Nabonidus chronicle, col ii, lines 1-4).

The Medes according to archaeology

If the Greek, Assyrian, and Babylonian texts provide a picture of the Medes as seen by outsiders, the archaeology of the area can tell us how the Medes themselves used their material culture—their architecture, their pottery, their weapons, and even their livestock and crops—to create the communities that defined them as Medes. Until the 1960s there were virtually no archaeological sites that could be identified as Median. In 1965, archaeologists Cuyler Young and David Stronach set out to change that by embarking on an archaeological survey of the central western Zagros with the goal of identifying Median sites to excavate. The two sites that they eventually selected, Tepe Nush-i Jan and Godin Tepe, changed not only our understanding of the Medes but of the entire prehistory of Western Iran. Since that time, other sites have added additional information to a growing sense of how communities thrived in the Zagros Mountains.

Tepe Nush-i Jan

Nush-i Jan is located at the edge of the Malayer Valley, some 60 kilometers south of Hamadan, right in the heart of Media. Perched on top of a natural shale outcrop some 37 meters high, Nush-i Jan is one of the best-preserved sites excavated in the past 50 years. As David Stronach and his team began excavation at the site in 1967, they removed what they thought was a preserved floor only to come down on what appeared to be an underlying massive deposit of shale (Stronach and Roaf 2008). It was only after a week's excavation that they realized that the "floor" was a ceiling and the shale was deliberately-laid fill that preserved an intact temple (Figure 2). The temple had apparently been carefully filled with stone when it was abandoned, presumably to ensure that it was not ritually polluted even after it was no longer in use. The preserved ceiling—a one-in-a-million archaeological find made possible only by the ritual in-filling of the building—was vaulted with mud-bricks, the earliest example of mud-brick vaulting yet discovered and testimony to the engineering expertise of the temple builders. The walls of the building were decorated by a repeating series of triangular and cross-shaped niches that seem to have been designed to create patterns of shadow and light across the surface of the wall. The temple had been stripped of almost all portable artifacts before it was abandoned, but in the central room a stone platform about one and a half meters square bore a 25-centimeter round depression on top that was still filled with ash when the excavators removed the shale fill above it. This apparent fire altar is reminiscent of later Zoroastrian tradition, but the preserved fire bowl is too shallow to allow for the perpetual fire required by Zoroastrian cult practice. The excavators have suggested that this temple belonged to a Median religious tradition of fire worship, perhaps already associated with Zoroastrian Mazdean worship, but not yet fully fitting within the dictates of later Zoroastrianism (Stronach and Roaf 2008).

Surrounding the temple at Nush-i Jan were several other large buildings, including storage magazines, an older temple, and most notably a columned hall—one of the earliest examples of the form that came to define Achaemenid Persian palatial architecture. The roof of the 300-square-meter hall was supported by three rows of four columns and a wide bench or platform was placed against the back wall. The function of this hall in association with the temple isn't clear, but by analogy to other such structures it can be assumed that the large roofed space was intended for groups of people, perhaps the congregants of the temple, to assemble: to eat, drink, discuss, celebrate, mourn, maybe even sleep.

Godin Tepe

Like the temple complex at Nush-i Jan, the Median remains at Godin were perched on top of a 30-meter-high hill, but unlike the rock outcrop at Nush this mound was made up entirely of the remains of human settlement (Gopnik and Rothman 2011). Godin Tepe was first settled about 7,000 years ago and was pretty much continuously occupied until about 500 BCE. At the top of the eroded detritus of thousands of years of mud-brick structures, a Median community built a single impressively large building that at its prime enclosed a space of almost 5,000 square meters. The Godin citadel included storage magazines, kitchens, banqueting rooms, and perhaps bedrooms on the second floor (Figure 3), but it was the large columned hall at its center that was built first and remained the raison-d'être of its construction (Gopnik 2011). Although it is likely that the building with its thick surrounding wall and five watch towers, was originally intended in part as a defensive fortress, by its final years the arrow slots had been allowed to fill up with garbage such that the yearly plastering that kept the mud-bricks waterproof had to stop some half-meter from the wall base (Figure 4). The artifacts found in the building bear no signs of military intent; the only weapons were two iron arrowheads that could have equally been used for hunting. Instead, several large garbage dumps in the back corners of the storage rooms and on the kitchen floor contain abundant remains of eating and drinking on an impressive scale. Thousands of pieces of cooking pots, small drinking bowls, and fine-ware serving bowls; the bones of young pig, sheep, and goat; and the seeds of barley, wheat, herbs, and grapes, all testify to the feasting that must have been one of the main activities in this central meeting place. It seems more than likely that this citadel was the home base of one of the Median *bēl-ālāni* whom the Assyrians had such a hard time controlling. It is possible that a succession of leaders occupied the space since there is considerable evidence for rebuilding and renovation of the building over time. It was finally peacefully abandoned and let to fall to ruin before a family of farmers moved into the remains some years later and built a small house there.

The columned hall at Godin was well preserved and probably reflects the typical layout of these reception rooms (Figure 5). Laid out in five rows of six columns, the columns would have been made of wood (which of course does not survive in the archaeological record) and would undoubtedly have been plastered and probably painted. A row of plastered mud-brick benches, some painted red, lined the side and rear walls of the hall with a raised seat against the rear wall that was clearly intended as a seat of honor, presumably for the *bēl-āli* who presided over the congregation. In front of the seat of honor was a hearth on a platform, a necessary feature given the cold winters of the Zagros Mountains. Significantly, this main hall was complemented by a small side room that was also equipped with benches and a seat of honor, the location for one-on-one meetings with supplicants or diplomats such as the Assyrian "magnates" mentioned in the governors' letters.

Although we have few surviving examples from this earlier period, the columned hall was one of the defining features of Median communities. In the narrative relief sculpture in the palace of Sargon II, where artists went to some trouble to pepper their illustrations with local detail, the Median "city" of Ḫarḫar is clearly depicted with a columned structure at its center (Figure 6), presumably a distinctive feature of Median architecture and the precursor to the later Persian columned halls at Pasargadae, Persepolis, and Susa (Gunter 1982). Interestingly, smaller versions of these halls have been found very far from Median influence on the Oman peninsula of Arabia, and we have to imagine that the form was more widespread than archaeology has so far revealed (Magee 2001, Boucharlat and Lombard 2001). I have suggested elsewhere (Gopnik 2010) that the proliferation of the columned hall in the mid-first millennium BCE is not tied to the spread of a specific ethnic group, aesthetic trend, or architectural technique—roofing a large space with columns would require no particular technical expertise and the idea is a simple one—but rather to the peculiar effectiveness of these halls as places of congregation. Architectural structural elements (e.g., columns, piers, and arches) are usually used to define and shape people's experience of the space that lies between or among them. In a cathedral for example the piers divide the nave from the aisles, creating a focal axis on the altar as well as drawing the visitor's eye upward to the soaring space of the vaulted ceiling (an allusion to the heavenly sphere). The evenly spaced columns of the Iron Age columned halls, however, seem to deliberately confuse the space of the hall so that it is difficult to assess the overall size of the room, or even the number of people crowded into the space. The columns emphasize structure over space, and instead of leading the visitors in a single direction as did the uniaxial throne rooms of Mesopotamian monarchs, the axes of vision and movement are multiplied to the point of disorientation. Although this seems like an odd layout for a throne room—and indeed it is seldom used in world architecture in spite of the obvious technical ease of roofing a large room in this way— it is a particularly effective means to express the power of congregation (Khatchadourian 2016). If the goal of these halls was to demonstrate the strength in numbers of the community who supported the local *bēl-āli*, and the Assyrian governors' letters indicate that this was indeed a large measure of their power, then the multiple rowed columned halls may have been designed to reinforce the impression of the crowd. In fact the columns themselves may have been intended to represent the assembled masses; this visual metaphor became a central part of the visual program of the later Achaemenid Persian Empire, as seen for example in Darius's tomb at Naqsh-i Rustam where the subjects of the empire are depicted as columns supporting his throne.

Archaeological Surveys

Although several archaeological surveys have been conducted in Media over the past fifty years (Young 1975, Levine 1987, Howell 1979, Stronach and Roaf 2008) so far none have found any architectural remains or ceramic sherd concentrations that might suggest the presence of anything remotely resembling a city. The largest sites identified measure only about 3-4 hectares—the size of a small village. At the same time, monumental architecture identified on surface surveys and excavated at Nush-i Jan, Godin, Gūnespān (Naseri et al. 2016), and Ozbaki Tepe seems to be reserved for single-purpose sites rather than constructed within a larger settlement. It is difficult to reconcile this archaeological picture with the *bēl-ālāni* system of "city leaders" we read about in the Assyrian documents. The most likely explanation for this disjuncture is that the Assyrians themselves just didn't get it. Faced with a political system of regional leaders who didn't fit their models of kings or tribal chiefs (for whom they reserved the term nasīkāni), the Assyrians looked to the city as a local political system that was familiar to them. If the Medes organized themselves as congregations of people who came to central locations for decision-making and negotiation, then these centers may have seemed to be the defining feature of government to the Assyrians. The Median bēl-ālāni seem to have derived their authority from a variety of socio-political arenas including religion, dispute regulation, military force, and trade, and each ruler may have had a different power base. It is likely that one of their primary sources of power, as well as vulnerability, was dealing with the imperial demands of the Assyrians; it is possible, in fact, that the structure of the Median polities developed in part in direct response to imperial pressures.

Anthropologist James C. Scott (2010) has argued that in Southeast Asia, highland groups deliberately adopted a non-literate, shifting settlement pattern in order to avoid or obstruct the encroaching lowland states around them. Given the Assyrians obvious difficulties in controlling the Medes using the imperial tactics of deportation and tribute, it seems likely that the Medes were able to exploit the bēl-ālāni system of on-demand government to dodge rather than confront the Assyrian imperial administration.

The location of the few Median congregational centers that we can identify—and there must have been many more judging from the number of Median "cities" mentioned in the texts—seems to support the notion of a diversified base for the bēl-ālāni's authority; all are located on the edge of valleys where they would be accessible to both lowland agriculturalists and highland pastoralists, and on travel routes where they could be both accessible to and in control of the trade through the mountains. The Malayer valley, for instance, has four identified centers (Nush-i Jan, Gūnespān, and two found on survey) (Stronach and Roaf 2008), located at the four entry points into the valley.

Was there ever a Median Empire?

Finally, we return to the question of the Median Empire. Is it possible that so disjointed a people—Liverani's "destructive and untamable force"—were capable of forming an empire of their own as Herodotus claimed?

New archaeological evidence may contribute to our understanding of this issue. New research at the Urartian site of Erebuni (Stronach et al. 2010, Deschamps et al. 2011), located in southwestern Armenia, has shown that a columned hall that had been dated to the Achaemenid Persian period by the original excavators, was probably actually built toward the end of the seventh century, during the exact period after the fall of Assyria when the Medes would have begun their expansion northward according to Herodotus. A similar columned hall at Altıntepe, a site in eastern Turkey, may also be dated to this period (Karaosmanoğlu and Korucu 2012). The spread of the columned hall form before the advent of the Achaemenid Empire suggests some form of influence from Media in the late seventh or early sixth centuries BCE, but the nature of that influence depends very much on the nature of Median polities at that time.

The last mention of Median bēl-ālāni comes from an inscription of Ashurbanipal that recounts a campaign of 656 BCE, in which three Median *bēl-ālāni* rebelled and were captured and brought back to Nineveh (Radner 2003). If Herodotus's version of the rise of the Median Empire is essentially correct, then Deioces's transition to kingship would have to have occurred in the final decades of the Assyrian empire when Assyrian power was on the wane (Tuplin 2004). This does not leave space for the succession of Deioces's son Phraortes nor for the Scythian interlude before the rise of the historically attested Cyaxeres/Umakištar. Presumably, something was lost in the transmission of this story. It is possible that the Deioces story had been passed down as an account of the political structure of Media—authority through arbitration and consensus (however manipulated)—and that Herodotus transformed it into the rise of a single king in order to create a Median dynasty. Deioces, Phraortes, and Cyaxeres may have instead been contemporaneous *bēl-ālāni*, whether allied or competing.

If, however, the political structure of Media that relied on negotiation, multiple spheres and sources of authority, and periodic congregation was partly developed to resist Assyrian imperial demands, we can posit that the withdrawal of that threat may have encouraged the abandonment of these tactics in favor of centralization. As it became conceivable for a united Media to defeat Assyria and assume her mantle of power in the region, the impetus to unite may have been stronger than the competitive forces dividing the *bēl-ālāni*. The peaceful abandonment of both Godin and Nush-i Jan may have been tied to this move toward centralization under one king—whether Deioces, Phraortes or Cyaxeres/Umakištar—with the early capital city at Ecbatana (Hamadan) simply buried and/or destroyed by the substantial subsequent occupation of the site. In this case, the spread of the columned hall to Erebuni and Altıntepe could have been a form of direct imperial control—the establishment of secondary courts and throne rooms in two critical regions.

If instead, Herodotus invented the story of unification to fit his model of successive empires, we are left with Cyaxeres/Umakištar as a general and a leader, but perhaps only the nominal head of an alliance of Median *bēl-ālāni*—regional rulers who far from being "untamable" were in fact experts at the power of negotiation (Waters 2011). Certainly our present models of "empire" would normally require a single governing authority, if not a king then a unified central government, but if we think of empire instead—as we do in the modern model of the "American Empire"—as the deliberate export of cultural ideas in order to exert control over a wider sphere, we can reconstruct a Median "empire" that never moved fully to kingship but rather retained its tradition of alliances and congregational authority while reaching out to a wider world. The columned halls outside the center might then have been built by other regional leaders with their own power bases, seeking alliance with the by this time large and militarily powerful Median league.

The Medes present us with a challenge to traditional historical models. They were a nation without a country, and an empire without a king. They built new forms of government based on consensus and negotiation yet left a legacy in one of the largest and most powerful empires the world has ever known. The Assyrians didn't understand them, the Greeks conjured them with Greek images, and modern scholarship has tried to fit them into conventional models of leadership. It is only by stretching boundaries and remaining flexible, as the Medes did, that we may be able to understand the Median phenomenon.

Figure. 1. Najafabad Stele, Sargon II. Courtesy of the Royal Ontario Museum.

Figure. 2. Reconstruction of Temple at Nush-I Jan. Courtesy of David Stronach.

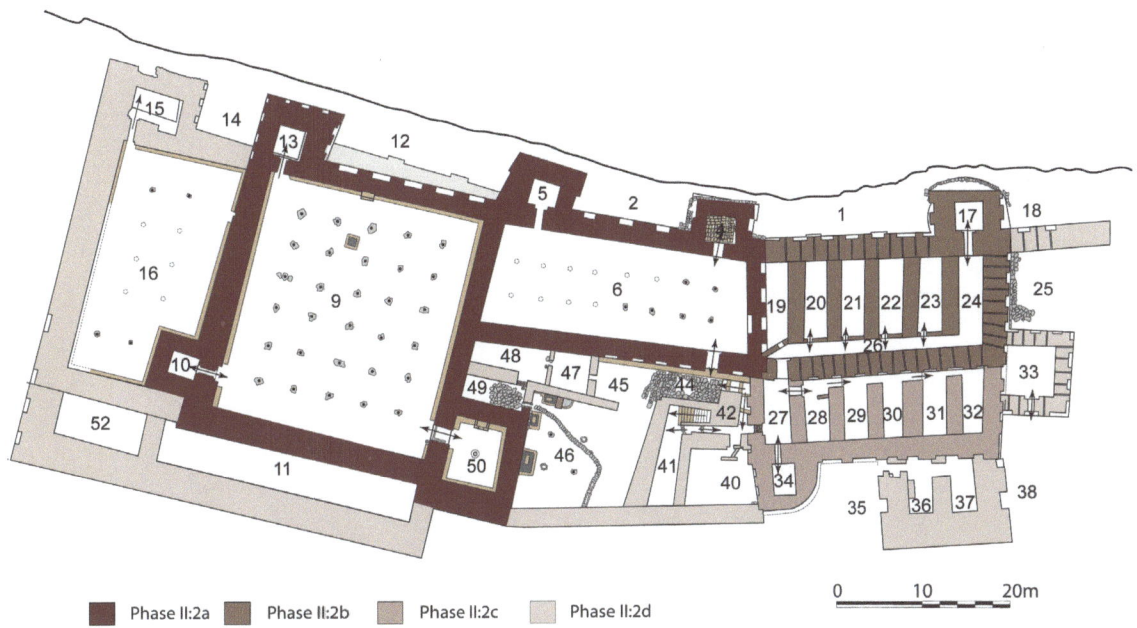

Phase II:2a   Phase II:2b   Phase II:2c   Phase II:2d

0   10   20m

Figure. 3. Plan of Godin Tepe

Figure. 4. Arrowslots at Godin Tepe showing successive lines of plaster

Figure. 5. Reconstruction of the Godin Tepe columned hall

Figure. 6. The Median city of Harhar

Further Reading

Gopnik, H. 2011. "The Median Citadel of Godin Period II." In *On the High Road: The History of Godin Tepe, Iran*, edited by H. Gopnik and M. Rothman, pp. 285–364. Toronto: Royal Ontario Museum.

Khatchadourian, L. 2016. *Imperial Matter: Ancient Persia and the Archaeology of Empires.* Oakland CA: University of California Press.

Radner, K. 2003. "An Assyrian View on the Medes." In Lanfranchi et al. (Eds.), *Continuity of Empire (?)Assyria, Media, Persia:* 119-130. Padova: S.a.r.g.o.n. Editrice E Libreria.

Stronach, D. and M. Roaf. 2008. *Nush-i Jan I: The Major Buildings of the Median Settlement.* London: British Institute of Persian Studies.

Waters, M. 2011. "Notes on the Medes and their "Empire" from JER 25:25 to HDT 1.134" In G. Frame (Ed.), *A Common Cultural Heritage: Studies on Mesopotamia and the Biblical World in Honor of Barry L. Eichler*: 243-253. Bethesda, Md.: CDL Press.

Bibliography

Boucharlat, R. and P. Lombard. 2001. "Le Bâtiment G De Rumeilah (Oasis d'Al Ain). Remarques Sur Les Salles À Poteaux De L'âge Du Fer En Péninsule d'Oman." *Iranica Antiqua* 36: 213-238.

Brown, S. 1986. "Media and Secondary State Formation in the Neo-Assyrian Zagros: An Anthropological Approach to An Assyriological Problem." *Journal of Cuneiform Studies* 38: 107-119.

Crawley, R. and J. Gavorse. 1934. The Complete Writings of Thucydides : The Peloponnesian War. New York: Modern Library.

Deschamps, S., F. de Clairfontaine, and D. Stronach. 2011. "Erebuni: The Environs of the Temple of Haldi During the 7th and 6th Centuries BC." *Aramazd* 6 (2): 121-140.

Fales, F. M. 2012. After Ta'Yinat : The New Status of Esarhaddon's Adê for Assyrian Political

History. *Revue d'Assyriologie* 106: 133-158.

Fuchs, A. and S. Parpola. 2001. *The Correspondence of Sargon II, Part III: Letters from Babylonia and the Eastern Provinces* (State Archives of Assyria, 15). Helsinki: Helsinki University Press.

Gopnik, H. 2003. "The Ceramics From Godin II in the Late 7th to Early 5th Centuries BC." In *Continuity of Empire (?) Assyria, Media, Persia.* Edited By G.B. Lanfranchi, 249-267. Padova: History of the Ancient Near East Monographs V,.

Gopnik, H. 2005. "The Shape of Sherds: Function and Style at Godin II." *Iranica Antiqua* 40: 249-270.

Gopnik, H. 2010. "Why Columned Halls?" In J. Curtis and S. J. Simpson (Eds.), *The World of Achaemenid Persia: History, Art and Society in Iran and the Ancient Near East*: 195–206. London: I.B. Tauris.

Gopnik, H. 2011. "The Median Citadel of Godin Period II." In *On the High Road: The History of Godin Tepe, Iran,* edited by H. Gopnik and M. Rothman, pp. 285–364. Toronto: Royal Ontario Museum.

Grayson, A. K. 2000. *Assyrian and Babylonian Chronicles (Texts from Cuneiform Sources).* Winona Lake: Eisenbrauns.

Grayson, A. K. 1996. *Assyrian Royal Inscriptions. Vol. 3: Assyrian Rulers of the Early First Millennium BC II (858-745 B.C.).* Toronto: University of Toronto Press.

Greene, D. (Trans.). 1987. *The History, Herodotus.* Chicago: University of Chicago Press.

Gunter, A. 1982. "Representations of Urartian and Western Iranian Fortress Architecture in the Assyrian Reliefs." *Iran* 20: 103-111.

Howell, R. 1979. "Survey of the Malayer Plain," *Iran* 17: 156-57.

Huff, D. 2005. "From Median to Achaemenian Palace Architecture." *Iranica Antiqua* 40: 371-396.

Karaosmanoğlu, M. and Korucu, H. 2012. "The Apadana of Altıntepe in the Light of the Second Season of Excavations." In A. Çilingiroğlu and A. Sagona (Eds.) *Anatolian Iron Ages 7: The Proceedings of the Seventh Anatolian Iron Ages Colloquium Held at Edirne, 19–24 April 2010*: 131-148. Leuven: Peeters.

Khatchadourian, L. 2016. *Imperial Matter: Ancient Persia and the Archaeology of Empires.* Oakland CA: University of California Press.

Lanfranchi, G., M. Roaf, and R. Rollinger (Eds.). 2003. *Continuity of Empire (?): Assyria, Media, Persia.* Padova : S.a.r.g.o.n. Editrice e Libreria.

Lanfranchi, G. 2003. "The Assyrian Expansion in the Zagros and the Local Ruling Elites." In Lanfranchi et al. (Eds.), *Continuity of Empire (?)Assyria, Media, Persia:* 79-118. Padova: S.a.r.g.o.n. Editrice E Libreria.

Leichty, E. 2011.*The Royal Inscriptions of Esarhaddon, King of Assyria (680-669 BC)* Royal Inscriptions of the Neo-Assyrian Period 4. Winona Lake, IN: Eisenbrauns.

Levine, L. D. 1972. *Two Neo-Assyrian Stelae from Iran.* Toronto: Royal Ontario Museum .

Levine, L. D. 1973. Geographical Studies in the Neo-Assyrian Zagros. *Iran* 11: 127.

Levine, L.D. 1987. "The Iron Age." In Hole, F. (Ed.), *The Archaeology of Western Iran. Settlement and Society from Prehistory to the Islamic Conquest.* Washington DC: Smithsonian Institution.

Liverani, M. 1995. "The Medes at Esarhaddon's Court." *Journal of Cuneiform Studies* 47: 57-62.

Liverani, M. 2003. "The Rise and Fall of Media." In Lanfranchi et al. (Eds.), *Continuity of Empire (?)Assyria, Media, Persia:* 1-12. Padova: S.a.r.g.o.n. Editrice E Libreria.

Luukko, M. 2013. *The Correspondence of Tiglath-Pileser III and Sargon II from Calah/Nimrud* (State Archives of Assyria, 19). Helsinki: Helsinki University Press.

Magee, P. 2001. "Excavations at the Iron Age Settlement of Muweilah 1997-2000." *Proceedings of the Seminar for Arabian Studies* 31:115-130.

Majizadeh, Y. 2000. "Excavations at Ozbaki: First Preliminary Report 1998." *Iranian Journal of Archaeology and History* 13: 57-81

Majizadeh, Y. 2001. "Excavations At Ozbaki: Second Preliminary Report 1999." *Iranian Journal of Archaeology and History* 14: 38-49.

Mcintosh, S.Keech. 1999. "Pathways to Complexity: An African Perspective." In *Beyond Chiefdoms: Pathways to Complexity in Africa.* Cambridge: Cambridge University Press.

Medveskaya, I.N. 1992. "The question of the identification of 8th-7th century Median sites and the formation of the Iranian architectural tradition," *Archaologische Mitteilungen aus Iran* 25: 73-79.

Naseri, R., M. Malekzadeh, and A. Naseri. 2016. Gūnespān: A Late Iron Age Site in the Median Heartland. *Iranica Antiqua* 51: 103-139.

Parpola, S. 2003. "Sakas, India Gobryas and the Median Royal Court." In Lanfranchi et al. (Eds.), *Continuity of Empire (?)Assyria, Media, Persia:* 339-350. Padova: S.a.r.g.o.n. Editrice E Libreria.

Radner, K. 2003. "An Assyrian View on the Medes." In Lanfranchi et al. (Eds.), *Continuity of Empire (?)Assyria, Media, Persia:* 119-130. Padova: S.a.r.g.o.n. Editrice E Libreria.

Radner, K. 2013. Assyria and the Medes. In D. Potts (Ed.) *The Oxford Handbook of Ancient Iran.* Oxford: Oxford University Press. DOI: 10.1093/oxfordhb/9780199733309.013.0032

Rollinger R. 2003. The Western Expansion of the Median "Empire" In Lanfranchi et al. (Eds.), *Continuity of Empire (?)Assyria, Media, Persia:* 321-326. Padova: S.a.r.g.o.n. Editrice E Libreria.

Rossi, A. 2010. "Elusive Identities in Pre-Achaemenid Iran: The Medes and the Median Language." In C.G. Cereti (Ed.), *Iranian Identity in the Course of History:* 289-330. Rome: Istituto Italiano per l'Africa e L'Oriente.

Root, M. 1997. *The King and Kingship in Achaemenid Art.* Leiden: E.J. Brill, 1979.

Scurlock, J. 2012 "Getting Smashed at the Victory Celebration, or What Happened to Esarhaddon's So-called Vassal Treaties and Why." In N. May (Ed.) *Iconoclasm and Text Destruction in the Ancient Near East and Beyond:* 175-186. Chicago: University of Chicago Press.

Scott, J. C. 2010. *The Art of Not Being Governed: An Anarchist History of Upland Southeast Asia* (Yale Agrarian Studies Series). New Haven: Yale University Press.

Starr, I. 1990. *Queries to the Sungod: Divination and Politics in Sargonid Assyria (State Archives of Assyria, 4).* Helsinki: Helsinki University Press.

Stronach, D., H. Thrane, C. Goff, and A. Farahani. 2010. "Erebuni 2008–2010." *Aramazd: Armenian Journal of Near Eastern Studies* 5(2): 98–133.

Stronach, D. 2003. "Independent Media, Archaeological Notes from the Homeland." In Lanfranchi et al. (Eds.), *Continuity of Empire (?)Assyria, Media, Persia:* 233-248 . Padova: S.a.r.g.o.n. Editrice E Libreria.

Stronach, D. and M. Roaf. 2008. *Nush-i Jan I: The Major Buildings of the Median Settlement.* London: British Institute of Persian Studies.

Tadmor H. and S. Yamada. 2011. *The Royal Inscriptions of Tiglath-Pileser III (744-727 BC) and Shalmaneser V (726-722 BC), Kings of Assyria.* Royal Inscriptions of the Neo-Assyrian Period 1. Winona Lake, IN: Eisenbrauns.

Tuplin, C. 2004. "Medes in Media, Mesopotamia, and Anatolia: Empire, Hegemony, Domination or Illusion?" *Ancient West & East* 3 (2): 223-251.

Venturi, R. 1977. "Complexity and Contradiction in Architecture." New York: Museum of Modern Art,.

Waters, M. 2011. "Notes on the Medes and their "Empire" from JER 25:25 to HDT 1.134" In G. Frame (Ed.), *A Common Cultural Heritage: Studies on Mesopotamia and the Biblical World in Honor of Barry L. Eichler:* 243-253. Bethesda, Md.: CDL Press.

Witzel, M. 2013. "Iranian Migration." In D. Potts (Ed.) *The Oxford Handbook of Ancient Iran online.* DOI: 10.1093/oxfordhb/9780199733309.013.0050.

Young, T. C. Jr. 1967. "The Iranian Migration into the Zagros." *Iran* 5: 11-34.

Young, T. C. Jr. 1975. "An Archaeological Survey of the Kangavar Valley." In F. Bagherzadeh (ed.) *Proceedings of the Third Annual Symposium on Archaeological Research in Iran:* 23-30, Tehran.

Zadok, R. 2002. "The Ethno-Linguistic Character of Northwestern Iran and Kurdistan in the Neo-Assyrian Period." *Iran* 40: 89-151.

THE ACHAEMENID EMPIRE
Lloyd Llewellyn-Jones

In 2005 the British Museum in London produced a major exhibition on the history and culture of the first Persian empire, that ruled by the Achaemenid dynasty (Curtis and Tallis 2005; Curtis and Simpson 2010). Despite boasting such luminaries as Cyrus the Great, Darius the Great and Xerxes, the exhibition was entitled "Forgotten Empire" in an attempt to emphasize the notion that while the Achaemenid empire was the largest and most influential empire in the pre-Alexander period – a true world empire in fact – its impact on later history and scholarship has been (and continues to be) seriously misunderstood and undervalued.

Before the nineteenth century, the popular image of the first Persian Empire, that ruled by the Achaemenid dynasty, was predominantly drawn from two diverse sources: the Hebrew Bible (or "Old Testament") and the works of Classical Greek and Roman authors (Olmstead 1948; Allen 2005a). By and large, the Hebrew Bible texts championed the Persians, because it was the Great Kings of Persia who freed the Jews from their Babylonian exile and allowed them to return home to build a new (second) temple in Jerusalem on the site of Solomon's original place of worship (Yamauchi 1990). The Classical authors, however, tended to depict Persia in a negative light. Great Kings are shown as lustful, capricious, and mad tyrants, and the Persian empire was regarded as an oppressive challenge to the Greek love of Freedom. The Persians were crafted by the Greeks as the barbarian "Other": cowardly, scheming, effeminate, vindictive, and dishonorable.

The "authentic voice" of ancient Persia has been either ignored or mistreated and we engage with the ancient Persians as either the champions of the Hebrew nation (the biblical slant), or the oppressors of the free world (the Classical tradition). Moreover, today it is difficult to comprehend that the land we now call Iran once lay at the heart of a magnificent empire; its importance as an ancient world power and a cultural axis has been almost completely eclipsed by the Western media's obsession with the changes that have taken place within Iran since the Islamic revolution of 1978/1979.

Thus, in the West, ancient Persia is best remembered for its war with Greece and its later invasion and ultimate defeat by Alexander of Macedon. For the Persians themselves, the Greco-Persian Wars were little more than tiresome border skirmishes which took place over 2,000 miles from the heart of the empire in Iran (Llewellyn-Jones & Robson 2010). Yet so much of our understanding of Persian history is filtered through ancient Greek sources, especially the influential "histories" of Herodotus, Xenophon, Arrian, Plutarch and Ctesias of Cnidus, that we find it difficult to separate the Greek fabrication of Persian history and culture from its reality. The Greek perspective on the history and nature of the Achaemenid empire pits Greek freedom and democracy against "Oriental" (i.e. Persian) tyranny and despotism.

The image propounded in the ancient Greek sources still dominates in modern popular Western culture. Several recent Hollywood movies exemplify the trend in which the Persian empire is only viewed as a negative stereotype of "Otherness." Oliver Stone's movie *Alexander* (2004) displays all the familiar Orientalist notions about the inferiority and picturesqueness of Eastern societies. So much so, indeed, that in terms of its portrayal of East–West relationships, *Alexander* has to be seen as a stale cultural statement and a worn-out reflection of the continuing Western preoccupation with an imaginary exotic Orient. More interesting, however, is *300*, Zack Snyder's 2007 film version of the graphic novel by Frank Miller and its 2014 prequel, *300: Rise of an Empire*. Snyder's take on the Thermopylae story and the slaughter of the 300 Spartans at the hands of the Persian army and his version of the Battle of Salamis are fantasies; they are created as the battles would have looked in the minds of the Greeks as they mythologize the stories of the sacrifice of the Greeks in their struggle for "freedom." This is not history, and the "Persians" of the films are a bizarre blend of sadomasochistic, effeminate, ninja-like cartoon villains (as equally bizarre in their way as are the Spartans' oiled and pumped-up porn-star bodies). However, *300* and *300: Rise of an Empire* do nothing to promote the quest to locate and understand the real Persian empire.

However, there is a very different version of Persian history and culture emerging from the decipherment of the cuneiform language known as Old Persian. Finally, the Achaemenid monarchs are able to speak for themselves for the first time since antiquity. The Old Persian inscriptions, although somewhat repetitive in ideological statements, nonetheless proclaim the heroic and militaristic qualities of the kings of Persia and place their reigns within the shadow of Ahuramazda, the great god of the ancient Iranians. Other cuneiform texts in Babylonian, Elamite, and Akkadian strengthen our knowledge of Persian history, and Egypt has also offered up information on Persian rule in hieroglyphic and demotic texts (Kuhrt 2007).

The first Persian Empire, created and maintained by the Great Kings of the Achaemenid dynasty, was a global empire of vast proportions. Before the conquests of Alexander of Macedon, the Achaemenid empire was the largest empire the world had ever seen, stretching from Libya to Pakistan. The period 559-465 BCE saw the rapid expansion of the empire under a series of conquering-kings, and thereafter the empire matured and continued to flourish until its conquest by Macedon (Briant 2002; Brosius 2006). The Achaemenids divided their vast empire into numerous satrapies to ensure efficient administration and the ability to levy taxes and tribute. Communication and trade was facilitated through excellent road systems. While the Persians adopted a tolerant position towards their conquered peoples, they could also be ruthless overlords, quelling opposition with startling swiftness and brutality.

The Achaemenid Empire was a true world empire. Throughout its 230-year history, it was in a constant state of flux: provinces were added through force or coercion and were lost from Persian control through wars, rebellions and uprisings. Yet in spite of revolts, succession crises and regicide, the vast empire held together as a coherent unit for 230 years. It showed no signs of internal weakness or stagnation at the time the last Achaemenid king, Darius III, lost his throne to Alexander of Macedon.

Establishing Empire: Cyrus of Anshan and the first Persian Kings

Cyrus (Old Persian "Kuruš") was born around 600 BCE, the son of Cambyses I, in a small southwestern Iranian kingdom known in western texts as Persia (Greek "Persis"), located in the modern province of Fars. The first king of the Persian dynasty had been Teispes, and he and his royal successors, including Cyrus, frequently styled themselves kings of Anshan, an area clinging to the foothills of the Zagros Mountains once ruled by the powerful and culturally sophisticated Elamites (Stronach 1997b). It would seem that the earliest Persian monarchs regarded themselves as the rulers of Elamite lands and perhaps even saw themselves as the natural inheritors of Elamite culture (which remained highly influential in Persia throughout the Achaemenid period in terms of language, administration, and court organization). The archaeology of early Fars (1150-650 BCE) shows a steady decline in populated settlements, but from the latter half of the seventh century BCE, during the reigns of the early Persian kings (ca. 650-559 BCE), evidence suggests that a massive resettlement of the area had taken place (Potts 1999; 2010; 2011). This suggests a growth in stability in the area, but knowledge of this period is scanty and nothing can be said about early Persian history with security.

When Cyrus II ascended to the throne of Persia there were four major empires in the Near East: Egypt, Babylonia, Lydia, and Media. Cyrus was to have an impact on each of them. During the reign of Cambyses I, if we follow the account offered by the Greek historian Herodotus (*Histories* 1. 101) the Persians were one of several Iranian tribes, each of which were vassals to the Medes, whose powerful kingdom was ever-growing in the north of Iran to the point where Median military aggression was focused on the wealthy area of Babylonia. The city of Babylon was saved from attack when in 550/49 BCE, some nine years after becoming king, Cyrus II, supported by a coalition of south Iranian tribes, marched north to attack the Median king, Astyages. The Greek accounts of Herodotus and Ctesias of Cnidus interpret Cyrus's action as a bid to break the yoke of Media, and they tie together the account of Cyrus's defeat of Astyages with tales of Cyrus's youth and character.

The Birth of Cyrus: Legend or Fact?

Legends of Cyrus the Great were no doubt common in the rich storytelling tradition of ancient Iran and in the Achaemenid period itself people probably told stories of the birth, reign, and greatness of their first imperial monarch. Herodotus reports that he knew of at least three legends about Cyrus's birth and upbringing, although he chooses to cite in full one whereby Cyrus's father had been married to Astyages's daughter, Mandane (*Histories* 1.95-130). Following the marriage, Astyages was plagued with nightmares in which he saw that his future grandson would take over his throne. When Mandane gave birth to her son, Astyages ordered it to be a slain, but one of his generals, Hapargus, smuggled the infant to safety in the countryside where he was raised by a herdsman. The child Cyrus grew to maturity and developed into an outstanding youth, overshadowing his friends and showing royal qualities of leadership until news of his kingly attributes reached Astyages, who invited Cyrus to court. Upon seeing the boy, the king immediately recognized his grandson and allowed him to return home to Persia to his noble parents. Cyrus began to play with the idea of seizing power from Astyages. He persuaded a number of the Persian tribes to side with him to throw off the yoke of Astyages and the Medes.

An alternative story tells of how the child Cyrus survived in the wild reared by a wild dog. Another version says that Cyrus was not related to Astyages at all, and yet another variation names Cyrus's father as Atradates, a thief, and his mother as Argoste, a goatherd.

These stories form part of the Founding Legends of Cyrus the Great, and follow a much older Near Eastern storytelling tradition of the humble birth of great leaders. King Sargon of Akkad and the Hebrew leader Moses share similar Founding Legends with Cyrus and all take their inspiration from the same forms of popular storytelling or political propaganda.

The conflict between Astyages and Cyrus can be considered either a piece of romantic fiction or the first documented fact in Achaemenid history. Certainly the war is attested in several Greek texts and other Near Eastern sources. A brief account of the conflict is given in contemporary inscriptions of the last Babylonian king – as the "Nabonidus Chronicle" (ca. 550/49 BC) recalls:

> [Astyages] mustered his troops and ...[m]arched on king Cyrus of Anshan ... The army of Astyages revolted against him, captured him, and deliv[ered] him to Cyrus. Cyrus <marched> on Ecbatana, the royal residence, and took to Anshan the silver, gold, goods, [and] valuables...

Cyrus's Conquests

Following the overthrow of the Medes and the sack of Ecbatana, Cyrus turned his attention towards northern Media, including the ancient kingdom of Urartu in the area of Lake Van. The chronology of this period is hazy, but it is possible that Cyrus also occupied Elam and claimed possession of Susa. Ctesias suggests that Cyrus also undertook a campaign in Bactria, although Herodotus passes off the Bactrian war as a minor skirmish (*Histories* 1.153).

More well-known is the Persian campaign against the wealthy and powerful kingdom of Lydia in Asia Minor (*Histories* 1.69-91). The Lydian king, Croesus, had brought the cities of Ionia under his rule and his capital, Sardis, benefited from extensive trade routes with Mesopotamia. Only Greek sources record the fall of Lydia, but its sack meant that Cyrus was able to take other important cities along the Ionian coast, which were placed under the control of Persian governors and administrators.

By 540 Cyrus was ready to march on Babylon and moved his army into Mesopotamia, marching first on Opis and then on Sippar. He entered into Babylon on 29 October 539, having already taken king Nabonidus prisoner. Apparently meeting no military resistance, Cyrus appointed his son, Cambyses, as the city's regent, although he maintained the status quo by allowing Babylonian officials to continue in their governmental and religious offices: he appointed a Babylonian named Ugbaru as the city governor.

In the years following the conquest of Babylonia (538-30 BCE) Cyrus was occupied gaining a truly international empire: Aria, Parthia, Sogdinan, and Margiana fell to him on the eastern front, while near the River Jaxartes he founded a city which the Greeks called Cyropolis. In the west, Cilicia, Syria, and Palestine came under Cyrus' rule and while he never held Egypt, he had clearly marked it out for conquest.

In 530 BCE Cyrus died on the battlefield in a war against the Massagetae. His legacy cannot be overemphasized: he swiftly founded a world empire of great cultural diversity. The Babylonian priests recognized him as Marduk's representative, the Jews saw him as God's anointed, and the Greeks regarded him as a supreme statesman and beneficent ruler, while among modern Iranians, Cyrus is a cult figure and his tomb is still a place of veneration for millions of people.

The Cyrus Cylinder: The First Bill of Human Rights?

The Cyrus Cylinder is a clay barrel-shaped foundation deposit written in Akkadian. It was found in excavations at Babylon in 1879 near the sanctuary of the god Marduk and was presumably composed on Cyrus' orders. The whole document is written from a Babylonian point of view in traditional Babylonian terms but was perhaps inspired by the inscriptions of the Assyrian king Ashurbanipal. As a piece of imperial propaganda, the Cylinder attempts to legitimize Cyrus's conquest of Babylon: it emphasizes how the wickedness of Nabonidus has driven the gods out of the city, while the Babylonians themselves are forced into heavy labor for his vainglorious building programme. Marduk looks down from heaven for a champion, and finds him in Cyrus who is presented as the city's savior: he returns order to Babylon, brings the corvée to an end, and allows deported peoples to return to their lands; he worships the gods piously and correctly:

> "Marduk, the great lord, was well pleased with my deeds and sent friendly blessings to myself, Cyrus, the king who worships him, to Cambyses, my son..., as well as to all my troops, and we all praised his great godhead."
>
> Cyrus "signs" himself:
>
> "King of the world, great king, legitimate king, king of Babylon, king of Sumer and Akkad, king of the four rims of the earth...descendant of Teispes... of a family which always exercised kingship, whose rule [the gods]... love."

Because of its references to the restoration of deported peoples, the Cylinder has been referred to as a bill of human rights; many modern Iranians take pride in the claim that Cyrus was a humanitarian. The image is enhanced by the Jewish praise for Cyrus's deeds which are found in the prophecies of Isaiah in the Hebrew Bible, for it was Cyrus who allowed the Jews to return from their Babylonian exile back to their homeland. As such, he is the only gentile to receive the honor of the title "Messiah" ("Lord's Anointed"): "Thus says the Lord to His anointed, to Cyrus, whose right hand I have held to subdue nations before him and loose the armor of kings, to open before him the double doors, so that the gates will not be shut" (Isaiah 45.1).

But the concept of "human rights" would have been completely alien to Cyrus and his contemporaries. In fact the Cylinder says nothing of human rights, and while it is true that the Jews were allowed to return home, other peoples did not fare so well under Cyrus: the citizens of Opis were massacred *en masse*, and, following the fall of Lydia, the population was deported to Nippur in Babylonia, where a community of Lydians is later attested.

Cyrus was clearly a pragmatic ruler. This is demonstrated in his appropriation of the worship of local gods. There is no acknowledgement in the Cylinder that Cyrus himself worshipped the Iranian god Ahuramazda. In the Akkadian text he is the tool of Marduk, just as in the Hebrew Bible he is presented as the servant of the God of the Jews.

Pasargadae: Cyrus's Paradise

Pasargadae (Old Persian Pâthragâda) in modern Fars was chosen by Cyrus as the site for his palace, probably because he had tribal connections to the area: two small stone structures (built by Lydian stonemasons) incorporating a residential area and an *apadana* or columned throne hall were built on his orders (Stronach 1978; 1997a; Matheson 1972). The walls of the palace were decorated with painted stone reliefs inspired by earlier Assyrian models. One well-preserved male figure (a semi-divine being) borrows motifs from all over the empire: an Elamite garment, Assyrian-style wings, and an Egyptian crown.

Pasargadae was planted with a formal garden. Cyrus incorporated a myriad of irrigation channels in the land surrounding the palace to insure his gardens were well watered. The result was nothing short of a desert paradise, the modern word being derived from the Persian word for a garden – *pairidaêza* (Greek *paradeisos*). At the edge of his garden, not far from the palace, Cyrus erected his simple tomb: a gabled building on a simple platform, inspired by Lydian funerary monuments.

Cambyses II: A Mad King?

Prince Cambyses had been trained for the succession by his father (he had been appointed governor of Babylon), and upon Cyrus's death he ascended peacefully to the throne. A Babylonian text dated 31 August 530 BCE names Cambyses as "king of Babylon, king of lands." At his accession Cambyses appointed his younger brother, Bardiya (known in Greek texts variously as Smerdis, Tanaoxares, or Tanyoxarkes), as a governor of Media (or, as some sources suggest, Bactria).

Cambyses's greatest achievement as king of Persia (530-522 BCE) was the conquest of Egypt in 525 BCE, following the death of the pharaoh Amasis, whose heir was defeated in battle at Pelusium. Cambyses was crowned pharaoh according to ancient rites at Memphis with the throne-name Mesuti-Re. Following the conquest of Egypt, the neighboring countries of Libya and Cyrene offered submission to the Persian forces. Cambyses marched south, down the Nile, stationing a Jewish garrison on the island of Elephantine near Aswan to protect Persian interests in the south, before advancing and conquering at least a part of Nubia.

Greek sources, Herodotus in particular, tend to portray Cambyses as a mad despot, tyrannically oppressing and even murdering his subjects, committing unnatural sexual acts, and impiously debasing the religious traditions of his conquered nations. He is accused of destroying Egyptian temples and even slaughtering the sacred Apis bull, the animal incarnation of the god Ptah. Much of this slander emanates from the accounts of Egyptian priests who were opposed to Cambyses's attempts to reduce their power and wealth.

Archaeological evidence from Egypt suggests that Cambyses adopted a policy of religious tolerance – inscriptions from the Serapeum in Memphis (524 BCE) confirm that he honored the death of a sacred bull with due rites and rituals. Like Cyrus in Babylon, Cambyses co-opted the support of Egyptian nobles to maintain his sovereignty. One text celebrates the reverence shown by Cambyses to the goddess Neith:

> Cambyses came to Sais... to the temple of Neith. He touched the ground before her very great majesty as every king had done, he organized a great feast... for Neith... That His Majesty did because I had caused him to know the importance of her majesty; for she is the mother of Re himself. (Brosius 2000)

Other similar texts confirm that Cambyses II was sensitive to Egypt's religious and cultural traditions and that Herodotus's image of him as a mad autocrat is unwarranted.

Darius's Court Coup

Cambyses's death, which occurred in Egypt in the summer of 522 BCE, is shrouded in mystery: he may have died naturally, or from a wound, or he might have committed suicide. According to the account Darius created in his Bisitun Inscription, Cambyses had secretly killed his brother Bardiya, but a *magus* (Median priest) named Gaumata claimed to be prince Bardiya and seized the throne. Cambyses, Darius maintained, killed himself. For six months the pretender Gaumata ruled Persia as Bardiya; no one was prepared to challenge him. The one detail that makes Darius's account (followed by Herodotus a century later) particularly suspect- almost farcical- is his claim that Gaumata looked exactly like Bardiya, to such an extent that even his harem of wives could not tell him apart from the murdered prince (Balcer 1987).

Events came to a head when Darius, son of Hystapses, the governor of Parthia, with six other Persian nobles conspired together to oust Gaumata from the throne. In a palace coup of 29 September 522 BCE, the impostor was slain and Darius ascended to the Persian throne.

High above the Royal Road near Ecbatana in north Iran, carved deep into the rock face of Mount Bisitun (Old Persian "Bagastāna," "Place of the Gods") towers Darius the Great's monument to kingship: his account of his accession to the throne and its immediate aftermath. Almost 66m below, on the mountain slope, are the remains of Sikayuvatish, the Median fortress where Gaumata was killed by Darius and the other six co-conspirators.

The inscription that tells the dramatic (if distorted) story of Darius's accession is written in three cuneiform languages, Elamite, Babylonian, and Old Persian, in regular columns carved into the rock face. A huge raised relief (probably once painted) dominates the surface of the stone; it can be read as a separate account of the literary texts that border it. The relief shows Darius, richly bearded and wearing a crown, standing at the head of a line of rebellious kings, each one fettered to the next by a rope, their hands tied behind their backs; at the end of the line, and added at a later date, is the figure of Skunkha, the rebel from Scythia, wearing a distinctive pointed cap. Darius is depicted on a larger scale than the other figures on the relief and he places his left foot upon the belly of the prostrate figure of Gaumata who lifts his arms in supplication. In his left hand Darius clutches a bow, a symbol of his military authority, which is echoed by the presence of two armed guards standing to his rear. Darius's right hand is raised in adoration at the figure in the winged disk at the centre of the scene: this is probably Ahuramazda, the supreme god of the Persians, who offers Darius the kingship in the form of a ring (Root 1979). Throughout the inscriptions, Darius confirms his devotion to the "Wise Lord" Ahuramazda and lays his success at the will of the god:

> Ahuramazda bestowed the kingdom upon me. Ahuramazda brought me aid until I had held together this kingdom. By the favour of Ahuramazda I hold this kingship.

Darius also cites his genealogy and stresses his right to the throne by claiming a common ancestry with Cyrus the Great, both of whom, he insists, are descended from Achaemenes. But like much else in the Bisitun Inscription, this is propaganda: Darius was not a member of the house of Cyrus and his ancestors, the kings of Anshan; and his succession to the throne had no legitimacy.

It is generally accepted that Darius's account of events is pure fabrication and that it actually serves as a cover-up for the fact that Darius himself had killed Cyrus's rightful successor. To legitimize his claim to the throne he invented a common ancestry between Cyrus and himself – Achaemenes, the eponymous founder of their "shared" dynasty.

Like Bardiya before him, Darius also consolidated his throne by marrying the daughters of Cyrus, Atossa and Artystone, and Parmys the daughter of Bardiya himself. He allied himself to the houses of the six nobles who had aided his bid for the throne by marrying their daughters or giving his female relatives to them in marriage (Brosius 1996). Why would Darius have needed to do this? Darius needed to keep his powerful nobles in check, and what better way to do so than to incorporate them into his family. He gave the six magnates his promise that they would have access to his person for a royal audience at any time, apart from those hours he spent with his women. By intermarrying with the Persian elite, Darius also ensured the expansion of the Achaemenid bloodline.

Not everybody accepted his rule so easily; rebellions broke out across the empire: in Babylon, Media, Armenia, Scythia, and even in Persia (led by a man claiming to be *another* Bardiya). Darius was ruthless in suppressing the revolts and bringing the empire to heel, an act that he accomplished in little more than a year. He captured and executed the rebel leaders and for the rest of his reign was never threatened with an uprising again (Lincoln 2007).

Darius the Administrator and Builder

In 518 BCE, after confirming his hold on the empire, Darius was able to expand its borders as far as the Sind (and possibly the Punjab) in India; in 513 he attempted to conquer the Scythians north of the Black Sea too. In Darius's reign the empire extended from Libya to Bactria. His brilliant administration divided the empire's territories into twenty satrapies (provinces), each governed by a satrap usually drawn from the royal family. Each satrapy was assessed for its wealth and was taxed accordingly in the form of annual tribute, which had to be paid to the central administration. It was Darius who also introduced coinage into the empire. To aid communication and prompt payment of taxes, Darius constructed the royal road from Susa to Sardis and disseminated his royal edicts along it in multiple languages, including Old Persian, a written form of the Persian language created at his behest.

Darius was also concerned with building and engineering projects: in Egypt he was responsible for the creation of a canal between the Nile and the Red Sea, as well as for building temples to Egyptian gods at Hibis. On the temple walls he is depicted in full pharaonic regalia. In the Iranian heartland, Susa, Ecbatana, and Pasargadae were expanded and embellished by Darius and he started the building program at Persepolis.

Darius at Susa

The ancient and celebrated Elamite city of Susa was afforded a new lease of life by Darius's ambitious building programme (Perrot 2010). He chose Susa as his administrative capital because he probably had Elamite ancestry: his mother was probably a woman named Idabama (an Elamite name), who appears frequently in the cuneiform sources of Darius's reign (Llewellyn-Jones 2015). On the acropolis at Susa Darius erected a large palace with an impressive *apadana* (throne hall) where glazed colored brick reliefs showed bodyguards standing in strict formation. Finds from the site include an over-life-size statue (once one of a pair of statues) of Darius probably made in Egypt and brought to Susa to adorn the palace. A foundation inscription from Susa records how Darius enlisted workmen from all over the empire to build and decorate his palace. The text was meant to advertise natural resources and labor at the king's command:

> The cedar timber, this was brought from a mountain named Lebanon. The Assyrian people brought it to Babylon; from Babylon the Carians and the Greeks brought it to Susa... The gold was brought from Lydia and from Bactria, which here was wrought. The precious stone lapis lazuli and carnelian... was brought from Sogdia... Precious turquoise... was brought from Chorasmia... The silver and the ebony were brought from Egypt. The ornamentation with which the wall was adorned, that from Greece was brought. The ivory... was brought from Nubia and from India... The men who wrought the wood, those were Lydians and Egyptians. The men who wrought the baked brick, those were Babylonians. The men who adorned the wall, those were Medes and Egyptians. Darius the King says: At Susa a very excellent work was ordered, a very excellent work was brought to completion.

Persepolis

Rising out of the sands of the Marv Dasht, the citadel of Persepolis (Old Persian *Pârsa*, modern Persian *Takht-e Jamshid*) is one of the great sites of antiquity, and one of the best preserved royal palaces of the ancient Near East (Schmidt 1853, 1957, 1970; Mousavi 2012). Darius the Great began the construction of the palace and ceremonial centre around 515 BCE, and it was greatly added to by Xerxes I who, in an on-site inscription records, "When my father Darius went away from the throne [i.e. died], I became king on his throne by the grace of Ahurmazda. After I became king, I finished what had been done by my father, and I added other works". After Xerxes, Artaxerxes I and each of the successive Achaemenid monarchs added to Persepolis's glory. It was still in the process of being built when, in 330 BCE, Alexander of Macedon burned it to the ground in retaliation, he claimed, for Xerxes's sack of Athens in 480 BCE. The buildings were built of locally quarried stone, although the craftsmen who worked on the site were drawn from all over Persia's vast empire – the 30,000 cuneiform tablets (the so-called Persepolis Fortification and Treasury texts) attest to the presence of different peoples of the empire, all of whom received payments in food stuffs for their labors – all of which was meticulously recorded by palace scribes (Potts 2008).

But what was Persepolis used for? First excavated by Ernst Herzfeld and the Oriental Institute of Chicago in 1931, Persepolis was found to consist of a vast complex of military quarters, treasuries and storerooms, private living quarters, large reception rooms, vast audience halls, and hill-cut royal tombs. Yet Persepolis was not inhabited by the Great King and his court continually: the court moved between Susa, Babylon, and Ecbatana annually, coming to rest at Persepolis, it is assumed, for the festivities of *Nou Rouz* (the spring equinox on March 21) (Llewellyn-Jones 2013; Tuplin 1996). It would seem that Darius planned Persepolis as a showcase of empire, for it was here that ambassadors from all over the Persian world, from Ethiopia to Elam, would congregate each year to offer tribute to the Great King; the sculptors working at the site recorded the scenes of imperial gift-giving in loving detail on the palace stairways: each group of tribute bearers wears "national dress" and brings gifts of precious metals, textiles, foodstuffs, and livestock to the palace. The treasury, a large multi-roomed building, was begun by Darius to safeguard the gold, silver and other costly materials gifted to the Great King as tribute. From the Fortification Texts we know that in 467 BCE, some 1,348 people were employed in the royal treasury.

The palace complex was divided into public and private spaces. Ambassadors, nobles and courtiers would, by and large, find themselves in the formal spaces, the Outer Courts, of the palace such as the Apadana, or throne room, a vast 20-meter high pillared hall in which the Great King held audience and received the obeisance of his court, or the Hall of a Hundred Columns – a huge indoor banqueting room built by Xerxes. Enormous courtyards were able to accommodate thousands of dignitaries and guards as they stood waiting to see the king, while impressive stairways and entrance gates such as Xerxes's Gate of All Lands, guarded by colossal sculpted human-headed winged bulls.

Courtiers and servants with close connections to the Great King, like his advisers and eunuchs, as well as members of the royal family, made up the Inner Court and they occupied living spaces at the rear of the palace complex, away from the eyes of strangers. A series of small banqueting rooms, council chambers, and terraces have been identified at Persepolis, and it is also possible to locate the private suites of the Great King – including his bedroom and bathroom. At the far end of the private wing of palaces is a large L-shaped building, which possibly served as the residential quarters of the royal harem – some of the wives, children, and even royal siblings were no doubt housed here when the king was in residence. One large section of this block- with its own pleasant courtyard – may have been occupied by the family as a group for social events.

Despite its scale, it is clear that the whole court could not have lived on the Persepolis terrace itself. The number of servants needed to look after the needs of the immediate members of the royal family would have run into huge figures alone, while the Great King himself was said to have had no less than 360 royal concubines, all of whom required accommodation. So where did the majority of people at court reside? There is archaeological evidence for a series of small palace structures surrounding the main palace platform, but even these would accommodate only a few hundred people at most. The majority of the court was housed in tented accommodation scattered around Persepolis for several miles, for the Persian court was, by nature, peripatetic and frequently lived out of huge and ornate tents. This would explain how so vast an infrastructure as the Persian court could leave so little trace in the archaeology of the landscape.

Of all the iconographic tropes found within the palace complex, the scene of a lion clinging onto and biting the back-quarters of a bucking bull is the most commonly found image at Persepolis. It is located in conspicuous spaces – such as on the stairways leading up to the Apadana of Darius - and is, without doubt, one of the most powerful and captivating images in Achaemenid art. But what does it mean?

It is possible that the motif confirms the message that even the strong bull cannot overcome the strength of the lion – the lord of beasts. In other words, it would be futile for any country within the empire to challenge the supremacy of the Great King. Instead they should offer him regular homage in the form of tribute and not arouse his hostility or anger.

On the other hand, some scholars interpret the motif as an astrological symbol, pointing to the constellation of Taurus giving way to that of Leo, thereby indicating the Spring Equinox and the celebration of *Now Rowz*, when Persepolis was used by the King and court for the New Year Festivities.

From Darius to Xerxes

Late in his reign Darius came into contact with the Greeks, and while he may have had ambitions to incorporate Greece into the empire and was certainly keen to punish Athens for its interference in Persian affairs, Herodotus's account of Greco-Persian tensions probably exaggerates the Persian response to the Greek resistance. Before he could launch a Greek campaign Darius died in the winter of 486 BCE and was buried in a tomb at Naqsh-i Rustam, near Persepolis. It was left to Xerxes to punish the Greeks.

Xerxes (486-465 BCE; Old Persian *Xšayāršā*) was the son of Darius I and Atossa, daughter of Cyrus the Great. Because the Persians followed no laws of primogeniture, he was appointed as Crown Prince by Darius despite not being the king's eldest son. Xerxes acknowledged this in an inscription he had carved at Persepolis: "Says Xerxes the king: other sons of Darius there were, (but) this was Ahumramazda's desire – Darius my father made me the greatest after himself."

Before his accession to the throne, Darius already had a harem of wives. His first-born son, Artobazanes, was one of three children born to Darius by the (unnamed) daughter of Gobryas, and hence from one of Persia's leading noble families. A reason for Darius's championship of Xerxes as heir can be found in the idea that had Darius promoted Artabazanes to the throne, then Gobryas's bloodline would have been greatly empowered and the Achaemenid branch of the family would have been weakened. Yet there is another aspect to the demotion of Artobazanes and the promotion of the younger son. Xerxes was born after Darius had ascended the throne, which perhaps gave him a better claim to the kingship. Moreover, as the son of Atossa and therefore the grandson of Cyrus the Great, Xerxes represented the physical embodiment of Darius's propaganda strategy played out in the Bisitun Inscription of uniting his bloodline with that of Cyrus. Herodotus, however, credits Xerxes's rise to the throne simply to the fact that "Atossa had all the power" (*Histories* 7.3) and that she fought against rival claimants to the throne. The struggles in which rival wives pushed their sons forward to gain the position of Crown Prince or King demonstrates the importance of the harem as a political institution in the Achaemenid court (Llewellyn-Jones 2013).

Xerxes took control of the throne around October 485 BCE, and in all essentials, he continued in his father's policies, although it must be noted that knowledge of Xerxes's reign is almost totally confined to the western periphery of the empire, due to the Greek sources. Moreover, evidence for the events of the latter years of his reign is sparse and mainly conjectural. Because of his aggressive policy towards the Greek lands, Classical sources depict Xerxes as a hubristic megalomaniac, but this is probably very far from the truth.

We know very little of his family life, save that he took as his chief queen a noblewoman named Amastris (her reputation among Greek historians suffered as much as that of her husband). Her father, Otanes, had been one of the nobles who had aided Darius. Accordingly, his family was honored with a political marriage: Otanes married a sister of Darius, who gave birth to Amestris, who was therefore Xerxes's cousin. She bore Xerxes at least three children: Artaxerxes (I), Darius, and Achaemenes.

A Troubled Empire

Xerxes's first task was coping with a rebellion in Egypt, which had begun just before Darius's death (Herodotus *Histories* 7.1). He appointed his brother Achaemenes as satrap of Egypt, a policy frequently adopted by the Achaemenid kings whereby close family members held important satrapal positions, so much so that the running of the empire became a family concern (Tuplin 1987).

In 481 BCE Babylonia erupted in revolt, led by a pretender "king" named Bêl-shimmani. Again Xerxes drew on his close relatives for aid: the rebels were subdued by Megabyzus, Xerxes's cousin and son-in-law (he was married to Xerxes's daughter Amytis). Afterwards Megabyzus became one of the supreme commanders during Xerxes's campaign against Greece. Xerxes responded to the revolt by dividing the satrapy of Babylonia into two: "Babylonia," embracing all of modern Iraq and Syria and "Beyond the River," including Syria-Palestine and lands west of the Euphrates (Dandamanev 1989).

One aim, in which Xerxes ultimately failed, was to force the mainland Greeks to acknowledge Persian power. From the perspective of Persia's long-term Aegean policy, extending a measure of control to European Greece was logical and the importance of this Persian expansion is signaled by the fact that Xerxes himself led the expedition to try to bring the Greeks under Persian control.

Xerxes punishes Babylon

As Xerxes was marching his army into Greece in 480 BCE, a second revolt in Babylonia broke out led by "king" Šamaš-eriba. The renewed unrest in Babylon would explain Xerxes's rapid departure from Greece. His rapid intervention in Babylonia was successful, since the province did not revolt again. However, according to Arrian (*Anabasis* 7.17.2), Xerxes punished the city by razing the temple of Marduk to the ground and removing the god's statue from the city. Is there any truth to this? Certainly, Babylonian documents from Darius's period are numerous, but from Xerxes's reign there are very few dated sources. The royal titles found in Babylon also show a demotion in status of the city in the titulary of the King from "Xerxes, King of Babylon, King of Lands" in year 3 to just "Xerxes, King of Lands" in year 5. But there is no archaeological evidence to suggest that Xerxes destroyed Babylon's temples. Babylonia was not treated with kindness after two revolts, but exactly what form Xerxes's punishment took we do not know; its sanctuaries and cults suffered no noticeable decline and the New Year Festivals of Marduk went uninterrupted.

Xerxes in the Hebrew Bible

The Hebrew Bible's Book of Esther is set in the royal court of Susa, and follows the exploits of the Jewish maiden Esther who enters, as a concubine, into the harem of King Ahasuerus – to be identified as Xerxes - whom she eventually marries. She uses her prestigious rank to secure the safety of the Jews from annihilation by the courtier Haman. Court intrigues form the background to the story, which is packed with incidental detail about Persian court life and palace protocol. Why is the Book of Esther so *au fait* with Persian law, custom, and language? It is generally held that Esther was composed in the Achaemenid era, and that its author was very familiar with Persian institutions. The style of Esther indicates a date of composition of approximately 400 BCE, only a few decades after the reign of Xerxes. There are a considerable number of Persian and Aramaic words and idioms used in the text, although there are no Greek words used at all, a fact that clearly points to a pre-Hellenistic date for its composition (Llewellyn-Jones & Robson 2010).

Xerxes's Death to Darius II

In August 465 BCE, Xerxes and his crown prince, Darius, were murdered in a court coup. The events are obscure, but the plot seems to have been hatched by another of Xerxes's sons, Artaxerxes, in cahoots with some powerful eunuchs. Certainly, when he was crowned the next king, Artaxerxes I posed as the avenger of his father and brother by executing the supposed eunuch assassins publicly.

Upon Artaxerxes's succession to the throne, and taking advantage of the chaos surrounding Xerxes's murder, Egypt broke away from Persian rule through an uprising led by an Egyptian dynast from the Western Delta named Inarus. We are dependent completely upon Greek sources for a narrative of the events of the revolt and so we cannot say with confidence how the Persians regarded the uprising or precisely how they managed its impact. But certainly for five years beginning in 460/59 BCE, Inarus successfully drove the Persians out of the Nile Delta and captured the capital city, Memphis. But Persian forces focused on Egypt and by 451 BCE the rebellion was brought to an end with the execution of Inarus. The campaign's success can be attributed to Megabuzus, a princely general who became something of a legend in his own lifetime and whose popularity and charisma was, clearly, seen as a threat by Artaxerxes who, according to some accounts, had him exiled.

Artaxerxes brokered a peace with Athens, the most troublesome of the Greek city-states. The so-called Peace of Callias was agreed on certain terms: the Greek cities of Asia Minor gained their autonomy on condition that the Athenians would make no further forays into the Great King's realm. However, the date and terms and even the historicity of the Peace are all questioned by scholars, and the reality of any form of treaty between Athens and Persia remains open to debate. Similarly, Artaxerxes's involvement with the resettlement of the Jews and the reconstruction of the Temple in Jerusalem is open to debate too. The biblical books of Ezra and Nehemiah suggest that Artaxerxes was instrumental in this move, but the accounts may be ahistorical.

After a forty-five-year reign (465-424 BCE), Artaxerxes I died and the throne passed smoothly to his son Xerxes II whose reign lasted only 45 days before he was murdered in a court coup. He was succeeded by a half-brother, Ochus, who ascended to the throne and took the name of Darius II. He took as his principal wife his half-sister, Parysatis, who proved to be a formidable presence at court and in the fortunes of the dynasty.

The reign of Darius II was conspicuous for frequent revolts, led partly by satraps who had acquired a power base in regions where their families had ruled for generations. The Greek historian Ctesias mentions a revolt by Darius's full brother, Arsites, assisted by Artyphios, son of the satrap Megabyzus, who had mounted a revolt during Artaxerxes I's reign. The revolt of the satrap Pissouthnes at Sardis was crushed, probably in 422 BCE, by Tissaphernes, who bribed Pissouthnes's Greek mercenary troops to abandon their commander. The Paphlagonian eunuch Artoxares, who had once helped Darius II to become king, also attempted a coup at an uncertain date. In addition, Ctesias's novella-like tale of the insubordination of the nobleman Teritouchmes, married to a daughter of Darius II, may well mask a more serious threat to the throne. There is evidence of trouble in Egypt in 410 BCE, a prelude to a successful revolt in 404 BCE while, in the heart of the Empire, the crushing of a Median revolt was followed by a campaign against the Cadusii.

Far from being a time of stagnation as historians have traditionally proposed, the late Achaemenid period actually witnessed a new spate of military activity and an expansionist policy, which resulted in the re-conquest of rebellious territories. The succession in 405/404 BCE from Darius II to his eldest son, Arses, who assumed the throne-name Artaxerxes II, seems to have been smooth.

However, Artaxerxes's younger brother, Cyrus the satrap of Lydia and Phrygia Minor, nursed ambitions for the throne – geared on by the king's mother, the influential Parysatis. Cyrus the Younger gathered a group of Persians aided by troops from his satrapy and a force of Greek mercenaries, including the Athenian soldier Xenophon, who, in his *Anabasis*, has left us a valuable description of Cyrus's ill-fated revolt. The rebellious army met with Artaxerxes's troops at Cunaxa in Babylonia in 401 BCE and Cyrus was killed. His bid for the throne had failed to gain more widespread support among the Persian nobility and Artaxerxes II's power remained unshaken.

The *coup d'état* of Cyrus the Younger heralded decades of trouble: a revolt by Evagoras of Cypriot Salamis between 391 and 380 BCE, by the Phoenicians ca. 380 BCE and, most alarmingly, in the western satrapies in the 360s and 350s BCE (led by prominent rebels such as Datames of Cappadocia, Ariobarzanes of Phrygia, and Autophradates of Lycia). And throughout all of this time (certainly from the period of Tissaphernes's sojourn in Asia

Minor, which signalled the start of intensified Persian interference in Greek affairs during the Peloponnesian war), major players were the Greek city-states and, subsequently, the growing strength of Macedon. Moreover, Egypt's secession from the Empire between 405 and 343 BCE was a major blow to the finances and morale of the Persian Great Kings, and Achaemenid history for the next fifty-six years is dominated by the continuous efforts to regain control of this important province. The Persians turned their attention to ensuring that Syria-Palestine and Asia Minor remained under firm control.

Artaxerxes II was the longest reigning of all the Achaemenids (405-359 BCE) and it is a pity that we know so little about him - although the Greek historian-moralist, Plutarch, provides us with a largely sympathetic sketch in his *Life of Artaxerxes:* he portrays him as a generous ruler, anxious to make himself accessible to his subjects, a loving husband and a courageous warrior prepared to share the hardships of his soldiers.

Harem Politics

Royal women played a key role in the politics of the empire and although they could not rule in their own right, they had access to power through their intimate relationships with the Great Kings, as mothers, wives, daughters, sisters, or concubines (Llewellyn-Jones 2013; Brosius 1996). Royal mothers of the dynasty are often attested in the Greek sources as being active in defending the royal family from external or internal threats. However, the favor they showed to one child over another could have disastrous consequences: it is clear that Parysatis encouraged her much-loved younger son, Cyrus, to rebel against his elder brother, Artaxerxes II. Clearly a woman of great drive and ambition, she is credited with executing and poisoning several court nobles and even poisoned her daughter-in-law, Artaxerxes's wife, Stateira, because she recognized in Stateira ambitions for power as great as her own.

The Greek fixation with the cruelty of the royal women might be read as a literary trope for certain, and these stories no doubt served an important moralistic purpose in the Greek-speaking world, but it is crucial to set the Greek tales of harem-based rivalries, intrigues, double-dealings, murders, and executions within the context of *bone fide* Achaemenid dynastic politics. Persia was controlled by an absolute ruler – that is not Orientalist cliché, it is a fact – and absolute monarchies are open to a particular form of political tension which usually focuses on the royal family and on the noble families who surround the king, and within such institutions the women of the ruling family often rise to positions of political agency, not through any formal route to power, but by other, less recognized means. Achaemenid royal women had considerable political influence, at times even influencing the succession (Scheidel 2009).

This is not unusual: recent studies of harem politics at the Ottoman Turkish court have illuminated a world in which domestic rivalries among the harem women had a direct impact upon Ottoman imperial policy. Across time and space, harem women of countless court societies went head-to-head with one another to secure their own status (and even their lives) but primarily to solidify the status and ambitions of their sons. The royal harem of Persia felt the tensions of the disputes as keenly as any other court society and the women of the Achaemenid court utilized methods of gaining or securing power as ruthlessly as the women of any other imperial dynasty.

Artaxerxes III and the re-conquest of Egypt

Long reigns like that of Artaxerxes II often create problems when it comes to the question of succession with several mature and experienced sons ready to jockey for position. Three of Artaxerxes II's sons, including Crown Prince Darius, died violent deaths, and another son, Ochus, who eventually succeeded as Artaxerxes III (in 359 BCE), is credited with engineering the fatalities.

The major achievement of his reign was the re-conquest of Egypt in 343 BCE, after hard campaigning, which had been preceded by the crushing of a revolt in Phoenicia, headed by the ruler of Sidon, Tennes, who had sent a substantial Greek mercenary force sent to him from Egypt. Artaxerxes's punishment of Sidon was swift: Tennes was executed, some of the city was destroyed, and a part of its population deported. This is recorded in a Babylonian chronicle:

> The fourteenth [year] (i.e. 345 BCE) of Umasu, who is called Artaxerxes: in the month Tishri (September/October) the prisoners which the king took [from] Sidon [were brought] to Babylon and Susa. On the thirteenth day of the same month a few of these troops entered Babylon. On the sixteenth day the... women prisoners from Sidon, which the king sent to Babylon - on that day they entered the palace of the king.

With the recapture of Egypt, Artaxerxes's reputation for harshness and cruelty was confirmed. A seal of the king depicts him crushing his enemy and leading prisoners on a leash.

Court Coups and the Clash of Empires

Artaxerxes III and most of his family died in a veritable bloodbath (338 BCE) masterminded by a eunuch, Bagoas, who then raised the sole surviving young son of Artaxerxes, Arses, to the throne; he again took the name Artaxerxes (IV). But after only two years, he was murdered by Bagoas, who now supported the claims of a member of a collateral branch of the Achaemenid family, Artashata, to the kingship – a man who had a reputation for exceptional physical bravery. Once Artashata was firmly established on the throne, having adopted the royal name Darius (III), he had Bagoas executed.

Darius III's reputation has suffered badly; fated to be the opponent of Alexander of Macedon, whose brilliant military victories, comparable to those of Cyrus the Great in their breathtaking sweep and speed, spelt the end of the Achaemenid dynasty, he has gone down in history as a weak-kneed coward. In reality, Darius was a brave soldier who posed a serious threat to Alexander's dreams of glory. He met Alexander in battle at Issus in 333 BCE, but was forced to flee the field, leaving Alexander to capture the royal harem. Darius met Alexander in battle again at Gaugamela in 331 BCE; but once again Darius was defeated. He fled to Ecbatana to try to raise fresh troops, but was pursued by Alexander, who was anxious to take him alive. The Great King fled to Bactria where he was killed not by Alexander but by his satrap Bessus in July 330 BCE. Alexander gave Darius an honourable funeral and to help legitimize his claim to the Achaemenid throne, he married Darius's daughter, Stateira as well as a daughter of Artaxerxes III.

King and Gods

In Achaemenid iconography the Great King shares his appearance with that of the supreme Iranian deity, Ahuramazda. Created under imperial auspices for predominately Persian spectators at the heart of the Empire, the monumental Bisitun relief (dated to just before 519 BCE) is a vivid depiction (although not necessarily a "portrait" as we might use the term) of Darius the Great, who, bow in one hand, lifts his other hand in a gesture of salutation to Ahuramazda, who hovers over the scene and offers a ring, representing kingship, to Darius. Just as the king and the god share close intimacy of space, so they share a physical form. The Great King encodes in his appearance the best physical attributes of the anthropomorphic divinity Ahuramazda; the Great King is the deity's doppelganger. They adopt the same hair-style and beard-shape, the same crown, the same garment-type, and they "emit" the same *xvarnah* or "brilliance," "luminosity," or "glory." The iconography stresses that reciprocity between king and god is guaranteed, and thus in an inscription from Susa, Darius can state with confidence that "Ahuramazda is mine; I am Ahuramazda's." Even if Persian kings were not gods, they could be understood only in their intimate relationships with the divine (Lanfranchi & Rollinger 2010).

We have already seen that Xerxes attributed his success in the succession struggle which followed the death of Darius I to the divine favor and celestial support of Ahuramazda: "by the grace of Ahuramazda I became king on my father's throne." But who exactly was Xerxes's helpful deity? The earliest reference to Ahuramazda ("the Wise Lord") is actually found in an eighth-century BCE Assyrian text, in which *as-sa-ra ma-za-aš* is named as one god in a list of many gods. It is clear that Ahuramazda was one of the Elamite pantheon, although it is difficult to know for sure if he was Cyrus the Great's god. Nevertheless, there are numerous references to this deity in the Achaemenid royal inscriptions, and especially those of Darius the Great, who lauded the god as Creator: "A great god is Ahuramazda, who created this earth, who created yonder sky, who created man, who created happiness for man." In other words Darius envisaged the Wise Lord as a Creator only of what is good and he expresses over and over again his faith in Ahuramazda and his belief that he serves the god as a divine instrument for establishing order and justice on earth: "When Ahuramazda saw this earth turbulent, then he bestowed it on me ...By the will of Ahuramazda I set it again in its place" and, "After Ahuramazda made me king in this earth, by the will of Ahuramazda all (that) I did was good."

It is little wonder that the Greeks mistook the Great King's intimate relationship with Ahuramazda to mean that the king himself was divine. The Great King held, by virtue of his office, a position mystical and he was, if less than a god, still more than a man. Therefore in his tragedy *Persians*, Aeschylus calls the dead Darius *isotheos*, "equal to the gods," *theion*, "divine," and *akakos*, "knowing no wrong," and while the Athenian playwright must not be taken literally on these points, he was capable, nonetheless, of thinking of the kings of the Achaemenid dynasty in this way. Indeed, some Greeks described the Great King as having a divine *daimon*, or spirit. This Greek belief in the king's *daimon* is a reasonable interpretation of the Persian belief in the *fravashi*, or "soul" of the monarch.

It is clear that Ahuramazda was conceived of as the king's god *par excellence* and the intimate relationship between the two is reiterated repeatedly; the king was expected, under the auspices of the Magi (priests), to carry out the prayers and rituals in Ahuramazda's honor, or to tend to the god's sacred fire. In the early Achaemenid royal inscriptions Ahuramazda alone is named, although occasionally he is mentioned alongside "all the gods" or as the "greatest of the gods." On one of the Elamite tablets from Persepolis he appears with "Mithra-(and)-the Baga" (i.e., "gods") and at the end of the Achaemenid period Artaxerxes III again makes this solicitation (Henkelman 2008). The Persepolis texts amply testify to the presence of "the other gods who are" and show how the royal administration supplied cultic necessities for the worship of numerous Iranian, Elamite, and Babylonian deities. In addition to Ahuramazda, the Persepolis texts name other gods worthy of ritual offerings, including Zurvan (a weather god), Mizduši (a fertility goddess), Narvasanga (a fire deity), Hvarita (Spirit of the Rising Sun), and Visai Baga (a collective entity of deities).

It was Artaxerxes II who conspicuously invoked a new triad in the official inscriptions of his reign: "Ahuramazda, Anahita, and Mithra" and these latter two gods proved to be popular in the Sasanian period alongside the ever-present Ahuramazda. Artaxerxes's texts suggest that they stood close to Ahuramazda in the monarch's esteem, probably for good reason: Mithra was a sun-god and a deity closely associated with horses, while Anahita was an important water-goddess as well as a warrior and fertility deity, likened by the Greeks to Athene, Artemis, and Aphrodite.

Titles and qualities of kingship

When in the Bisitun Inscription, Darius states that "I (am) ... the Great King, King of Kings, King in Fars, King of the Countries, Hystaspes's son, Arsames's grandson, an Achaemenid," he utilises the full panoply of titles available to any Persian king (Old Persian, *xšayaθiya,* hence Middle/New Persian, *šāh* - "king"). The monarch's three pre-eminent titles, found time and again in official rhetoric, were "King of Kings," "Great King," and "King of the Countries" (or its variations: "King of the Countries Containing All Races" and "King of the Countries Containing Many Races"), to which can be added another, lesser-used but nonetheless instructive title: "King on this (Great) Earth (Even Far Off)," suggesting a development in the Achaemenid conception of their own territorial expansions.

Unsurprisingly, in foreign territories under their control, Great Kings adopted and adapted indigenous titles for their own use; thus in Babylon Cyrus II claimed for himself the grandiose Babylonian title "King of the Universe, the Mighty King, King of Babylon, King of Sumer and Akkad, King of the Four Quarters of the World," while Darius I portrayed himself as the legitimate pharaoh of Egypt by adopting a series of important and ancient hieroglyphic titles including "King of Upper and Lower Egypt," "Lord of the Two Lands," "Supreme Ruler of the World," "Son of Amun," and "Living Image of Rē."

The topic of the ideology of ancient Persian kingship (Old Persian, *xšaca*) has attracted much attention. Contemporary scholars now have little doubt that Mesopotamian ideologies of kingship helped to inspire certain Achaemenid traditions, but into the mix we must now place other influential components: first, an indigenous Iranian element, secondly, a pharaonic Egyptian ideology that had an increasing hold on the Persians following Cambyses's conquest of the country in 525 BCE, and finally, and most significantly, some important Neo-Elamite elements (Lanfranchi & Rollinger 2010; Root 1979). These had entered early into the developing Achaemenid ideological thought-processes and scholars are increasingly recognizing Elamite cultural and theological ideologies as a key to understanding early Persian conceptions of monarchy. As kings of Anšan, the early Persian rulers of southwestern Iran, were easily pulled into the culturally dominant orbit of the sophisticated Elamites, and scholars are becoming increasingly aware of a geopolitical interdependency that emerged between Elam and southern Iran in the immediate centuries before the growth of Persian power in the Near East. There can be little doubt that the Elamites form the "missing link" in the chain of Persian royal ideological development and that the Persians have now been revealed as the true heirs of the Elamites, and not of the Medes as has long been supposed. But, nonetheless, this must not overshadow the fact that the Persians also had their own distinct identity. In the royal texts Persian uniqueness is repeatedly emphasized and the Great King is shown to be a Persian, the descendent of generations of Persians, ruling over Persians and the conquered lands beyond Persia. For its part, Persia is shown to be "good, containing good horses and good men" and under the especial care and attention of the king: "If the Persian people are protected, for a long time unending happiness will rest upon this (royal) house."

It was the Persian king's duty, under the auspices of Ahuramazda, to bring order out of potential chaos. It was his obligation to uphold Truth (Old Persian, *arta*) and dispel the Lie (Old Persian, *drauga*), which was best represented by the chaos of rebellion and insurgence against the throne (or, in purely visual terms, in the king's guise as "Persian Hero" slaughtering a lion or hybrid monster that represents the essence of chaos). In an Old Persian inscription on the façade of his tomb at Naqš-i Rustam, Darius I confirms that his Empire was won by military prowess: "the spear of a Persian man has gone far; then shall it become known to you: a Persian man has delivered battle far indeed from Persia." This is the logical conclusion to the first official pronouncement of Darius's reign, contained on the Bisitun monument in which his initial fight for Empire is inscribed. His tomb contains another interesting statement, which focuses on the strength of the king's body and his ability as a warrior-king and is, incidentally, the most verbose surviving Achaemenid text:

> This is my ability: that my body is strong. As a warrior, I am a good warrior. At once my intelligence holds its place, whether I see a rebel or not. Both by intelligence and by command at that time I know myself to be above panic, both when I see a rebel and I do not see one. I am furious in the strength of my revenge, with both hands and both feet. As a bowman I am a good bowman, both on foot and on horseback. As a spearman I am a good spearman, both on foot and on horseback. These are the skills which Ahuramazda has bestowed on me and I have had the strength to bear them.

Darius depicts himself as a rational and considered monarch, he never acts in haste or in panic, and it is his sheer force of personality that guarantees his Persian subjects will receive the benefit of his considered and learned judgements. But while ethical and moral qualities are central to the ideology of the tomb inscription, brute force is stressed there as well. Darius is strong enough to endure the hardships of campaigning on horseback and on the march, and his arms have strength to draw the bow and wield the lance, and these skills, he emphasizes, come *directly* from Ahuramazda. Near Eastern texts frequently suggest there was a special connection between the king's weapons and the deity, for after all, it was the god who made powerful the royal weapons and imbued the royal body with strength enough to wield them, and at Darius's insistence, in his inscription Ahuramazda is portrayed as the god who empowers the king with martial valour. Although Great Kings did not necessarily regularly participate in battle, imperial royal ideology propounded that Great Kings were skilled fighters: "as a warrior, I am a good warrior" is Darius's bold claim. In order to be an effective ruler, the king had to be thought of as a brave soldier first, and court propaganda (later picked up in Classical traditions) reiterated the image for successive Achaemenid monarchs.

For the elites of successive courts and noble houses, the hunt became an elaborate ritual encrusted with jargon and ceremonial that served to validate the aristocratic credentials of the hunters, for the court hunt had nothing to do with providing for economic necessity - it was predominantly a political and ideological activity (Allsen 2006), and the countless depictions of the hunt on Achaemenid seals demonstrate the centrality of the image in Persian thought.

An interesting nexus existed between warfare and hunting, as it was through this display of chivalric bravery that the Great King was able to demonstrate his manhood, for the same skills were necessary for both events and thus monarchs had to be leaders in war and hunting. Hunts took place in *paradeisoi*, vast game reserves which represented the Empire in miniature, given that they were planted with flora from across the royal territories and stocked with game captured from across the length and breadth of the king's realm.

Pax Persiaca

The longevity of the Empire is testimony to the Achaemenid policy of tolerance towards its conquered peoples and ruthlessness in maintaining power. Royal inscriptions (disseminated widely across the empire) emphasized that all conquered nations were united in service to the Great King, whose laws they were required to obey. The king was championed by the god Ahuramazda, who granted the monarch the gift of kingship. The royal texts frequently used the notion that rebellion was linked to cosmic disorder and that the king was the champion of Truth (*arta*) and therefore crushed rebellious subjects so that order could triumph. Rebellion against Persian authority was therefore seen as a revolt against divine rule.

Darius I divided the empire's territories into administrative satrapies in order to maintain the levy of tribute required from each region. Darius's Bisitun Inscription provides the oldest extant list of the constituents of the empire. It begins with two core lands, Persia and Elam. Then the order roughly follows the map of the empire in a clockwise fashion, first referring to the western provinces or satrapies, then those in the northern part, followed by the lands in the east of the empire. The ordering of the provinces of the empire here is interesting, since lands lying closest to the imperial centre are privileged in the text over those at the periphery of empire, suggesting an Achaemenid ideology of hierarchy: proximity to Persia signifies a higher level of civilization.

When in the Bisitun Inscription, Darius I states that "I (am) ... the Great King, King of Kings, King in Fars, King of the Countries..., an Achaemenid," he utilises the full panoply of titles available to any Persian king. The monarch's three pre-eminent titles, found time and again in official rhetoric, were "King of Kings," "Great King," and "King of the Countries," or its variations – "King of the Countries Containing All Races," to which can be added another, lesser-used but nonetheless instructive title: "King on this (Great) Earth (Even Far Off)." Unsurprisingly, in foreign territories under their control, Great Kings adopted and adapted indigenous titles for their own use; thus in Babylon Cyrus II claimed for himself the grandiose Babylonian title "King of the Universe, the Mighty King, King of Babylon, King of Sumer and Akkad, King of the Four Quarters of the World," while Darius I portrayed himself as the legitimate pharaoh of Egypt by adopting a series of important and ancient hieroglyphic titles.

Art of Empire

Achaemenid art is essentially an eclectic mix of styles and motifs drawn from different parts of the empire, but fused together to produce a distinctive and harmonious look which is distinctly Persian. Egyptian and Assyrian motifs (like winged disks and winged *genii*, pediment designs, and even cannons for depicting the human figure) are frequently melded together, so that Achaemenid art can be said to reflect in material form both the diversity and unity of the empire as a whole.

The art of the Achaemenid empire serves a primary purpose: it confirms the royal ideology of the unity of the empire and promotes the image of the monarch. In a way, all Achaemenid art is royal art since the motifs created for the glorification of the king are found time and again in almost all Persian material artefacts. These range from vast rock cut sculptures – such as those found at Bisitun or the tombs of the kings at Naqsh i-Rustam and Persepolis – to miniscule engravings found on gemstones.

The Great King is often the central focus: he is shown as a warrior, bow or spear in hand, trampling on his enemies or as a great mythic hero, a kind of Gilgamesh figure, who slays monstrous beasts, the representatives of chaos, with his sword or dagger. Alternatively, the Great King is depicted at a fire altar piously adoring the figure of Ahuramazda, the supreme god of the Persians, who takes on human form and resides in a winged disk above the altar. The Great King is also shown in state, wearing the lavishly decorated royal robes, progressing through his palace with parasol-bearers and fly-whisk bearers in attendance; he is also shown seated on his high-backed throne as he receives courtiers in audience.

A particularly interesting motif shows the great king elevated on a thronelike platform that is raised up high by individuals from across the empire, and each person is identified by ethnic dress and features as a representative of a different province. In his tomb inscription at Naqsh i-Rustam, Darius I encourages the reader to look at the accompanying reliefs to understand the vastness of the empire:

"If now you shall think that 'How many are the countries which King Darius held?' look at the sculptures [of those] who bear the throne, then shall you know, then shall it become known to you: the spear of a Persian man has gone forth far; then shall it become known to you: a Persian man has delivered battle far indeed from Persia."

The theme is also found in three-dimensional form in the sculpture of Darius found at Susa in 1972. Carved in Egyptian style, it shows Darius in Persian court robes standing on a rectangular pedestal which is carved with keeling individuals who raise up their hands to support the figure of the king above them. As on the tomb relief, each person is dressed in local costume and is named. In effect the statue is a three-dimensional empire list, a sculpted enumeration of nations subject to the Great King.

The interest in the ethic make-up of the empire is also apparent on the staircases leading to the Apadana at Persepolis. Here representatives of the empire are depicted in loving detail bringing tribute to the court of the Great King: curly-haired, dark-skinned Nubians carry elephant tusks and lead an okapi on a leash; Ionians with hooked noses and turbans carry silver tableware and ornamental armlets; and Elamite nobles lead in a lioness and her cubs. The detailing of every delegate, every courtier, and every soldier is overwhelming – while the personality of a Bactrian camel is clear in the rendering of its face, and a testimony to the skills of the ancient artists.

Theatre of Royalty: court ceremony and etiquette

Achaemenid court ceremonial was used by the dynasty as a form of self-definition since it maintained and reinforced hierarchy within the elite and delineated power relations between courtiers, the royal family, and the monarch himself (Llewellyn-Jones 2013). Persian monarchs relied upon formalized etiquette and court ceremony to create a special aura around the throne. A deliberate separation and distancing of the king from the gaze of his subjects, even from much of his court, meant that elaborate rituals were enacted through which courtiers and visitors might get limited access to the royal personage during a tightly controlled and stage-managed audience ceremony (Esther 1.14 highlights the notion of having privileged access to the royal presence). Therefore we might think of the Great King, costumed in his finery, as an actor in a great royal drama (and his courtiers as part-players and spectators) because events at court, like coronations and investitures, royal audiences, and imperial parade-reviews, were clearly focused on a kind of "performance," since they were set far apart from everyday life by being "scripted" or turned into ceremony (Allen 2005b).

Narrative accounts of audiences with the Great King form a significant corpus in Greek and biblical writings on the Persian court but nothing remotely comparable exists in the Achaemenid literary tradition; instead we must turn to a rich stratum of iconography for information on the intricacies of the ceremony. Representations of the royal audience come in the form of numerous seal - and gemstone - images, a small painted image on a sarcophagus, and from the sculptured monumental doorjambs at Persepolis, although the finest surviving examples come in the form of two big stone reliefs once located at the staircases to the Apadana (later moved to the Treasury) (Kaptan 2002). The Great King is shown in audience in a "frozen moment"; he wears a court robe and crown and holds a pomegranate blossom and a sceptre; he is accompanied by the crown prince, who is depicted wearing the same garb as the king, and who is given the prerogative of holding a pomegranate blossom too. Also in attendance are high-ranking members of the court and the military. Two incense-burners help to demarcate the royal space (and accentuate its sacredness), as does the dais upon which the throne is placed and the baldachin, decorated with an image of Ahuramazda, which covers the scene. The theatrical paraphernalia of the throne room and the awesome setting of the Apadana were intended to instil fear and wonder in suppliants; the figure of the king, the protagonist of the drama, must have been an impressive, almost overwhelming, sight.

Interestingly, what appears to be a female audience is depicted on a cylinder seal from an unknown (but possibly Levantine) provenance. The parallel with the king's audience is explicit and is proof of the high regard in which royal women – possibly in this instance the king's mother – were held. The high social rank of royal females, like that of the Great King himself, was stressed by their conspicuous invisibility (although this must not be confused with any kind of "Oriental seclusion") and formal audiences only served to heighten their significance at court.

At the centre of the Treasury Relief, a courtier dressed in a riding habit – possibly the chiliarch or vizier – performs a ritual gesture of obeisance to the monarch which, *prima facie*, is associated to the *sala'am*, or formal greeting, used in later Muslim courts. Formalized gestures were a hallmark of Persian social communication and the Achaemenids readily seem to have transformed the gestures of "real life" into a rarefied form of court etiquette. Known to the Greeks as *proskynesis*, the exact nature of the ceremonial obeisance is debated, but when Herodotus says that one should perform *proskynesis* to a superior while prostrating oneself or bowing down, the term must describe an act performed once one is bowed or prostrate, which is, as on the Treasury Relief, kissing from the hands.

The Court on the Move

Administrative documents from Persepolis attest to the systematic criss-crossing of vast swathes of the Empire by the Great King and his court who traversed the realm not just for pragmatic reasons of state, but also to satisfy a deep-set instinct in the Persian psyche: for the Achaemenids were essentially nomads and a regular itinerant pattern of movement-settlement-movement can be located in the routine peripatetic practices of the court as they shifted locations between Ecbatana, Susa, Babylon, Persepolis and many other locales in the central part of the Empire – and sometimes far beyond.

The best surviving description of the Achaemenid peripatetic court is preserved by the Roman historian Quintus Curtius Rufus (3.3.8-16, 20-27), who probably reiterates earlier Greek observations on the royal procession. All Classical accounts agree that the king travelled with his insignia of power - religious banners, fire altars, and an entourage of priests – and with a vast military force, treasury porters, and multitudes of servants and kinsmen – even the royal harem was transported, under guard, in covered wagons (*hamamaxae*) and on horseback.

The logistics of the court shifting locations required enormous organization and colossal resources since many thousands of people would have been affected by, or responsible for, the move. Members of the royal family might travel independently of the king, taking with them their own courts-in-miniature and here too precision in planning would have been tantamount. For instance, Irdabama, the mother of Darius I - and thus the highest-ranking female at court - was economically active and had the authority to issue commands to the administrative hierarchy at Persepolis. She is well attested in the Persepolis texts overseeing her vast personal estates, receiving and distributing food supplies, and commanding an entourage of workers; she is verified at the ceremonial cities of Persepolis and Susa, and even at Borsippa in Babylonia.

When the imperial procession came to a halt, a camp was set up. Tents were erected and a royal city of cloth, leather, and wood appeared. Indeed, the king's tent was a collapsible version of a palace throne-hall, and it is reasonable to conceive of the Apadanas at both Persepolis and Susa as a stone version of the royal tent. As a mark of favour and as a display of royal largess, the Great King might gift a favored courtier with a splendid tent, often richly furnished with couches, textiles, gold plate, and slaves. The tent was a visible emblem of imperial authority.

Satraps and Governance

The administration of the Achaemenid empire was in the hands of a group of men drawn exclusively from the highest echelons of the Persian aristocracy, very often from the royal family itself. These "satraps" enjoyed the privilege of being the Great King's representative. They were responsible for the collection of taxes and tribute and raising armed forces when occasion required and, at a regional level, satraps were required to make all governmental decisions. For matters of international importance, however, satraps were obliged to consult the king and his chief ministers. As a representative of the king, satraps kept court and maintained court ceremony based on that at the heart of the empire.

Every satrapy covered an extensive area, ruled from a capital (which also acted as an administrative centre) where the satrap had a palace. These regional capitals were used to store taxes which were paid in both coin and kind, the latter including foodstuffs used to maintain the vast satrapal court and its dependents. However, taxation payments in precious goods and metals were widely used. The palaces were also centres for provincial administration; here royal orders were delivered to the satrap from the central authority. Royal decrees, identifiable by the king's seal, have been found as far afield as Nippur, Samaria and Artašat in Armenia and at Elephantine in Upper Egypt, athough the biggest horde of royal seals was discovered at Daskyleion in Anatolia. Archives were kept of all royal and satrapal decrees so that they could form future reference.

The satraps relied on a healthy interaction with local elites. In pursuing good inter-regional relationships, the institutions of marriage and concubinage should not be overlooked. Although we have very little information about the wives of satraps (let alone those of lesser-ranking Persian commanders and officials), there certainly were marriages between Persians and local women. Likewise, the marriage of the Paphlagonian prince, Otys, to the daughter of the Persian noble, Spithridates, recorded by Xenophon (*Hellenica* 4.1.6-7) attests to the reverse practice of elite men taking Persian brides. Such alliances gave the local elite a foothold in the Persian honor system. In addition, both kings and satraps took women from among subject peoples into their harems as concubines. According to Herodotus, "every man has a number of wives, a much greater number of concubines" (*Histories* 1.135), and while this scenario of empire-wide polygyny cannot be taken at face value, it may well be representative of privileged members of Iranian society. Persian nobles, especially satraps, certainly imitated the royal polygynous custom: Pharnabazus, satrap of Phrygia, kept a court full of concubines at Sardis. The Great King's 360 concubines were, so to speak, physical manifestations of the Persian realm.

The Persian system depended very much on cooperation with local power-holders and they frequently used well-established regional administrative systems to work for them. Additionally, Persians often employed individuals who were au fait with localized government to work with them. The Egyptian nobleman Udjahorresnet is a case in point: a former naval commander under the last indigenous pharaohs of the Saite dynasty, he was stripped of his military rank under Cambyses but was accorded the privileged title of king's "friend" along with a high rank in the temple of Neith at Sais. In other words, Udjahorresnet was denied any effective military power, but retained in royal service in an honorific position and he could operate as a royal adviser.

The same system can be seen at work with the lesser-kings and local dynasts. A good example is the use the satrap Pharnabazus made of the local rulers of Dardanus. When Zenis, the long-serving pro-Persian client-king of Dardanus, died, Pharnabazus had planned to bestow the satrapy to someone else. But Zenis's wife, Mania, petitioned Pharnabazus to bestow the province on her. The satrap took the unusual step of appointing a woman to the post to keep it within Zenis's family. Pharnabazus was delighted to find that Mania paid the tribute into the satrapal treasury just as regularly as her husband had done. These events illustrate the advantage of employing local elites to defend Persian interests. Conversely, dependence of the local dynasts on the satrap, and his power to strip the family of rank, kept them in check.

The smooth-running of the empire was facilitated by an excellent infrastructure (Potts 2008). First-rate roads connected the main satrapal centres of the empire with the imperial core. The most important of these highways was the Royal Road, which connected Sardis to Persepolis via Susa and Babylon; an eastern branch led first to Ecbatana and thence onwards to Bactra and on to Pashwar, while another road connected Persepolis to Egypt via Damascus and Jerusalem. The roads were measured in 6-km (3.7-mile) intervals (*parasangs*) and road-stations were set up around every 28 km (17.4 miles) of the route to accommodate the quick change of fresh horses for any imperial messenger carrying official documents. Herodotus estimated that the distance from Susa to Sardis, 450 *parasangs*, could be covered in ninety days (*Histories* 5.53).

The Persians displayed no desire to impose their language or culture upon the conquered nations; the Great Kings utilized local languages for their decrees and employed Aramaic as a form of *lingua franca* throughout the imperial territories to help facilitate effective communication. In the realm of religion, too, the Persian kings were careful to appear as active upholders of local cults, if only to ensure control of the wealthy sanctuaries and the adherence of powerful priesthoods. Even in small administrative regions, like Jerusalem and Magnesia-on-the-Maeander, the Persians granted temple privileges and acknowledged the support their local gods had given them.

However, this seemingly *laissez-faire* attitude towards cultural autonomy needs to be balanced by the fact that the Persians could prove to be merciless overlords if crossed

(Lincoln 2007). Rebellious subjects and states were treated with ruthlessness: populations were uprooted and deported across the empire, and their holy shrines were burned and destroyed. Artaxerxes III's reputation for harshness and cruelty is perhaps justified by his treatment of Sidon, while his violent re-conquest of Egypt is recorded on the stela of an Egyptian nobleman named Somtutefnakht: "The Asiatic... slew a million at my sides," he recalls. The Persians could inflict savage punishments on their foes.

The Immortals

The empire was founded and maintained by military might. The army consisted of infantry, horse cavalry and camel cavalry, and elite charioteers. The Persians also routinely incorporated subject and mercenary Greeks in their army, each of whom received a monthly wage (a gold *Daric* per month in 401 BC). By the time of Alexander, these mercenaries had become a regular part of the army and their leaders had even been incorporated into the Iranian aristocracy. Other areas of the empire sent men to bolster the Imperial army: Scythian charioteers and bowmen and Bactrian camel-riders are well attested.

The size of the imperial army was never as large as the Greeks suggested and historians now estimate that Xerxes's forces for the Greek campaign numbered around 70,000 infantry and 9,000 horsemen, while the army of Artaxerxes II at Cunaxa was probably around 40,000 in number. Darius III's troops at Gaugamela amounted to about 34,000 cavalry and some infantry. The army was led by a supreme commander, who was either the Great King himself or a close relative. Next in command was an officer in charge of a division of 1,000 men, subdivided into ten battalions. The most famous of the army units was the crack fighting team known as the Ten Thousand (or "Immortals"), a division of which served as the royal bodyguard.

The Immortals (Greek *athánatoi* – lit. "those without deaths") is the name of an elite corps of 10,000 Achaemind Persian infantry soldiers. Much of our information about the Immortals derives from Herodotus's *Histories*, although later attestations are found in Athenaeus's *Deipnosophistai* 12.514c (quoting Heracleides of Cumae), Hesychius's *Lexicon*, and Procopius (1.14.31).

The Herodotean passages are our most valuable source for the Immortals' involvement in Xerxes's Greek campaign of 480–479 BCE. Herodotus's first mention of the Immortals (7.83) follows his list of the generals of the six main corps of Xerxes's infantry (7.82); he states that Hydarnes was the commander-in-chief (Old Persian *azabaritēs*, or perhaps *hazarapatiš*) of the 10,000 select troops. Herodotus calls them a "body of picked Persian troops" and glosses the name "Immortals" by ascertaining that "it was invariably kept up to strength: if a man was killed or fell sick, the vacancy he left was at once filled, so that the strength [of the group] was never more or less more than 10,000."

The Immortals were regarded as standing apart from the common Persian soldiery. Herodotus (7.61) describes their appearance:

> the dress of these troops consisted of the tiara, or soft felt cap, embroidered
> tunic with sleeves, a coat of mail looking like the scales of a fish, and trousers;
> for arms they carried light wicker shields, quivers slung below them, short

spears, powerful bows with cane arrows, and short swords swinging from belts beside the right thigh.

In the *Histories* 7.83, Herodotus notes that "every man glittered with gold," that they accompanied the purdah-carriages of the royal concubines, and that they were provided with special food, brought to them separately from the rest of the army on camel and mule wagons. However, at no point does Herodotus use the adjective *athánatoi* here, so it cannot be confidently assumed that he is describing the appearance and duties of the Immortals. Confusion occurs in the *Histories* 7.40-41 too: here Herodotus describes Xerxes's march from Sardis to the Hellespont. The Great King rode at the centre of the army, preceded by 1000 horsemen and 1000 spearbearers carrying their spear points downwards; the butt-ends of the spears were decorated with golden pomegranates. Behind the king was another group of 1000 chosen Persian spearbearers carrying their spears upright; their weapons were decorated with golden apples (this might have seemed strange to Herodotus because Greek spears had a large blade on top and a short utilitarian spike at the other end). The spearbearers were followed by a further 1000 horsemen and then 10,000 infantry. Again, although the word *athánatoi* is not used here, these 10,000 must be the Immortals. Herodotus's description continues: "of these, 1000 had golden pomegranates instead of spikes on the butt-end of their spears, and they were arrayed around to circle the other 9,000, whose spears had silver pomegranates." From this it would appear that there existed a regiment of spearbearers (whom Heracleides calls "Applebearers") separate from the 10,000 Immortals and perhaps chosen from the ranks of the Immortals themselves because of their blood nobility (we know that Darius I served as a spearbearer to Cambyses II). It is possible that this regiment – the elite of the elite – marched in two columns in front of and behind the monarch, which has confused Herodotus into thinking of them as two separate regiments.

Whatever their exact make up, the Immortals played a particularly important role at the Battle of Thermopylae. They were brought into the action on the fifth day of battle after a Median regiment had failed to secure the pass of Thermopylae or to overcome the small Spartan force defending it. "Their place was taken," says Herodotus, "by Hydarnes and his hand-picked Persian troops – the king's Immortals – who advanced in full confidence of bringing the business to a quick and easy end" (7.211). However, it was not until the Greek Ephialtes betrayed the Spartans by alerting the Persians to a mountain path to the narrow pass that the Immortals were able to help secure a victory for Xerxes.

When the King began his withdrawal from Greece, following the Persian defeat at Salamis (and possibly to put down a revolt in Babylonia), Mardonius was instructed to stay behind in Thessaly to continue the Greek campaign the following spring. His impulse was to command the Immortals to remain with him, without Hydarnes, because the nobleman, "refused to be separated from the King" (8.113). However, given that the Immortals make no (obvious) appearance in Herodotus's description of the campaigns of 479 BCE, it is probable that they returned to the Persian heartland with Hydarnes and the King (acting as his bodyguard).

The bona fide Persian sources for the Immortals are elusive. It is generally assumed that the bearded and richly liveried soldiers represented in the beautiful faience tiles from the Achaemenid palace at Susa and the wall reliefs at Persepolis represent the Immortals, but there is nothing to categorically support this idea.

More importantly, there are no references to a corps of Immortals in the Persian written sources. Probably, Herodotus heard the Old Persian word *anûšiya* ("companions [of the King]"), which certainly is located in Persian texts, but confused it or associated it with the phonetically similar Persian word *anauša* ("Immortals"). All in all, there are more questions surrounding this special corps of the Persian army than there are answers: their exact tasks, and even their Iranian name, remain unknown because authentic Achaemenid sources with this information do not exist.

Concluding Thoughts: the Achaemenid Empire Today

There can be no doubt that the first Persian empire was of enormous significance for the development of the idea of "empire." It made possible the first significant and continuous contact between East and West, and prepared the ground for Alexander the Great's vision of what an empire could be.

Within Iran itself, the debate on what the Achaemenid empire means in a modern framework is very much alive. Mohammed Reza Shah's obsession with the Achaemenid dynasty during the 1970s led to a backlash against the study of, and engagement with, the Persian past throughout the formative period of the Islamic Revolution. Yet today the monuments of ancient Iran are both studied and enjoyed by the Iranians, who appraise the Achaemenid empire as being at the apex of the history of Iranian civilization. Cyrus the Great is particularly revered as a visionary leader of great moral integrity and brilliance and the Cyrus Cylinder is frequently claimed as the first Bill of Human Rights. In Iran the Achaemenid dynasty is remembered with enormous pride.

In the West, the study of the Achaemenid empire continues to expand and change, and, despite today's political tensions, the dialogue between Western and Iranian scholars is flourishing as never before. Textual studies of indigenous Persian sources continue to appear, and the archaeology of the empire is still producing unexpected finds which constantly force scholarship to rethink and re-mold their definitions of empire. Are the ancient sources on Persia really as Hellenocentric as they are often presented as being? Can we study the ancient Persian empire without forcing the subject to be viewed through the prism of Orientalism? Achaemenid studies stands at the threshold of new and interesting debates.

Recent scholarship, based on a new understanding using ancient textual sources from all parts of the empire, together with the sophisticated study of Achaemenid art and archaeology, has recognized that Classical authors with specific and focused agendas displayed a heavy bias against Persian culture and society. We can now determine however that, in spite of revolts, succession crises, and even endemic regicide, the vast Persian empire nevertheless held together as a coherent unit for two hundred thirty years and showed no signs of internal weakness or stagnation at the time when the Macedonians took over power from the last Achaemenid king, Darius III. It is wrong to think of the Achaemenid Empire as the "Forgotten Empire"; let us relabel it the "Misrepresented Empire."

Figure. 1. Drawing of the so-called Winged Genius, from Cyrus's Palace in Pasargadae

Figure. 2. The back of Cyrus's tomb in Pasargadae

Figure. 3. Darius's relief and inscriptions at Behistun

Figure. 4. Headless statues of Darius with hieroglyphic inscriptions found in Egypt

Figure. 5. The "Gate of All Nations" in Persepolis

Figure. 6. Details of a relief from Persepolis

Figure. 7. Doorway relief of a king killing a lion, Persepolis

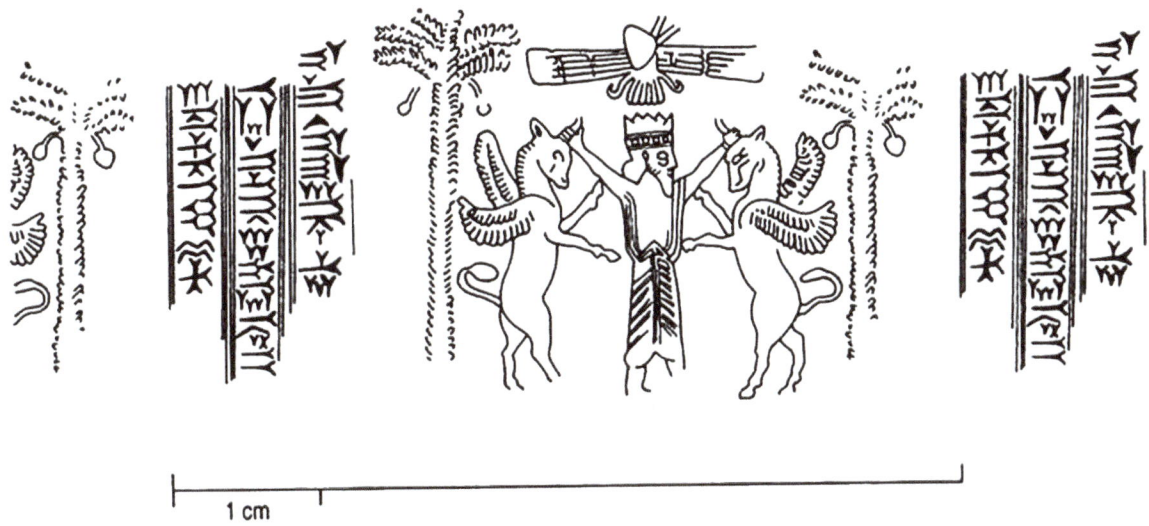

Figure. 8. Drawing of a seal impression bearing the name of Darius

Figure. 9. The king with the fire altar and the winged icon, from Darius's tomb in Naqsh-e Rostam

Figure. 10. King with attendants, from a relief at Persepolis

Figure. 11. Modern drawing of a relief of Darius I granting an audience

Figure. 12. Tomb relief of Darius I

Figure. 13. Camel head from a relief at Persepolis

Figure. 14. Drawing of the relief of a Queen with attendants

Figure. 15. Achaemenid soldiers on a relief from Susa

Bibliography

Allen, L. 2005a. *The Persian Empire*. London.

Allen, L. 2005b. "Le Roi Imaginaire: an Audience with the Achaemenid King" in O. Hekster & R. Fowler (eds.), *Imaginary Kings. Royal images in the Ancient Near East, Greece and Rome*. Munich. 39-62.

Allsen, T.T. 2006. *The Royal Hunt in Eurasian History*. Philadelphia.

Balcer, J.M. 1987. *Herodotus & Bisitun. Problems in Ancient Persian Historiography*. Stuttgart.

Balcer, J.M. 1993. *A Prosopographical Study of the Ancient Persians Royal and Noble, c. 550 -450 BC*. Lampeter.

Boardman, J. 2000. *Persia and the West. An Archaeological Investigation of the Genesis of Achaemenid Art*. London.

Briant, P. 2002. *From Cyrus to Alexander. A History of the Persian Empire*. Winona Lake.

Brosius, M. 1996. *Women in Ancient Persia (559-331 BC)*. Oxford.

Brosius, M. 2000. *The Persian Empire from Cyrus II to Artaxerxes I*. Lactor 16. Cambridge.

Brosius, M. 2006. *The Persians. An Introduction*. London

Cook, J.M. 1983. *The Persian Empire*. London.

Curtis, J. & Simpson, S. (eds.). 2010. *The World of Achaemenid Persia*. London.

Curtis, J. & Tallis, N. (eds.). 2005. *Forgotten Empire. The World of Ancient Persia*. London.

Curtis, V.S. 1993. *Persian Myths*. London.

Dandamanev, M.A. 1989. *A Political History of the Achaemenid Empire*. Brill.

Dandamanev, M.A. & Lukonin, V.G. 1989. *The Culture and Social Institutions of Ancient Iran*. Cambridge.

de Jong, A. 2010. "Religion at the Achaemenid Court" in B. Jacobs & R. Rollinger (eds.), *Der Achämenidenhof/The Achaemenid Court*. Stuttgart. 533-58.

Driver, G.R. 1956. *Aramaic Documents of the Fifth Century BC*. Oxford.

Harrison, T. 2002. (ed.), *Greeks and Barbarians*. Edinburgh.

Harrison, T. 2010. *Writing Ancient Persia*. London.

Henkelman, W.F.M. 2008. *The Other Gods Who Are. Studies in Elamite-Iranian Acculturation Based on the Persepolis Fortification Texts. Achaemenid History XIV*. Leiden.

Kaptan, D. 2002. *The Daskyleion Bullae: Seal Images from the Western Achaemenid Empire*. II Vols. Leiden.

Koch, H. 2001. *Persepolis*. Mainz Am Rhein.

Krefter, F. 1971. *Persepolis. Rekonstruktionen*. Berlin.

Kuhrt, A. 2007. *The Persian Empire. A Corpus of Sources from the Achaemenid Period*. II Vols.

London.

Lanfranchi, G.B. & Rollinger, R. (eds.). 2010. *Concepts of Kingship in Antiquity*. Padua.

Lincoln, B. 2007. *Religion, Empire and Torture. The Case of Achaemenid Persia, with a postscript on Abu Ghraib*. Chicago.

Lindenberger, J.M. 2003. *Ancient Aramaic and Hebrew Letters*. Atlanta.

Llewellyn-Jones, L. 2012. "The Great Kings of the Fourth Century and the Greek Memory of the Persian Past" in J. Marincola, L.Llewellyn-Jones & C. Maciver (eds.), *Greek Notions of the Past in the Archaic and Classical Eras. History Without Historians*. Edinburgh. 317-46.

Llewellyn-Jones, L. 2013. *King and Court in Ancient Persia 559-331 BCE*. Edinburgh.

Llewellyn-Jones, L. & Robson, J. 2010. *Ctesias' History of Persia. Tales of the Orient*. London.

L'Orange, H.P. 1953. *Studies in the Iconography of Cosmic Kingship*. Oslo.

Matheson, S.A. 1972. *Persia: An Archaeological Guide*. London.

Mousavi, A. 2012. *Persepolis. Discovery and Afterlife of a World Wonder*. Berlin.

Olmstead, A.T. 1948. *History of the Persian Empire*. Chicago.

Perrot, J. (ed.). 2010. *Le palais de Darius à Suse. Une résidence royale sur la route de Persépolis à Babylone*. Paris.

Potts, D.T. 1999. *The Archaeology of Elam. Formation and Transformation of an Ancient Iranian State*. Cambridge.

Potts, D.T. 2008. "The Persepolis Fortification Texts and the Royal Road: Another Look at the Fahliyan Area" in P. Briant, W. Henkleman, W. & M. Stolper (eds.), *L'archive des Fortifications de Persépolis*. Paris. 275-302.

Potts, D.T. 2010. "Monarchy, Factionalism and Warlordism: Reflections on Neo-Elamite Courts" in B. Jacobs & R. Rollinger, eds., *Der Achämenidenhof/The Achaemenid Court*. Stuttgart. 107-37.

Potts, D.T. 2011. "The Elamites" in T. Daryaee (ed.), *The Oxford Handbook of Iranian History*. Oxford. 37-56.

Root, M.C. 1979. *The King and Kingship in Achaemenid Art: Essays on the Creation of an Iconography of Empire*. Leiden.

Scheidel, W. 2009. "Sex and Empire. A Darwinian Perspective" in I. Morris & W. Scheidel (eds.), *The Dynamics of Ancient Empires. State Power from Assyria to Byzantium*. Oxford. 255-324.

Schmidt, E.F. 1953. *Persepolis I*. Chicago.

Schmidt, E.F. 1957. *Persepolis II, Contents of the treasury and other discoveries*. Chicago.

Schmidt, E.F. 1970. *Persepolis III, The royal tombs and other monuments*. Chicago.

Spawforth, A.J.S. 2007a "The Court of Alexander the Great" in A.J.S. Spawforth (ed.), *The Court and Court Society in Ancient Monarchies*. Cambridge. 82-120.

Stronach, D. 1978. *Parsagade*. Oxford.

Stronach, D. 1997a. "Darius as Parsagadae: a neglected source for the history of early Persia". *Topoi*, Supplement 1. 351-63.

Stronach, D. 1997b. "Anshan and Persia: Early Achaemenid History, Art and Architecture on the Iranian Plateau" in J. Curtis (ed.), *Mesopotamia and Iran in the Persian Period: Conquest and Imperialism 539-331 BC*. London. 35-53.

Stronach, D. 2011. "Court Dress and Riding Dress at Persepolis: New Approaches to Old

Questions" in J. Álvarez-Mon & M.B. Garrison (eds.), *Elam and Persia*. Winona Lake. 475-87.

Tilia, A.B. 1972. *Studies and Restorations at Persepolis and Other Sites of Fārs* I. Rome.

Tilia, A.B. 1978. *Studies and Restorations at Persepolis and Other Sites of Fārs* II. Rome.

Tuplin, C. 1987. "The administration of the Achaemenid Empire" in I. Carradice (ed.), *Coinage and Administration in the Athenian and Persian Empires. BAR International Series* 34. London. 109-166.

Tuplin, C. 1996. *Achaemenid Studies*. Stuttgart.

Wiesehöfer, J. 1996. *Ancient Persia from 550 BC to 650 AD*. London & New York.

Wiesehöfer, J. 2009. "The Achaemenid Empire" in I. Morris & W. Scheidel (eds.), *The Dynamics of Ancient Empires. State Power from Assyria to Byzantium*. Oxford. 66-98.

Wilber, D.N. 1969. *Persepolis. The Archaeology of Parsa, Seat of the Persian Kings*. Princeton.

Yamauchi, E.M. 1990. *Persia and the Bible*. Grand Rapids.

SELEUCID IRAN

Omar Coloru

The history of Seleucid Iran begins after Seleucus I (r. 312-281 BCE) had recovered Babylon in 312, where he had been satrap until his enemy, Antigonus The One-Eyed, had forced him to seek refuge at Ptolemy's court in Egypt in 315. Once he was settled again in his former satrapy, Seleucus decided to launch a campaign to conquer the whole of the so-called Upper Satrapies, i.e., the territories of the former Achaemenid empire lying to the east of Babylon. The Iranian territories, however, were still in the hands of Antigonus, who, as expected, tried to oppose the ambition of Seleucus. If we put together the patchy information provided by the Babylonian astronomical diaries, the Babylonian historiographical text known as the *Diadochi Chronicle* (Del Monte 1997: 183-194; Finkel and van der Spek: online), and the accounts of the classical authors as well (Diodorus 19.90-92; Appian, *Syr.* 55), we learn that several battles took place in Babylon between Seleucus's forces and Antigonus and his officers in the years from 310 to 308 (Wheatley 2002: 39-47). Seleucus gained an important victory along the river Tigris against Nicanor, the satrap of Media, who had gathered an impressive army of 10,000 men and 7000 cavalry from Media, Persis, and the neighbouring regions. Nicanor had to flee with a few companions, while Evager, the general in charge of the Persian detachment, was killed together with other officers. The final battle was fought on August 10, 309 when Seleucus inflicted a severe defeat to the troops of Antigonus (*Diadochi Chronicle*, Reverse, col. 4, left edge, l. 2; Polyaenus, 4.9.1). The possessions of Antigonus in the east were definitively lost, and Seleucus could add to his dominion the satrapies of Media, Susiana, and the bordering areas.

Since 308, Seleucus was occupied in conquering the easternmost satrapies including Bactria and Sogdiana, and then he crossed the Hindu Kush to fight the Indian king Chandragupta (r. ca. 324-298 BCE), founder of the Mauryan dynasty. The details of this eastern campaign are almost lost, as we do not have anything more than a list of regions of the eastern Iranian world, which were successfully subdued by Seleucus: Hyrcania, Parthia, Tapouria, Bactria, Sogdiana, and Arachosia (Appian, *Syr.* 55; Justin 15.4.10; Trogus, *Prologi* 15). The latter, however, together with other territories south of the Hindu Kush range, was left to Chandragupta after the peace treaty with Seleucus at an uncertain date between 305 and 302 (Capdetrey 2007: 39-48; Kosmin 2014: 32-37). The conquest of such an extended territory within a relatively short time span suggests that Seleucus did not meet with any serious opposition along the way. Numismatic sources shed some light as far as Bactria is concerned: there, Seleucus may have confronted a local dynast called Sophytos, who ruled the area between ca. 315-305 (Bopearachchi and Flandrin 2005: 195-201).

At the beginning of the third century, Seleucus had become master of most of Alexander's empire. In 294, in an effort to consolidate his territorial gains, the king appointed his son Antiochus I as co-ruler and governor of the eastern half of the empire. The two first Seleucids took great care to secure and settle their Iranian possessions, as they were located far from the centre of power represented by Antioch in Syria. The long distance that separated them demanded a good organization of logistics in order to make the presence of the Seleucid authority felt and to protect the Upper Satrapies from the incursions of the nomadic populations. The choice of appointing Antiochus as co-ruler went exactly in that direction. Moreover, the fact that his mother was the Bactrian princess Apama may have increased the loyalty of his Iranian subjects. Hence, Antiochus was the living example of the policy of cultural fusion between Greeks and Iranians which Alexander the Great had tried to promote during his lifetime (on the interplay between Greek and Iranian culture under the Seleucids see Iossif 2011: 229-291; Canepa 2015). Seleucus I and, to an ever greater extent, Antiochus, increased their control over these lands by founding or refounding a range of settlements: these could be forts and military colonies charged with the protection of certain districts such as the fortress in the area of Kermanshah, which controlled the great route linking Babylon to Ecbatana (Capdetrey 2007: 261-262; Rougemont 2012: 186-187; Kosmin 2014: 191), or the site of Kampyr-Tepe in Bactria built on the right bank of the Amudarya in order to watch over a ford (Cohen 2013: 277-279). They could be new cities such as Europos-Rhagai (modern Rey, see Cohen 2013: 209-210), Laodicea-in-Media (Nihavand, see Cohen 2013: 219-220), Antioch-in-Margiana (Merv, see Cohen 2013: 245-250), and Ai Khanum in Bactria (Bernard et al. 1973-2013; Cohen 2013: 219-244). Nevertheless, it must be said that at the beginning, these sites were generally small-scale settlements that could increase in size and importance depending on the commitment of the royal authority. The typology of the Seleucid settlements included indigenous towns that received colonists and, in many cases, a new name: for instance, an ancient Achaemenid centre such as Susa hosted a Greco-Macedonian community and was renamed Seleuceia-on-the-Eulaios (Martinez-Sève 2010: 47-50; Cohen 2013: 194-199). A fragmentary inscription seems to prove that Susa was also provided with the Macedonian institution of the *peliganes*, i.e., the elder council (Gatier 2013: 205-210). The settlement of Greek and Macedonian colonists was a major element of the Seleucid policy as it allowed the creation of a network of cities able to assure loyalty toward the dynasty, definition of the royal space, and control even in the remote parts of the empire. Settlers from Greece but especially from Asia Minor were involved in this process (Capdetrey 2007: 76-81; Coloru 2013: 30-44). For instance, it seems that the city of Magnesia-on-the-Meander had provided many settlers to several colonies in Iran and Central Asia: Antiochus I sent a group of Magnesians to populate the settlement of Antioch-in-Persis – probably modern Bushir – on the Persian Gulf (Rougemont 2012: n° 53, ll. 14-20), and colonists from Magnesia increased the Seleucid communities in Bactria to the point that in 206 even the king Euthydemus I could boast the Magnesian origins of his family during the peace conference with Antiochus III (Polybius 11.34.1). The two first Seleucids also organized expeditions in order to acquire a better knowledge of their eastern territories: the admiral Patrocles, for example, explored the coasts of the Caspian Sea (Strabo 11.10.1; Pliny the Elder 6.49.8-10), while Demodamas of Miletus was sent to Sogdiana where he crossed the Iaxartes river (modern Syrdarya) and set altars in honor of the Apollo of Didyma (Pliny the Elder 6.49.8-10).

After the death of Seleucus in 281, the extant historical sources do not record any relevant facts concerning Iran and Central Asia under the reigns of Antiochus I (r. 281-261) and Antiochus II (r. 261-246). During these decades, we have absolutely no information about the political situation in the Upper Satrapies. The only references to the Seleucid rule in Central Asia in this period are provided by two documents: the first one is an inscription from Hyrcania attesting the liberation of the slave Hermaios on behalf of Antiochus I, the queen Stratonike, and their descendants. It can be dated between 281 and 261 BCE (Sherwin-White and Kuhrt 1993: 81-82; Rougemont 2012: n° 76). The second document is a Babylonian tablet dated to the 24th day of the month of Addaru in the 38th year of the Seleucid Era (=March 26, 273). This document states that the satrap of Bactria had sent to Antiochus I twenty elephants that he presumably had to use in the First Syrian War (274-271) against Ptolemy II (Sachs and Hunger 1996: 345).

When Antiochus II died in 246, a dynastic crisis broke up: Seleucus II (r. 246-226), the elder son from his first wife Laodice, fought for his right to succeed to the throne against Berenice, Antiochus's second wife, who had given birth to another son also named Antiochus. Berenice and his son were murdered and that prompted Berenice's brother, Ptolemy IV of Egypt, to invade Syria and Mesopotamia to avenge their deaths. This difficult situation affected the stability of the eastern Iranian territories: Andragoras, the satrap of Parthia-Hyrcania, and Diodotus, the satrap of Bactria-Sogdiana, proclaimed their independence from the Seleucid Empire in the months following the death of Antiochus II, a sign that the two governors had long been meditating this move. It is likely that they had both been in charge of the administration of their satrapies for many years and had had the time to create a strong power base there. Andragoras might have been involved in the administration of Parthia-Hyrcania since the reign of Antiochus I, if he has to be identified with the officer mentioned in the aforesaid act of manumission of the slave Hermaios. In the following years, the new Bactrian kingdom of Diodotus annexed the bordering satrapies of Areia, Drangiana, and Margiana. On the other hand, Andragoras's rule was short-lived, as around 238 the Parni nomads under their chief Arsaces invaded Parthia and killed Andragoras. Then, Arsaces established his own dynasty laying the foundations of the Parthian empire (see e.g., Strabo 11.9.3; Justin 41.4.6-8). A few years later, Seleucus II launched a campaign to retake the lost territories. The details of this expedition are unfortunately lost and we only have fragmentary information: a copy of a royal letter possibly sent by Seleucus to his officer Herophantos (Rougemont 2012: n° 80 bis) would attest the presence of the king in a place called Baiseira, a toponym which is identical to that mentioned in two parchments from Avroman (Kurdistan) dated respectively to 88/87 BCE and 22/21 BCE (Rougemont 2012: n° 73 and 74), although it is not possible to conclude that we are dealing with the same place yet. Nevertheless, it seems that, during the campaign, the king received in this city a delegation from some villages devoted to horse breeding. These villages probably complained about their obligation of providing accommodation for the soldiers and passing dignitaries. On the other hand, the classical sources let us know that Seleucus confronted Arsaces several times and at first the Seleucid army was so successful in repelling the Parthians that Arsaces had to seek refuge among the nomads Apasiakai (Strabo 11.8.8). This positive course was interrupted by the severe defeat suffered by Seleucus in a memorable pitched battle, which the Parthians consider the true beginning of their independence (Justin 41.4.9-10). Nevertheless, it seems that this major defeat was not the only factor that forced Seleucus to withdraw his troops. It seems it was also caused by an uprising which Seleucus's aunt Stratonike stirred up in Antioch because the king had refused to marry her. Through this planned marriage, she aimed to start a war between Syria and Macedonia in order to take her revenge on her first husband, king Demetrius II, who had married the Epirote princess Phtia (Flavius Josephus, *Against Apion* 1.22).

For the years to come, the eastern frontier of the Seleucid Empire was represented by Media. This important region was at the centre of a new revolt against the Seleucids in the '20s of the third century. In 222, Molon, the satrap of Media, proclaimed himself king and with the support of his brother Alexander, satrap of Persis, marched against Antiochus III (r. 223-187), who was at that time still young and under the sway of his tutor and first minister Hermeias (Polybius 5.40-54). After a series of ineffective attempts by the Seleucid generals to stop Molon, in 220 Antiochus put himself at the head of his army and met Molon on the battlefield; as soon as the left wing of the rebel army saw Antiochus, it passed immediately on the king's side, throwing Molon and the rest of his troops into panic. Both Molon and his brother Alexander fled and committed suicide in order to avoid capture. The king, however, had the body of Molon crucified and ordered his officers to expose it at the beginning of the route leading into the Zagros as a warning against those who had thought to revolt (Polybius 5.54). Antiochus, who was now encouraged by his victory, decided to pursue the campaign by punishing those who had provided assistance to Molon. The main target was Artabazanes, king of Media Atropatene (roughly corresponding to northwest Iran), who being very old and fearing for his kingdom made a treaty on terms very favourable to Antiochus (Polybius 5.55). Once this matter was settled, Antiochus turned west to fight Ptolemy IV of Egypt in the Fourth Syrian War (219-217), and then to suppress the revolt of his cousin Achaeus in Asia Minor.

Almost a decade after the revolt of Molon, Antiochus was finally free to engage himself in an impressive campaign (from 212 to 205/4) to reassert Seleucid authority over the eastern satrapies. The first step consisted in marching against Xerxes, the dynast of Sophene – a district of the kingdom of Armenia, nowadays in southeast Turkey. Xerxes, and his father before him, had actually stopped to pay the tribute due to the Seleucids, quite probably by taking advantage of the crisis of their empire in the second half of the third century. At first, Antiochus laid siege to the capital Arsamosata, where Xerxes had shut himself in to oppose his overlord's demands. Soon, however, Xerxes began to be in fear of losing his entire possessions and preferred to come to terms with Antiochus. Although the friends of the king urged him to eliminate Xerxes and put his nephew Mithridates on the throne, Antiochus accepted the submission of the dynast, left him in his place and remitted to him most of the tribute he was expected to pay. In addition, the king gave him his sister Antiochis in marriage. In exchange, Xerxes provided Antiochus with 300 talents, 1000 horses, and 1000 mules (Polybius 8.25). This was a bold move on Antiochus's part, as dictating mild conditions and creating familial ties with the dynasty of Sophene allowed him to gain more influence in the area than if he had spent time and resources occupying it. A few years later, the same Antiochus will have his sister poison Xerxes for unknown reasons (John of Antioch fr. 122, ed. Roberto 2005). This fact shows that the choice of exerting a remote control over Sophene did not prevent the Seleucid king from deeply intervening in the affairs of this client kingdom. What is more, about 190, Antiochus had gained such a sway over the Armenian territories as to divide them in two parts: Sophene was assigned to Zariadris, while Greater Armenia went to Artaxias. These two local dynasts acted as *strategoi*, "governors," for the Seleucids (Strabo 11.14.15).

After obtaining the submission of Xerxes of Sophene, Antiochus marched to Ecbatana, where he gathered a huge force of 100,000 infantry and 20,000 cavalry (Justin 41.5.7). There, he took away 4000 talents in gold and silver from the temple of Anaitis to finance the expedition (Polybius 10.27.11-13; see Houghton and Lorber 2002: 455-464; Boillet 2013: 191-211).

The years 210-208 were devoted to fighting Arsaces II (r. 211-185), son and successor of the founder of the Arsacid kingdom, in Parthia and Hyrcania. The Parthians tried to slow the advance of the Seleucid army along the route, at first by trying to destroy the water wells in the desert between the Caspian Gates and the city of Hecatompylos, then by ambushing the army in the narrow pass of the Elburz range (Polybius 10.28-30). All of these attempts failed and Antiochus was able to make it into Hyrcania, where he camped in the town of Tambrax. Since the enemy had retreated to the nearby town of Sirynx, Antiochus decided to lay siege to it; the place was protected by an impressive defensive system, so that the king had recourse to his military engineers to undermine the walls, which eventually fell, despite the attempts of the besieged soldiers to hamper the construction of the tunnels. The soldiers of the Parthian garrison had no choice but to flee. However, before leaving the town under cover of darkness, they slaughtered all the members of the Greek community and took away the most valuable objects they could find. Antiochus sent a detachment of his army in pursuit of the fugitives; as the pursuers approached, the Parthians threw away the plunder and returned to Sirynx, but there they were forced to surrender (Polybius 10.31). After this episode, we lose track of the Seleucid military operations in Parthia-Hyrcania. A short reference in Justin (41.5.7) informs us that, after a series of battles, Antiochus decided to make peace with Arsaces II and concluded a treaty of alliance with him. We do not know its exact terms, but it is reasonable to suppose that it implied Arsaces's formal submission as a client-king of the Seleucids. The next phase brought the Seleucid army to Bactria, where Antiochus had to face the strong resistance of King Euthydemus I (Polybius 10.49). The first clash took place at the western borders of the Greco-Bactrian kingdom, while Antiochus and his army were engaged in crossing the river Arius (modern Hari Rud). There followed a fierce fighting against the Bactrian cavalry and Antiochus himself was wounded, but eventually the Seleucid army managed to repel the assault and Euthydemus withdrew to his capital Bactra (modern Balkh). Antiochus put the town under siege for two years, but we do not know the details, as the text of the historian Polybius, who narrated this part of the Seleucid campaign in the East, is totally lost. In another section of his *Histories*, Polybius (29.12) claims that the siege of Bactra was one of the most favourite subjects among the experts of military history and that it stood on an equal footing with the famous sieges of Tarentum, Corinth, Sardis, Gaza, and Carthage. However, numismatic evidence gives at least a rough idea of the movements of Antiochus during this period. It seems that the strategy adopted by the king was to weaken his enemy by taking places vital at both a strategic and an economic level; apparently, Antiochus may have gained control of Sogdiana, which had been lost to the Greco-Bactrian kings since the first years of their independence (Atakhodjaev 2013: 213-246). In the northeast, he took the important town of Ai Khanum with its irrigated farmland (Kritt 2015: 62-63). Much like what had happened with Arsaces, however, Antiochus, in 206, decided to come to terms with Euthydemus and concluded their alliance by guaranteeing the title of king to Euthydemus while Antiochus would receive a number of war elephants and supplies for his troops (Polybius 11.34.9-10). In addition, Antiochus promised one of his daughters in marriage to Demetrius, the son of Euthydemus. Afterwards, Antiochus continued his campaign to India, where he met the Indian king Sophagasenos with whom he renewed the treaty that his ancestor Seleucus I had concluded with King Chandragupta almost a century earlier (Polybius 11.34). He also received a tribute including more war elephants that, added to those given by Euthydemus, reached a total of 150. From there he moved through Arachosia and Drangiana, and set his winter quarters in Carmania. On the Persian Gulf, he made sure to strengthen the Seleucid authority on the islands of the gulf and the communities of the eastern coast of the Arabian Peninsula such as the Arab kingdom of Gerrha, whose capital is probably located at or near modern Thaj (Martinez-Sève 2010: 56-62). Then, he concluded his enterprise at Seleuceia-on-the-Tigris in 204.

The Seleucid control over their remaining Iranian territories began to show some signs of weakness after the Romans defeated Antiochus III at the battle of Magnesia in 189. The first repercussions of this event emerged in Elymais, a region occupying part of the modern Iranian province of Khuzestan, in the foothills of the Zagros. In 187, Antiochus decided to start a new campaign in order to reaffirm the Seleucid suzerainty in the east. The submission of the Elymaeans seems to have been among the primary objectives of this expedition; during these operations, whose development remains unknown, Antiochus took away the riches of a local Elymaean shrine of Zeus/Bel (Diodorus of Sicily 28.3 and 29.15; Strabo 16.1.18; Justin 32.2.1-2; Eusebius of Caesarea, *Chronicon* 1, p. 253; Jerome, *in Danielem* 11). Although anti-Seleucid sources have interpreted this action as a "pillage" aiming to obtain precious metal to pay the war indemnities demanded by the Romans, the reality seems to have been more complex. In fact, Antiochus did not need to enter a difficult and peripheral region of his empire to plunder a temple when he could have found wealthier shrines in more accessible areas. It is likely that by "pillaging" the temple of Bel, Antiochus sought to give tangible proof of his royal authority over the region (Capdetrey 2007: 186-187; Martinez-Sève 2014: 263-265). The troubles in that region had probably already begun before Antiochus had decided to attack the temple of Bel, but in the end the king lost his life during a battle against the Elymaeans, who had reacted to this provocation.

Elymais continued to be a problem for the Seleucids, so that the region became once again one of the targets of the military campaign in western Iran organized by Antiochus IV (r. 175-164) in the years 165-164. This time, the king tried, to no avail, to plunder a temple of Artemis/Nanaia (see e.g., Polybius 31.9.1-3; Flavius Josephus, *AJ* 12.358-359; Appian, *Syr.* 66 Porphyry, FGrHist 260 F 53 and 56; II *Macc.* 1.13-16 and 9.1-2; Potts [1999: 383-384] supposes that the shrine might be identified with the site of Masjid-i Soleiman), but he had to retreat to Persis, where he died not long after at Tabai (close to modern Isfahan). The similarity of this episode with that which had involved Antiochus III suggests that we are not dealing with a mere case of pillage, but with a deliberate policy which amounted to claiming royal authority over a territory through the confiscation of the treasure of a local shrine. Despite the dramatic conclusion of this expedition, Antiochus IV had nonetheless maintained the Seleucid control over Armenia, Media, Susiana, and the Persian Gulf. He might have also concluded an alliance with the king of Media Atropatene, sealed by a dynastic marriage between a Seleucid princess and the Median prince Ariobarzanes (Coloru 2014). As for the Persian Gulf, our sources seem to suggest that Antiochus IV was intensely active (Pliny the Elder 6.139, 6.147, 6.152; see also Martinez-Sève 2013: 305-325). The king may be credited with the refoundation of Alexandria-of-Characene, which he would rename Antioch after himself. This action was in line with a policy adopted since the beginning by the Seleucid dynasty in the Persian Gulf. It aimed to secure the area and affirm authority over the maritime trade routes and the populations of the coast as well as of the islands. Antioch-of-Characene, whose unexcavated site should lie in the vicinity of Khorramshahr (Cohen 2013: 109-116), was the capital of the Seleucid satrapy of the Erythrean Sea; and Antiochus appointed Hyspaosines, son of Sagdodonacus, as its governor. The Persian Gulf had been also the scene of a naval battle where Noumenius, the admiral of Antiochus, gained a victory against the Persians – quite probably a generic term, rather than the inhabitants of Persis, designating local populations living along the coast and practising piracy.

Persis was another region that tried to make itself independent from the Seleucid domination about that same time. Towards the end of the third century, Persis was administered in the name of the Seleucids by local dynasts, titled *fratarakā i bayan* i.e., "governors in the name of the gods/lords." The identity of those gods/lords is still debated; several solutions have been put forward (Callieri 2014: 97-100), but the possibility that the title alludes to a cult for the *fratarakā*'s illustrious ancestors, i.e., the Achaemenids, might fit well with the feeling of "national" pride, which at that time was growing strong among the Persian aristocracy (Callieri 2014: 89). In the first half of the second century BC, the *fratarakā* had gradually become independent from the Seleucids by taking advantage of the crisis of their empire (Wiesehöfer 2000: 195; alternative chronology, Engels 2013: 28-82). In fact, we learn that during this period, three thousand Seleucid military colonists were massacred by order of a King Oborzos – who can be identified with the *fratarakā* Wahbarz in his coin legends – because they had conspired against him (Polyaenus 7.40). What is more, it is likely that Wahbarz celebrated this event on the reverse of a commemorative drachm where a king, dressed in Achaemenid royal garments, is represented in the act of finishing off a Macedonian soldier (Alram 1987: 147-155; Shayegan 2011: 169-177; Wiesehöfer 2011:

113-114). The coin legend attributes to Wahbarz the title of *karanos*, "commander," which in the Achaemenid period designated a high-rank official exerting command over the military forces of a number of satrapies (Olbrycht 2013: 63-74). This is also the title assumed by Arsaces I of Parthia in some of his early issues. As a matter of fact, this was not a simple reference to the Achaemenid tradition: it was also the assertion of a new political status which was no longer that of a subordinated satrap but that of an independent ruler. The massacre of three thousand Seleucid colonists actually marked the first step of Wahbarz towards full independence from the Seleucid rule, although this process seems to have experienced alternate stages. After the conquest of Mithridates in 138, the *fratarakā* became vassals of the Parthians and after 133 we find that Persis is governed by a new dynasty of client rulers inaugurated by Dārāyān who gives up the old title of *fratarakā* in order to assume that of *shah* (king).

After Antiochus IV died in Persis, the throne went to his son Antiochus V. However, since he was still of a young age, he was assisted by his tutor Lysias. Both of them were however killed by Demetrius I (162-150), the representative of the main dynastic branch, on his return to Syria. He had escaped from Rome, where he was being held as hostage, to claim his rights to the succession. Thus, another Seleucid governor of Media, Timarchus (r. 162-161), took advantage of this difficult dynastic situation to revolt and proclaim himself king with the consent of the Roman Senate (Polybius 31.33, 32.2-3 and 13; Trogus, *Prologi* 34; Diodorus of Sicily 31.27; Appian, *Syr.* 47). The satrapy of Media again showed its geopolitical importance for the stability of the empire. After obtaining the support of the neighbour satrapies and having concluded an alliance with King Artaxias of Greater Armenia, Timarchus advanced toward the west and occupied Babylon. Demetrius I responded swiftly by marching with his army against the usurper, who was defeated and killed in Mesopotamia. Nevertheless, the Seleucid presence in Iran did not stay stable for long. In Parthia, the accession of the new king, Mithridates I (r. 165-132, revised chronology by Assar 2006: 88-98), inaugurated a phase of territorial expansion bound to turn the Parthian kingdom into an empire. After annexing territories in the east at the expense of the Greco-Bactrian kingdom - the satrapy of Tourioua and that governed by a certain Aspiones (Strabo, 11.9.2 and 11.11.2) – Mithridates turned to Media, where he had to face the Seleucid opposition, which for several years managed to stop, or at least to slow down, the Parthian advance. A dedication made at Behistun in June-July 148 by a Pantauchos, son of Hyakinthos, for the safety of Kleomenes, governor of the Upper Satrapies, is the last known document attesting Seleucid control over the region (Rougemont 2012: n° 70).

However, other areas of Seleucid Iran had been attacked. Around 147, the king of Elymais, Kamniskires I, occupied Susa, where he issued coinage in his name – in point of fact, Kamniskires was not a personal name, but rather the Greek rendering of the Elamite title *kap-nu-ish-kir-ra*, "treasurer" (Potts 1999: 386). The assassination of Alexander Balas (r. 150-145) in 145 as well as the civil war opposing Demetrius II (first reign 145-138, second reign 129-125) to Antiochus VI (r. 144-141) and his tutor Diodotus Tryphon (141-138) are likely to have given Kamniskires the opportunity to launch an attack against the Seleucid possessions in Mesopotamia. Between the autumn of 145 and the summer of 144, the troops of Kamniskires ravaged Babylonia, but they were finally driven back by the forces of

Tryphon (Potts 2002: 352-353). In the same years, Mithridates must have been concluding the occupation of Media. With this territorial gain, Mithridates now had direct access to Mesopotamia, and at the beginning of July 141 he took Seleuceia-on-the-Tigris and Babylon (Sachs and Hunger 1996: 130-139; Del Monte 1997: 102-103). Mithridates did not stay long in Mesopotamia, as he had to go back in order to repel the raids of nomadic people in Hyrcania. However, he left his generals on the spot with the task of submitting Elymais. The Parthians were able to occupy Susa and subdue most of Elymais in the years 140-138, but their control over the area was not strong enough to prevent a usurper named Tigraios (138-133) from ruling in Susa for five years. In addition, the Elymaeans continued to fight fiercely against the Parthians in the following years and allied themselves with Hyspaosines, the former governor of Characene, in southern Mesopotamia, who had begun to detach himself from the Seleucid authority around this period (Potts 1999: 390-391; Schuol 2000: 291-300). By 132, however, the Elymaeans had to surrender to the troops of Mithridates.

In 139, Demetrius II decided to march against Mithridates to recover the Upper Satrapies. According to his plans, those territories should have become the operational base allowing him to gain enough strength to fight back Tryphon and retake control over the whole of the Seleucid empire (Dąbrowa 1999: 9-17). After a series of successful battles, Demetrius was ambushed and taken as prisoner to Hyrcania by Mithridates, who nonetheless treated him according to his princely rank and gave him his daughter Rodogune's hand in marriage (Justin 38.9.3-9; Appian, *Syr.* 68). The captivity of Demetrius in Hyrcania lasted ten years, even though he had tried to escape twice. In 130-129, his brother Antiochus VII (r. 138-129) launched an imposing campaign against the successor of Mithridates, Phraates II (r. 132-127), in a bid to rescue Demetrius and retake the Upper Satrapies. In the hope of causing a dynastic conflict between the two brothers, Phraates released Demetrius, but Antiochus was already winning one victory after another and had taken Mesopotamia and Media until Phraates would have been left only with the territories of his ancestors (Justin 38.10.1-10; Diodorus of Sicily 34.15-19; Flavius Josephus, *AJ* 13.250-253). The Arsacid tried to start negotiations to avoid further territorial losses, but the demands of Antiochus were so heavy that Phraates had to keep on fighting. The ensuing confrontation, however, resulted in a terrible defeat for Antiochus, who lost his life on the field. This marked the definite end of the authority of the Seleucids over their Iranian possessions. Between 129 and 126, even Hyspaosines took on the title of king and founded the kingdom of Characene. He also renamed Antioch-of-Characene as Spasinou Charax, "The Garden of Hyspaosines." The kingdom of Characene may have continued to exist as a Parthian vassal state until the Sasanian conquest in the third century CE (Schuol 2000: 291-378).

None of the successors of Antiochus VII had enough power to oppose the Parthians because of the internal dynastic strife which had been gradually weakening the Seleucid kingdom. One of the last Seleucids, Demetrius III (r. 97/96-88/87) ended his days as a prisoner at the Parthian court (Flavius Josephus, *AJ* 13.384-386).

Figure. 1. Bronze head of Seleucus I, Roman copy from a Hellenistic original, location: Naples, National Archaeological Museum.
(License: http://creativecommons.org/licenses/by-sa/2.0/it/deed.en)

Figure. 2. Tetradrachm of Antiochus I (credits: Emporium Hamburg, Auction 76
Auction date: 12 May 2016 Lot number: 87) *(credits: Emporium Hamburg, Auction 76
Auction date: 12 May 2016 Lot number: 87).*

Figure. 3. Stater of Seleucus II (credits: CNG, www.cngcoins.com, Triton XIX Lot number:
284, Auction date: 5 January 2016).

Figure. 4. Tetradrachm of Antiochus III
Credits: Gemini, LLC, Auction II lot 134 11 January 2006. *(credits: Gemini, LLC, Auction
II lot 134 11 January 2006).*

Figure. 5. Marble head of Antiochus IV
Photo: Omar Coloru, location: Berlin, Altes Museum.

Figure. 6. Statue of Herakles with dedication to the Seleucid governor of the Upper Satrapies Pantauchos, location: Behistun, Iran.
Photo: Ron Frazier (original in color) https://creativecommons. org/licenses/by/2.0/legalcode

Figure. 7. Tetradrachm of Demetrius II (credits: Gorny&Mosch GmbH, Auction 130, Auction date: 8 March 2004, Lot number: 1291).

Figure. 8. Tetradrachm of Antiochus VII (credits: CNG www.cngcoins.com, Auction 102 Auction date: 18 May 2016 Lot number: 607).

Figure. 9. Drachm of Arsaces I of Parthia (Public Domain Mark 1.0, PD-US)

Figure. 10. Tetradrachm of Mithridates I of Parthia
(credits: CNG, license: www.creativecommons.org/licenses/by-sa/3.0/deed.en).

Figure. 11. Tetradrachm of Hyspaosines of Characene (credits: CNG www.cngcoins.
com : CNG 75, Lot: 603 Closing Date: Wednesday, 23 May 2007).

Figure. 12. Tetradrachm of Wahbarz (Oborzes) of Persis (credits: Dr. Busso Peus Nachf.,
Auction 400, lot 197, date 22 April 2010).

Time-line of the Seleucid presence in Iran

310/308 Seleucus I fights against Antigonus The One-Eyed in Mesopotamia.

Ca. 308-302 Seleucus I conquers the Upper Satrapies and makes a treaty with King Chandragupta in India.

294 Seleucus I appoints his son Antiochus as viceroy of the Upper Satrapies.

Ca. 246 Secession of Parthia and Bactria from the Seleucid Empire.

Ca. 238 Arsaces's invasion of Parthia and establishment of the Parthian kingdom.

Ca. 230s Campaign of Seleucus II against Arsaces.

222-220 Revolt of Molon, governor of Media.

212-204 Campaign of Antiochus III in the Upper Satrapies.

187 Antiochus III dies while fighting against the Elymaeans

165-164 Campaign of Antiochus IV in the eastern Seleucid territories.

162-161 Revolt of Timarchus, governor of Media.

147-138 Mithridates I of Parthia conquers Media, Elymais, and Babylonia.

139-138 Demetrius II campaigns against Mithridates and is taken prisoner.

129 Antiochus VII campaigns against Phraates II, end of the Seleucid presence in Iran.

Bibliography

Alram, M. 1987. "Eine neue Drachme des Vahbarz (Oborzos) aus der Persis?" *Litterae Numismaticae Vindobonenses*, 3: 147-155.

Assar, G. R. F. 2006. "A Revised Parthian Chronology of 165-91-BC." *Electrum*, 11: 87-158.

Atakhodjaev, A. Kh. 2013. "Données numismatiques pour l'histoire politique de la Sogdiane (IVe-IIe siècles avant notre ère)." *Revue Numismatique*, 170 : 213-246.

Bernard, P. et al. 1973-2013. *Fouilles d'Aï Khanoum*. Paris: De Boccard.

Boillet, P.-Y. 2013. "La production de l'atelier monétaire d'Ecbatane: mise en perspective historique et financière." *Revue Numismatique*, 170: 191-211.

Bopearachchi, O. and Flandrin, Ph 2005. *Le Portrait d'Alexandre le Grand: Histoire d'une découverte pour l'humanité*. Monaco: Éditions du Roche.

Callieri, P. 2014. "The Cultural Heritage of the Aristocracy of Persis." In T. Daryaee, A. Mousavi and K. Rezakhani (ed.), *Excavating an Empire. Achaemenid Persia in Longue Durée*. Costa Mesa (CA): Mazda Publishers, 88-121.

Canepa, M. P. 2015. "Seleukid Sacred Architecture, Royal Cult and the Transformation of Iranian Culture in the Middle Iranian Period." *Iranian Studies* 48/1: 71-97.

Capdetrey, L. 2007. *Le pouvoir séleucide. Territoire, administration, finances d'un royaume hellénistique (312-129 avant J.-C.)*. Rennes: Presses Universitaires de Rennes.

Cohen, G. M. 2013. *The Hellenistic Settlements in the East from Armenia and Mesopotamia to Bactria and India*. Berkeley-Los Angeles-London: University of California Press.

Coloru, O. 2013. "Seleukid Settlements: Between Ethnic Identity and Mobility." *Electrum*, 20: 37-56.

Coloru, O. 2014. "Antiochos IV et le royaume de Médie Atropatène: nouvelles considerations sur un mariage dynastique entre Séleucides et la maison d'Atropatès." In C. Feyel and L. Graslin-Thomé (ed.), *Le projet politique d'Antiochos IV*. Nancy: De Boccard, 395-414.

Dąbrowa, E. 1999. "L'expédition de Démétrios II contre les Parthes (139-138 av. J.-C.)." '*Parthica*, 1: 9-17.

Del Monte, G.F. 1997. *Testi dalla Babilonia Ellenistica. Volume I. Testi Cronografici*. Pisa-Roma: Istituti Editoriali e Poligrafici Internazionali.

Engels, D. 2013. "A New Frataraka Chronology." *Latomus* 72: 28-82.

Finkel, I. and van der Spek, R.J. *Babylonian Chronicles of the Hellenistic Period*. http://www.livius.org/sources/about/mesopotamian-chronicles/?#**

Gatier, P.-L. 2013. "Des péliganes à Suse." *Zeitschrift für Papyrologie und Epigraphik*, 184 : 205-210.

Houghton, A. and Lorber, C. 2002. *Seleucid Coins. A Comprehensive Catalogue. Part I. Seleucus I through Antiochus III.* New York – Lancaster (PA): ANS and CNG.

Iossif, P. 2011. "Apollo Toxotes and the Seleukids: Comme un air de famille." In P.P. Iossif, A.S. Chankowski and C.C. Lorber (ed.), *More than Men, Less than Gods. Studies on Royal Cult and Emperor Worship.* Leuven/Paris/Dudley (MA): Peeters, 229-291.

Kosmin, P. 2014. *The Land of the Elephant Kings: Space, Territory, and Ideology in the Seleucid Empire.* Cambridge (MA): Harvard University Press.

Kritt, B. 2015. *New Discoveries in Bactrian Numismatics,* Lancaster (PA): CNG.

Kuhrt, A. and Sherwin-White, S. 1993. *From Samarkhand to Sardis. A New Approach to the Seleucid Empire.* Berkeley-Los Angeles: University of California Press.

Martinez-Sève, L. 2010. "Suse et les Séleucides au IIIᵉ siècle avant J.-C. " *Electrum,* 18: 41-66.

Martinez-Sève, L. 2013. "Antiochos IV en Susiane, dans le Golfe Persique et en Élymaïde." In C. Feyel and L. Graslin-Thomé (ed.), *Le projet politique d'Antiochos IV.* Nancy: De Boccard, 363-393.

Martinez-Sève, L. 2014. "Les sanctuaires autochtones dans les mondes iraniens : quelques exemples." In Ph. Clancier and J. Monerie (ed.), *Les sanctuaires autochtones et le Roi dans le Proche-Orient hellénistique.* Lyon: Topoi 19/1, 239-277.

Olbrycht, M. 2013 [2014]. "The titulature of Arsaces I, king of Parthia." *Parthica,* 15: 63-74.

Potts, D.T. 1999. *The Archaeology of Elam. Formation and Transformation of an Ancient Iranian State.* Cambridge: Cambridge University Press.

Potts, D. T. 2002. "Five Episodes in the History of Elymais, 145-124 B.C.: New Data from the Astronomical Diaries." *Cahiers de Studia Iranica,* 25: 349-362.

Roberto, U. 2005. *Ioannis Antiocheni Fragmenta ex Historia cronica.* Berlin-New York: Walter de Gruyter.

Rougemont, G. 2012. *Inscriptions grecques d'Iran et d'Asie centrale. Corpus inscriptionum Iranicarum, Part II: Inscriptions of the Seleucid and Parthian periods of eastern Iran and central Asia. Vol. I: Inscriptions in non-Iranian languages, 1.* London: School of Oriental and African Studies.

Sachs, A. J. and Hunger, H. 1996. *Astronomical Diaries and Related Texts from Babylonia. Vol. 3. Diaries from 164 B.C. to 61 B.C.* Wien: Verlag der Österreichischen Akademie der Wissenschaften.

Schuol, M. 2000. *Die Charakene. Ein mesopotamisches Königreich in hellenistisch-parthischer Zeit.* Stuttgart: Franz Steiner Verlag.

Shayegan, M. R. 2011. *Arsacids and Sasanians. Political Ideology in Post-Hellenistic and Late Antique Persia.* Cambridge: Cambridge University Press.

Schuol, M. 2000. *Die Charakene. Ein mesopotamisches Königreich in hellenistisch-parthischer Zeit.* Stuttgart: Franz Steiner Verlag.

Wheatley, P. 2002, "Antigonus Monophthalmus in Babylonia, 310-308 B. C." *Journal of Near Eastern Studies* 61/1: 39-47.

Wiesehöfer, J. 2000. "Frataraka." *Encyclopaedia Iranica* 10/2: 195. (Online version updated in 2012 http://www.iranicaonline.org/articles/frataraka)

Wiesehöfer, J. 2011. "Frataraka rule in Seleucid Persis: a new appraisal." In A. Erskine and L. Llewellyn-Jones (ed.), *Creating a Hellenistic World.* Swansea: Classical Press of Wales, 107-121.

THE ARSACID EMPIRE
Leonardo Gregoratti

The Arsacid Dynasty was the name of the ruling household of the Parthian Empire (247 BC - AD 224), a state also referred to by modern scholars as the Arsacid Empire, from the name of its royal family. It was a major political actor, which ruled over a large portion of southwestern Asia. By the end of the second century BC, at the time of its maximal extension, the Parthian rule stretched from the Euphrates (Strabo, XVI, 1.28) to north-western India (Plin, *N.H.*, VI, 137), including Mesopotamia, Iran, and all the territories lying between the Persian Gulf and Indian Ocean to the south, and the Caspian Sea, Caucasus and the river Amu Darya, the ancient Oxus, to the north (Plin, *N.H.*, VI, 112). The Arsacid rule was established, a few decades after Alexander's death, in the satrapy of Parthia, one of the remotest provinces of the Seleucid kingdom, and lasted for almost five centuries until the rise of the Sasanians.

Sources

The Greek and Latin literary sources from Roman writers provide the largest amount of information concerning the political and military organization and the society of the Parthian empire (Hackl, Jacobs and Weber, 2010). The narration of Rome's political confrontation with the "barbarians" beyond the Euphrates occupies significant portions of the works of historians like Tacitus, Cassius Dio and Plutarch, among others. What is known about the history of the Parthian kingdom and its administrative structure is mainly based on the incomplete and largely stereotyped accounts drawn up by Roman and Greek writers, whose interest in the Arsacids was restricted to the provinces of this vast domain lying closer to the Roman borders and to the historical episodes more closely connected with Rome's policy.

It has recently been demonstrated (Lerouge 2008) that much of the information available from western writers is deeply influenced by an artificial idea, conceived and shared in the Roman empire, regarding the Parthians. In Roman imagination, the Arsacids were considered a mixture of elements that ancient Greek authors had in the past attributed to the Scythian people or Achaemenid Persians.

More unbiased, but scarce, information can be found in the reports of Chinese travelers

(Posch, 1998), the eastern neighbors of Parthia, in Talmudic treatises concerning Jewish communities of the empire (Neusner, 1984) and in late Armenian sources (Kettenhofen, 1998). Parthian and Aramaic inscriptions can shed light on local realities of the empire, for instance, the epigraphic texts from Hatra (Aggoula, 1991) and Osrohene in northern Mesopotamia or the administrative documents from Nisa, the early Arsacid capital in the northeastern part of the empire. Cuneiform documents from Babylonia (Sachs and Hunger, 1996) and later Syriac religious and historical texts can provide useful evidence for shedding light on the history of the Empire.

The coins issued by Parthian rulers as well as those minted by their client kings remain one of the most important sources of information (Alram, 1998). Normally, the issues have the portrait of the Great King on the obverse. On the reverse is a stylized figure sitting on a throne sometimes wielding a bow representing Arsaces the founder of the dynasty. In the legend the sovereigns adopt the crown name of Arsaces along with the royal titles of their Seleucid predecessors; thus the attributions of most of the coins to specific kings are based on their portraits and on the variations in their appearance. Proper names are used only in case of coexistence of two pretenders to the throne (Sellwood, 1980). Only with Vologases I does the king's name in Aramaic begin to appear. The dates follow the Seleucid reckoning. Most of the issues are silver drachms or tetradrachms; important mints were at Seleucia and Ecbatana. Some vassal kings had the right to have their own coinage. The most important issues are those of the kings of Characene, Elymais and Persis. It seems probable that the rulers of Hatra and Adiabene were also entitled to strike their own coins for some time (Walker, 1958; Milik, 1961; Slocum, 1977).

Furthermore, until the middle of the first century AD, the Greek metropolis of Selucia on the Tigris, along with the royal coins, also minted its own municipal coinage. These coins are of various types in accordance with the choices of the magistrates in charge of the city mint. During the rule of Artabanus II, a representation of the Great King enters among the types of city coinage for the first time (Le Rider, 1999, Gregoratti 2012a).

An increasing amount of data are also provided by archaeological excavations in Iran, Iraq and Turkmenistan. In the northeast of the empire, the capital city of Nisa has been extensively excavated. It consists of two separate fortified areas: a large settlement (New Nisa) and the royal citadel (Old Nisa, Mithradatkert), which probably played the role of ideological centre for the Arsacid dynasty. The monumental "Square House" and the "Round Hall" prove the influence of both Hellenistic and Central Asiatic architecture on the first Arsacid capital (Invernizzi, 1998).

Many of the most ancient cities of Mesopotamia seem to have enjoyed a period of prosperity under Arsacid rule. In Babylonia the Mesopotamian temples continued their existence along with Greek institutions. Similar scenarios seem to take place at Ninive and Assur, probably belonging to the kingdom of Adiabene (Reade, 1998; Hauser, 2011). Uruk was also an important centre as well as Nippur, where an imposing fortress was built (first-second century AD; Keall, 1975). One of the most important sites of central Mesopotamia was Seleucia on the Tigris, the largest, richest and most populous city outside Roman borders. Here a minority constituted by Greek leading-classes ruled over the local population despite a continuous influence from nearby Ctesiphon, seat of the Great King (Strab., XVI,

2. 5; Tac., *Ann.*, VI, 42).

The Polish scholar Josef Wolski (Wolski, 1993) deigned to distinguish in Parthian history a sequence of different evolutionary stages involving the social and administrative organization of the empire. According to him, a so-called "formation" phase was followed by a period when the kingdom was shaken by a sequence of changes which radically altered the nature of the relationship between the king and the nobility.

Origins

In the middle of the third century BC, the Parni, a tribe belonging to the confederation of the Dahi, a central Asian semi-nomadic people who lived along the Ochus River (now Tejen), moved southwards into the Seleucid satrapy of Parthia (Strabo, XI, 9.2). Soon its leader, Arsaces, defeated Andragoras, the Greek governor of Parthia, who had already made himself autonomous from the Seleucid authority, taking control of the whole region and choosing the year 247 BC as the first year of the Arsacid Era. According to another version, the Parthians were a Scythian tribe that moved and settled south in more ancient times, during Assyrian and Median domination. They remained obscure under the following Persian and Macedonian rule, until they managed to become strong enough to rebel against the Greek governors. Other accounts portray Arsaces as a man of uncertain origins leading a tribe of marauders (Pomp. Trogus/ Justin, 41. 4. 6-8), as a refugee from Bactriana (Strabo, XI, 9.3), as a young Achaemenid prince, a descendant of Artaxerses (Arr., *Parth.*, frgm., 1, Ross), or, along with all Arsacids, as a descendant of Andragoras, the Macedonian governor of Parthia, appointed directly by Alexander (Pomp. Trogus/ Justin, 12. 4. 2).

It seems evident that apart from Strabo's, most of the other versions concerning the origins of the Parthians and their ruling dynasty are an expression of the Arsacid royal ideology and aimed at legitimating their own rule. The purpose was to present the Parthians as an indigenous population in the attempt to push their Central Asiatic origins into the background. On the other hand, the Arsacid household is described as detached from the Parthian people and strongly connected with the Persian authority that preceded Macedonian conquest or with Alexander's rule. The Arsacid represented a mere continuation of the ancient dynasties that ruled western Asia.

The reason why the year 247 BC was chosen as the first year of the Arsacid era and therefore used along with the more traditional and popular Seleucid one in some documents is unclear. It probably indicated the moment when the satrapy of Parthia became independent of Seleucid rule.

The Seleucid kings achieved some military successes against the Parthians in the last decades of the third century BC. They were unable to recover all of the lost territories on the northeastern frontier of the kingdom, but they obtained a formal submission from the Parthian king, Arsaces II. The latter was appointed *basileus* after acknowledging the superiority of Antiochus III the Great. After the defeat of Magnesia (190 BC), the Seleucids ceased to constitute a threat to Parthian independence.

Expansion

With the weakening of the Seleucids, the Arsacid king Mithridates I of Parthia (r. 171-138

BC) was able to spread his control over large territories of Western Asia. Mesopotamia, Babylonia, and the metropolis of Seleucia on the Tigris were conquered in 141 BC, along with the small kingdoms of Elymais and Characene, on the Persian Gulf, whose monarchs submitted themselves to the Great King. Besides Hecatompylos, the first capital, several other residences were established at Mithradatkert (Nisa), Ecbatana, Seleucia, and Ctesiphon while the centre of gravity of the whole empire was quickly moving westwards (Dąbrowa, 2011).

The last attempt of Antiochus VII Sidetes to form an anti-Parthian coalition and regain the lost satrapies came to an abrupt end in 129 BC, when the Seleucid king, after some relevant military successes, was defeated and killed in battle. It was a fate similar to that shared by the great Kings Phraates II (r. 138-128 BC) and Artabanus I (r. 128-124 BC) when fighting the Scythian tribes (Saka) which had invaded Parthia's northeastern border (Olbrycht, 1998).

Mithridates I of Parthia (r. 124-90 BC) triumphed over the nomadic tribes and recovered the lost satrapies. In 121 BC, the Chinese Han emperor Wu sent a delegation to the Parthian court with the purpose of opening official trade relations with the Arsacids along the Silk Road. From that time on, silk, pearls, spices, and iron began to travel across the Parthian empire to reach the Roman market, while the Chinese purchased perfumes, fruits, exotic animals, and Roman glassware from the Parthians.

The Confrontation with Rome and the Crisis

The Arsacids maintained their neutrality during the wars that Mithridates IV, king of Pontus and his ally Tiridates of Armenia fought against the Romans. During an informal meeting between the Roman commander Sulla and Orobazos (Great King Mithridates II's envoy), the river Euphrates was chosen as the boundary between Parthia and Rome (Plut. *Sull.*, 5. 4-5).

After the death of Mithridates II, Parthia gradually entered a period of political crisis caused by the frequent struggles between brothers to gain the throne. In 58 BC Phraates III was assassinated by his two sons, Orodes II and Mithridates III, who soon found themselves at odds, both aiming at the throne of Parthia. According to Cassius Dio (Cass. Dio, XXXIX, 56. 2), the weaker of the two princes, Mithridates, besieged in Seleucia, asked for help, probably offering the submission of the portion of Parthia under his control to the Romans in exchange for the help he needed to gain the throne. But the Roman governor of Syria, who was already marching with his legions towards the Euphrates to rescue the prince, could not exploit the opportunity because of unexpected troubles in Egypt.

It was probably the concrete possibility to reduce the whole Parthian empire to a state that was *socius et amicus populi Romani*, and not only -- as contemporary and more recent sources tend to tell us (Cic., *De Finibus*, III, 75; Vell. Pat., II, 46. 2; App. *Bell. Civ.*, II, 18; Plut., *Crass.*, 15-16; Cass. Dio, XL, 12. 1; Floro, XIII, 4. 10) -- the mere desire for glory and wealth, that convinced the *triumvir* M. Licinius Crassus to launch his ill-fated invasion of Mesopotamia.

A few months later Crassus crossed the Euphrates with a large army seeking to reach Seleucia as soon as possible by the most direct route, along the Euphrates. There Mithridates was still opposing his brother with a strenuous resistance, as his coin emissions seem to suggest (54 BC) (Plut., *Crass.*, 20).

Forced to delay by the behaviour of Abgar, king of Osrhoene, who was probably in charge of buying time for Orodes, Crassus reached Carrhae in northern Mesopotamia only in the spring of 53 BC. Here in the steppe around the city, the Parthian general Surena, the chief of the noble family of the same name, managed to inflict one of the most devastating defeats the Romans suffered in the East. More than 20,000 Romans lost their lives and about 10,000 prisoners were taken. Only a small contingent of 10,000 men was able to cross the Euphrates and reach Roman Syria (Plut., *Crass.*, 31). Crassus was not among them. He met his death after the battle when fighting burst out during a meeting.

Taking advantage of that strategic victory, the Parthians twice invaded Roman lands, in 51 BC (Cic., *Ad familiares* 8.5-10; 15.1-4; *Ad Atticum* 5.18; 5.20-21; 6.1-8; 7.2) and a decade later in 41 BC, when a large-scale invasion led by Q. Labienus, a Roman general who had fought for the caesaricides Brutus and Cassius, and for Pacorus, the young Parthian prince and heir to the throne. Exploiting the internal Roman trouble that followed Caesar's assassination, Labienus and Pacorus invaded the whole of Syria and part of Anatolia and gained control of Judea. Both died in the failed invasion attempt when their contingents were defeated by Antony's man Ventidius Bassus (39-38 BC). The loss of Pacorus, heir prince of Parthia, increased the political crisis at the Arsacid court.

Towards the middle of the first century BC, Parthia entered a condition of social and institutional instability. The king's leadership had been in fact overruled. Monarchs were maintained with the sole intent to provide a formal legitimacy for power gained by one or the other among the aristocratic groups. Parthia was torn by competition between the main noble factions interested in weakening the crown to enlarge their power, thus enhancing their independence from the king.

During the "expansion" period, the nobility offered firm and undisputed political support to the king, who found himself in the condition to exert power without restrictions. The noblemen's collaboration was rewarded by granting them the ownership of large portions of conquered land. Noble families thus began gradually to build their own power on the large estates that they had received from the king. The king granted the noble chiefs large and fertile portions of land as fief. In return the noble landlords were obliged to give military support to royal political enterprises and wartime undertakings. General Surena's army, which defeated Crassus, was an aristocratic army, led by noblemen and mustered in the lands owned by the most powerful noble houses. These armies gradually assumed the characteristics of private militias of the noble houses, whose engagement at the king's side was influenced mainly by the political plans of their patrician commanders (Wolski, 1993).

Several years of political detente between the two superpowers struggling for supremacy in western Asia followed the failed attempt made by Antony to invade Media and to take the city of Praaspa (34-33 BC). In 20 BC, Octavian Augustus, at the time already acknowledged as *princeps* in Rome, decided to settle the situation in the East by diplomatic means. The Parthian Great King Phraates IV (r. 37- 2 BC) consented to return the legionary standards and the prisoners taken at Carrhae in order to reach an agreement with Rome, perceived as the natural ally by the opponents of royal authority. On that occasion, or immediately thereafter, Augustus gifted to Phraates IV an Italic slave girl named Musa, intended to enrich the number of royal concubines (Flav. Joseph., *Ant. Jud.*, XVIII, 38-43) Musa actively did her best to increase her power and influence within the royal palace and upon the king himself. The Great King, struck by her charm and beauty, elevated her to the rank of queen once she gave birth to a child. The monarch then sent his elder sons to Rome as hostages, choosing her as main queen, the mother of the only heir to the throne (Aug., *Res Gestae*, 32; Strabo, XVI,1. 28). The murder of the Great King opened the way to the crowning of her son, Phraataces (Phraates V, 2 BC- AD 4), a weak sovereign more subject to his mother's authority than his father was; as a result, she finally got the power she desired. In AD 2, she married her son, with whom (according to Flavius Josephus) she had a relationship, thus elevating herself to the rank of both Queen consort and Queen mother before being driven out by aristocratic opposition.

After some years of anarchy and internal strife during which Rome tried to impose its own candidates, chosen among the Arsacids living in Rome, onto the Parthian throne, Artabanus II came to power (r. AD 12- 38/41). The first concern of the new Great King was to exploit new sources of income in order to grant the Crown a certain level of economical power and thereby counteract the overwhelming influence of the aristocracy. Artabanus conceived and tried to build a new system of controlling the territory, based on a close relation with local political subjects like the Greek cities' leading classes, the vassal dynasties, and the Jewish communities. The aim of this more direct system of administering territories, alternative to the traditional hierarchical one, was to exclude the interference and the mediation by state officers of aristocratic origins. Artabanus II was the first to perceive the importance of finding new alliances to regain independence from the nobility (Gregoratti, 2015).

Artabanus tried to strengthen his influence on the autonomous Greek cities of the Parthian empire. He put into action a series of political initiatives aimed at gaining indirect control over Seleucia and its trade activity by favouring his supporters in the leading classes and moving large numbers of Jews, supporters of the crown, into the city.

An example of his policy towards the Greek cities is provided by the famous letter of Artabanus to the city of Susa. The king writes in Greek to the city council to advocate the case of one of his supporters there who was about to be appointed treasurer before the time prescribed by the city laws (Zambelli, 1963). This policy, successful as it seems to be with the minor Greek cities, finally provoked the upheaval of the Seleucians, who managed to free the city from royal control for seven years (Tac., *Ann.*, XI, 9) until the reign of Vardanes. Artabanus sought an allegiance with the Jewish communities of Mesopotamia, Nisibis, and Nahardea, as is shown by the episode of the two Jewish brothers Asinaeus and Anilaeus, who revolted against the local Parthian aristocrats and satraps and became outlaws. Artabanus invited them to his court and, despite the opinion of his noble councillors and generals, offered them hegemony over Babylonia, which enabled them to act as king's governors and to rule the region for fifteen years (Flav. Joseph., *Ant. Jud.*, XVIII, 310-79; Brizzi, 1995).

A Roman military offensive in Armenia, along with the attempt of one of the Arsacids living in Rome, to gain the throne with the support of the nobility against the Great King threatened Artabanus's rule (AD 35). Defeated in the west he was forced to seek refuge in the eastern satrapies. According to Tacitus, Artabanus, abandoned by nobles and courtesans, and together only with his bodyguard formed by mercenary raiders, "hurriedly fled to the remote districts adjoining Scythia; where he hoped that his marriage connections with the Hyrcanians and Carmanians would find him allies" (Tac., *Ann.*, VI, 36).

In the forests of Hyrcania, southeast of the Caspian Sea, he remained wandering in rags and providing food for himself with his bow. Artabanus went to the eastern satrapies looking for military support among the nomadic chiefs and the Hyrcanian aristocracy. He presented himself as a nomadic hunter imitating the "Scythian" Arsaces, the illustrious founder of the dynasty. He played the role of the nomadic warrior, able to survive in the wilderness far away from court leisure, relying only on his archery skills. The bow, the traditional weapon of Arsacid kings, which Arsaces wields on all Parthian coins, had in fact an important symbolic and propagandistic value. Soon after that, at the head of an army of Sacae and Dahae, he was able to regain the throne (Gregoratti, 2013a).

In his last years of reign, Artabanus became arrogant and ambitious towards Rome. He became confident enough, according to Tacitus, to "insist on the ancient boundaries of Persia and Macedonia, and intimate, with a vainglorious threat, that he meant to seize the country possessed by Cyrus and afterwards by Alexander" (Tac., *Ann.*, VI, 31).

This passage is often quoted by modern scholars in order to demonstrate the fact that the Arsacids were aware of the powerful Persian empire of the Achaemenids that preceded Alexander's conquest and that they considered themselves their legitimate successors.

Moreover, Artabanus seems to put also Alexander and the Seleucids among the ancestors whose territorial possessions he aims to regain. It must nonetheless be noted that the whole passage is characterized by a hyperbolic tone employed by the Roman historian to demonstrate the arrogance of Artabanus, which eventually brought him to insult the old emperor Tiberius. Reading it as an explanation of Arsacid ideology would probably take the interpretation of the text too far.

After Artabanus's death, the empire was again torn by internal strife for the throne. Two pretenders, Gotarzes II and Vardanes I, rulers in the east and in the west, confronted one another for supremacy. Vardanes was able to defeat his rival by conducting a swift military campaign straight into the core of his rival's power, the eastern satrapies, but fell victim to a conspiracy of the aristocratic opposition during a hunting party. Gotarzes's cruel rule lasted until AD 49/50.

The period of Renewal and the final Collapse
The successive rulers, Vologases I (r. AD 51- 77/78) and his son Pacorus II (r. AD 77/78 – 105/110) followed the plan traced by Artabanus. They detected a possible solution in the highly remunerative long-distance trade, which connected both by land and sea, East Asia and India with the Mediterranean coast, and passed through many of the most important Parthian cities. To apprehend this traffic and establish an efficient system for collecting taxes on exotic goods could have provided these kings with the financial sources they needed. They tried to entertain new political and institutional relationships with all the local subjects who were in the condition to exert control over long distance trade. Pacorus in particular also established intensive diplomatic relations with the Chinese Han court after a Chinese

envoy, Gan Ying, had attempted without success to cross the Parthian kingdom and reach the Roman territories by land in AD 97 (Hou *Hanshu*, c. 88. 2918; Gregoratti, 2012b).

Vologases I, son of Vonones II of Media, associated the throne with his two brothers, monarchs in Armenia and Media Atropatene, and thereby conferred stability to the top of the state structure and consolidated the whole empire (Tac., *Ann.*, XV, 2). This political solution enabled Parthia to successfully face a military confrontation with Rome for the rule of the kingdom of Armenia that Vologases had assigned to his brother Tiridates (AD 54-66) (Dąbrowa 1983).

The first major conflict began with the usurpation of the Armenian throne by Rhadamistus, the son of the king of Caucasian Iberia. Vologases interpreted the event as a violation of the previous accords between the two superpowers and felt free to invade the kingdom and claim the throne for his household.

The war was unavoidable and Gn. Domitius Corbulo, a general who has already demonstrated his skills in Germania, was appointed by the young emperor Nero to lead the military operations (Tac., *Ann.*, XII, 8). After some years of preparation often interrupted by diplomatic activity and by the unexpected revolt of the *filius Vardanis*, the Roman general was able to invade Armenia, take control of the major cities of Artaxata and Tigranocerta, drive away Tiridates, son of Vologases I and Arsacid king of Armenia, and install an allied king on the throne (AD 58-59) (Chaumont, 1976).

Tiridates, deprived of his kingdom, a vital element in the new state structure conceived by his father and Monobazos, and the loyal Arsacid client king of Adiabene, whose kingdom was now exposed to the raiding parties of the enemy, protested in front of the whole Parthian court, accusing the Great King of not doing enough to protect his servants (Tac., *Ann.*, XV, 1). The accusation was serious and threatened to ruin the trust between the Great King and his subjects, destroying the entire structure of government conceived by Vologases. The Great King was thus forced by circumstances to react. Having experienced Corbulo's extraordinary military skills, the cunning monarch managed to draw into a trap the newly appointed and arrogant governor of Cappadocia, L. Caesennius Paetus.

Paetus's army was forced to surrender at Rhandeia in AD 62. Following the Parthian victory, Tiridates was allowed to be king of Armenia, but forced to travel as far as Rome to obtain the crown from Nero's hands during a spectacular public ceremony (Tac., *Ann.*, XV. 31-32; Cass. Dio, LXIII, 1-7).

Such a solution to the Armenian problem, conceived by Gn. Domitius Corbulo, commander in chief of the Roman forces in the East, assured a long period of peace and prosperity for Parthia, interrupted only by the incursion of the Alan tribes in AD 72, which ravaged Armenia and Media, probably crossing the Caucasus range (Flav. Joseph., *Bell. Jud.*, VII, 244-251).

After half a century, the appointment of Parthamasiris to the Armenian throne by the Arsacids without Roman approval (AD 113-114), which was considered a violation of the Armenian peace treaty, acted as justification for the major invasion of Parthia, begun by the emperor Trajan. Roman legions quickly marched on Armenia in AD 114. At Elegeia (Cass. Dio, LXVII, 17-20), Trajan deposed Parthamasiris and announced the creation of the Roman province of Armenia. With the support of Abgar of Edessa and other minor north

Mesopotamian lords, in 115-116 imperial legions marched deep into Parthian territory with the purpose of also reducing Mesopotamia and the eastern bank of the Tigris to provinces of Rome (Guey, 1937; Lepper, 1948). Again Roman forces took advantage of the fact that the Arsacid empire was torn by internal strife between two candidates for the throne, Osroes and Vologases II. They took Seleucia on the Tigris and Ctesiphon, the seat of the Arsacid court, before being forced to withdraw to Syria by a major upheaval of the Babylonian population and the Mesopotamian Jewish communities, which allowed the Parthians to organize a successful counteroffensive (114-117 AD).

Despite the switching of sides of many Parthian vassal kingdoms -- including that of Attambelos of Characene, who welcomed the Roman emperor, allowing him to reach the shores of the Persian Gulf -- no firm occupation of Parthian territory could be assured. The idea that the network of different political subjects that constituted the structure of the Parthian state would collapse once Mesopotamia (the capital city and the centre of Arsacid policy and economy of that vast empire) had fallen into Roman hands proved wrong.

The composite nature of the Parthian rule and the bond that each of its many elements had established with the Great King, or better with the royal Arsacid house, explains the extraordinary capacity of Parthia to resist the hardest blows. Paradoxically, the most evident cause of weakness, the existence of two candidates to the throne, Osroes ruling Mesopotamia and Vologases ruling the East, constituted a key element in the emergency situation. Even if most of the satrapies in the west were lost and many western vassal kings deserted or were defeated, in the eastern satrapies, the ruling system that supported Vologases III remained intact as well as its conspicuous resources that could be used to regain lost ground.

A few years after the withdrawal of Trajan's legions, Vologases gained control of the whole empire, tightening the relationship between the crown and local kings through military occupation or by appointing a member of the Arsacid royal house to the throne.

In AD 147/148, with the ascendance of Vologases III, a new branch of the Arsacid family took power. As the first member of a new dynasty, Vologases's first concern was to affirm the control on the lesser kingdom that was becoming more and more important within the empire. In the kingdom of the Characene king Meredates, a son of the former Great King Pacorus II and the brother of Vologases's predecessor, was deposed through military intervention and replaced by Orabzes, probably a relative of the new Great King (AD 151). These events are attested in the famous bilingual inscription found on the statue of Heracles from Seleucia on the Tigris (Bernard, 1990).

Having consolidated the kingdom, Vologases launched an attack west of the Euphrates, which eventually resulted in a disastrous defeat at the hands of the emperor Lucius Verus's generals (AD 161-169), who were again able to reach and burn the Parthian capital (Luc., *Quomodo*). Following the successful invasion of the Roman legions, the town of Dura Europos fell into Roman hands. A small foundation of the Seleucids on the western bank of the Euphrates in the middle of a district rich in fertile lands, the town was conquered by the Arsacids in the second half of the second century BC, constituting for almost three centuries the only Parthian possession west of the Euphrates. During the period of Arsacid rule, as seen in Seleucia and Susa, the town was led by a family who claimed to descend from the first Greek colons and held the most important magistracies belonging to the

Greek municipal organization, which was maintained. During that period the town grew significantly: imposing walls were built, as well as temples, a main square, and an orthogonal street system. The settlement managed to attract an important community of Palmyrene merchants already in the early phase of Palmyra's economic expansion, and that group seemed to play an important role in the town's society until its conquest by the Sasanians. Rediscovered in the 1920s after being abandoned for almost seventeen centuries, the site of Dura Europos has been renamed the "Pompeii of the East" for the extraordinary richness of its archaeological findings.

The materials relative to the Parthian phase are in no way comparable to those belonging to the following Roman one; nonetheless the inscriptions, coins and papyri were fundamental in shedding light on the municipal life of the small Greek town at the western periphery of the Arsacid empire (Arnaud, 1986; Millar, 1998 add Gregoratti, 2016).

For the third time in the second century, Parthian Mesopotamia was invaded by Roman legions in AD 197. The military impact of the most powerful empire of the ancient world began to take its toll, irremediably weakening the structure of the Arsacid kingdom. The importance and the autonomy of the local dynasties increased exponentially. Around AD 208, a first major rebellion against the Arsacid rule was quashed with great effort.

The last Roman offensive, launched by the emperor Caracalla, which reached as far as Arbil and the territories beyond the Tigris, ended abruptly with the assassination of the emperor (AD 217). The newly acclaimed emperor, Macrinus, sought peace by paying two hundred million *denarii* to Parthia. This victory was not enough to restore the largely compromised internal situation of a kingdom on the verge of disintegration.

Ardashir I, the founder of the Sasanian dynasty, belonged to the local aristocracy of Persis, one of the southern client kingdoms of the Arsacid empire. Gaining the loyalty of the other local rulers, he was able to quickly extend his power far beyond Persis. In the end he became powerful enough to face the Great King Artabanus V, defeating his army and killing him at the battle of Hormozdgan (AD 224). That event marked the end of the Arsacid empire even though Artabanus's brother, Vologases V, continued to mint coins in Seleucia until AD 227/228, and an Arsacid dynasty continued to rule the kingdom of Armenia until late antiquity.

The new conquerors were partly responsible for the scarcity of local sources concerning the Parthian period. In the propaganda of the winners and new dynasts, the centuries during which the Arsacids, the *Ashkānīs*, were Great Kings were depicted in a very negative way. Considered the heirs of Alexander, they were weak rulers of the country, allowing the emergence of many local "petty kings" who threw the state into chaos and anarchy. Later historians speak of an "age of darkness" during which "demons and beasts assuming human shape were free to wander through the country, a time in which there was no religion or education but only corruption and disaster" (Al-Ṭabarī, *Tārīḫ*, I, pp. 704-707; 710-711, 823; *Tansar Letter* (§ 39).

Structure of the Empire

The figure of the king played a fundamental role in the power structure of the Arsacid empire; as descendant of the founder and leader of the state he was the maximal Parthian authority. Nonetheless, many times in the history of the Parthian empire, the royal institution came under discussion by noble leaders or various pretenders and usurpers. Even on these occasions, the real element of continuity appeared to be the royal household. No pretender without a blood connection to the royal clan could have any chance of being accepted as the Great King by the many noble families (Strab., XVI, 1. 28). In other words every pretender to the throne who wished to have success had to be able to demonstrate his blood connection with Arsaces, the founder of the dynasty. From there he would have derived his legitimacy. Furthermore, some ceramic documents from Nisa suggest that a sort of "cult of the ancestors" existed or that at least the memory of the first Arsacid kings was kept in high esteem.

Due to the nature of the Parthian state itself, its history and evolution, the Arsacid king amalgamated characteristics of Oriental/Persian Kings, nomadic tribal leaders, and Hellenistic sovereigns. Most probably a complex protocol regulated the royal ceremonies of investiture during which the Great King and his subjects reaffirmed the bond of allegiance that existed between them. Very little information in this regard is provided by the sources; we have the scenes of investiture in the reliefs of Elymais (Vanden Berghe and Schippmann, 1985), probably the investiture speech made by Tiridates, crowned in Rome (Cass. Dio, LXIII, 5), certainly the prestigious role reserved for the chief of the house of Surene as the only one allowed to put the crown on the head of the new Great King (Tac., *Ann.*, VI, 42.4), and also the royal *insignia* that the king of Adiabene was allowed to show (Flav. Ioseph., *Ant. Iud.*, XX, 54-69). These are all elements belonging to an intricate complex of power-sharing, power legitimization, and bonds of loyalty about which very little is known.

As a general rule, the older prince would gain access to the throne after his father's death. In some cases, the elder son was allowed to co-rule at the side of his elderly parent. The experience of Queen Musa and the occurrence of many cases of strife between brothers to gain the throne prove that this was not a strict rule. A Great King could change his mind or the right to the throne of the elder son could be put into discussion by members of the royal family or by the aristocratic groups.

According to Roman and Greek chroniclers, the Arsacid monarchs were cruel and despotic. Posidonius informs us about the ruthless treatment reserved for the "companions" of the king during official banquets (Lerouge, 2013). The respect subjects showed depended on the fear the Great Kings were capable of instilling (Pomp. Trogus/Justin, XLI, 3. 9). Other *topoi* regarding Parthian kings concerned their polygamy (often associated with an excessive sexual appetite [Pomp. Trogus/Justin, XLI, 3. 1; Plut. *Crass.*, 21, 7]) and intrigues at court between members of the ruling dynasty, which were closely connected with the supposed traditional political instability of all oriental kingdoms and of the Parthian kingdom as well.

Roman historians faced a difficult task having to provide the Western public with a representation of the only people daring to challenge Rome's supremacy over the whole known world. They found that the best solution was to provide a moral representation of the Parthians using the same stereotypes which the Greeks had conceived and handed down with regard to their enemies. A series of familiar ethnographic *topoi* were picked up and amalgamated in order to create a new artificial model for the Parthian people. Nonetheless, such a model proved useful in describing to the Romans this exotic people, capable of building a kingdom which, unlike all the others, Rome was not immediately able to subjugate, a kingdom which forced the greatest empire of that time to compromise. In general, the Roman explanation for the condition of political crisis in Parthia was ascribed to the very nature of the "barbarians." In the absence of a real historical investigation, the temporary weakness of the Arsacids was seen as a natural consequence of their whimsical and inconstant nature. The Parthians were seen to be politically unstable, because they were unfaithful, treacherous, and unable to consolidate a kingdom always on the brink to collapse. According to the Romans, the reality could not be different: the Parthian kingdom was weak because the nature of its monarchs and subjects was weak (Gregoratti, 2012c).

Pompeius Trogus (Pomp. Trogus/Justin, XLI, 2. 2) speaks of a "*probulorum ordo*," a group of councillors, dignitaries, and high officers among whom generals were chosen in time of war and magistrates in time of peace. Some scholars postulated the existence of a royal senate in charge of supporting the Great King's ruling activity (Strab., IX, 9. 3 quoting Posidonius of Apamea). Nothing seems to attest to the existence of such a political organ. Most probably, an aristocratic social group existed which expressed most of the high magistracies and played the role of a royal council, providing advice to the king and supporting his government activity. Greek and Roman writers, using familiar terms taken from the western political organization, thus offered the terms *synedrion* or *senatus* in an attempt to explain to their readers a particularity of the Parthian court.

Nonetheless a group of dignitaries, religious figures, and men close to the king or relatives to him seem to maintain a reference role in the periods of political instability.

The *ostraka* from Nisa help to shed light on Parthian administration (Lukonin, 1983). A series of officers' titles, whose exact duties and competences remain unclear, appears in the documents. There were satraps, governors of the provinces described by Isidoros of Charax in his *Parthian Stations* (Kramer. 2003), along with the *marzbān*, marquis, probably at the head of border districts, the *dizpat*, fortress commander, probably in charge of lesser districts, and chief of the cavalry. Other titles like *batēsa* and *hargapet* seem to be widespread over the whole Parthian cultural area and beyond. This, along with other Iranic cultural elements, like Iranic loanwords and personal names, which can be found outside the Parthian proper territory, for example, Armenia, north Mesopotamia, and Caucasus, suggested to Albert de Jong the idea of what he called the "Parthian Commonwealth," a geopolitical region that shared common elements of Iranic culture, thanks to a certain influence of Parthian authority (De Jong, 2013).

During the so called "expansion period," the Parthian kingdom was involved in a forceful expansive policy against the Seleucids. The situation required a strong royal authority supported by noble houses in its military effort. The collaboration of the aristocratic families was rewarded by granting them large estates in the conquered lands, including their populations and resources, which the conquerors exploited and considered their own private property. Moreover, king's governors were normally chosen among the noble houses who had most of the land in a satrapy, thus promoting the creation of autonomous territorial properties outside royal control. By conquering new lands, the Arsacid kings were able to obtain enough money to preserve their own independence from the aristocracy, in particular, in the context of the army. In this way, such an income made possible the recruitment of large numbers of central Asian tribesmen as mercenaries. Gradually these mercenaries became the only way the king had at disposal to exert control over the nobility and to raise an army quickly without recurring to the aristocracy.

By the end of Mithridates II's reign (about 88 BC), such a balanced situation began to change. New conquests occurred more and more rarely. In a kingdom like Parthia, so largely dependent on territorial acquisitions, this radically-changed circumstance along with the significant loss of income for the royal house made plain the enormous imbalance in the relative availability of money, and therefore of real power, between the king and the nobles. At the same time, the Arsacid candidates fighting each other for the throne saw themselves more and more often forced to rely almost entirely on aristocratic military power.

The absolute control over large sectors of Parthian territory -- and more specifically the power they exerted on local populations -- constituted the basis of noble families' military strength. Aristocratic members fought side by side with the monarch, leading into the battlefield huge personal armies rallied by recruiting soldiers among the subject populations living on their lands. Equipped and trained at their lords' expenses, these units constituted the backbone of a typical Parthian army. The feudal armies, conceived originally as the main expression of a landlord's loyalty towards the Crown and a substantial help for the king to maintain his dominant position, gradually assumed the characteristics of private militias, whose engagement at the king's side was influenced mainly by the political plans of their patrician commanders.

The situation could have been significantly different if only the monarch had been able to maintain that condition of economical autonomy that enabled his predecessors of the second century BC to hire mercenary contingents in large numbers.

Employing mercenary armies would have allowed the monarch to preserve his independence, but in order to do this, large sums of money were needed. The first concern of Artabanus II, once ascended to the throne in AD 12, was to find new financial sources in order to increase the economic relevance of the Crown in contrast to the power of the aristocracy. He detected a possible solution in the highly remunerative long-distance trade that connected, both by land and sea, East Asia and India with the Mediterranean coast, and passed through many of the most important Parthian cities.

The composition of the Parthian army has been the subject of discussion over the years. Pompeius Trogus (Pomp. Trogus/ Justin, XLI, 2. 5) refers to the troops recruited by the noble families among the populations living on their properties as *servi*, slaves.

According to Wolski, western sources should not be taken literally (Wolski, 1983). By using words well known to their readers, the chroniclers attempted to explain a social phenomenon peculiar to Iranic society. The people living in the territory of a nobleman who retained "feudal" rights to that land obtained from the Great King were bound to a relationship of dependence towards their lord similar to that between the King and his vassals. Such a relationship implied a series of duties and services for the local lord such as serving in the nobleman's militia. Pompeius, speaking of some four hundred freemen and fifty thousand *servi,* contributed to spreading the conviction that the Parthian army was constituted mainly by slaves. But the contradiction in Pompeius becomes evident when, continuing with the subdivision between *servi* and freemen, he maintains that only the freemen were allowed to ride horses (Pomp. Trogus/ Justin, XLI, 3. 4). Traditionally, the Parthian army was a mounted one, as seen in the description of the battle of Carrhae, where mounted archers were supposed to weaken the Roman units, forcing them to regroup to provide an ideal target for the smashing charge of mounted spearmen in full armor. Therefore the majority of the troops were trained in horse-riding.

It is evident that the generic term used by Pompeius included different categories of men in service. Plutarch, in fact describing Surena's army, introduces different types of *servi*, who outnumbered the freemen by nine times: *douloi, pelátai,* and *oikétoi* (Plut., *Crass.* 21 and 27). These represented different levels of dependent people corresponding to different services. It seems clear that the relations of dependence between lords and populations cannot be all assimilated with the traditional concept of slavery and were instead more similar to the institution of serfdom peculiar to high medieval Europe. Slavery as traditionally intended in the Classical world existed of course, but was limited to Mesopotamia and the regions where the presence of a Greek population was more relevant.

Since its very beginning, the Parthian empire was characterised by a strongly decentralised and composite nature. Extremely different realities coexisted within its vast borders. A structure of territorial government existed, organized through satrapies and similar to those of the Seleucid and Achaemenid empires. In the territories ruled by royal satraps, Jewish communities (Nehardea, Babylonia), Greek *poleis* (Susa, Seleucia on the Tigris), and aristocratic households (Surene, Karene) exerted some kind of local power. The Arsacid monarchs used to confer some of their royal prerogatives on local groups of power which were strongly rooted in the territory in order to assure the control of the most important districts.

In the land formally submitted to the Great King's authority there were also local dynasties, endowed with an independent political life and administrative organization (Plin, *N.H.*, VI, 112). These "client" kings were influenced in their activity, as were the provincial governors, by the oath of allegiance they took in favor of the Parthian king. These subordinated kingdoms included Armenia, Media Atropatene, Gordyene, Adiabene, Hatra, Osrhoene, Characene, Elymais, Persis, and, for a short period, Hyrcania and the Indo-Parthian states.

The kingdom of Armenia, ruled for many decades by the Artaxiads, became one of the leading vassal states after the appointment to the throne of Tiridates, brother of Vologases I. The Arsacid dynasty of Armenia lasted much longer than the main branch and fiercely opposed the Sasanians for a long time after the fall of the Parthian empire, until the fourth century AD (Kettenhofen, 1998).

The other kingdom that constituted the restricted leading council of Parthia according to Vologases I's reorganization was that of Media Atropatenes, the seat of a local dynasty since the fourth century BC. Starting from the first century AD and the reign of Great King Artabanus II, the kingdom was ruled by a branch of the Arsacid royal house (Schottky, 1991).

The kingdom of Adiabene, west of the Tigris, is famous for the conversion to Judaism of its powerful king Izates II, as reported by Flavius Josephus (Flav. Joseph., *Ant. Jud.*, XX, 17-68; *Bereshit Rabbah*, XLVI, 10). It played a major role in Parthian policy during the reign of Artabanus II. The queen mother, Helena, established direct contacts with the community of Jerusalem, where she built palaces and a royal tomb (Marciak, 2015).

The city of Hatra in northern Mesopotamia flourished during the second century AD and was an important religious and commercial centre. Its impressive archaeological remains include several monumental religious buildings and an imposing wall curtain. It resisted the assaults of the Roman legions three times, under Trajan and Septimus Severus, and was finally conquered by the Sasanian army of Shapur I in AD 241. Hatra was a relevant religious and commercial centre, its lords, *mary'*, ruled over most of the settlements and routes of North Mesopotamia (Altaweel and Hauser, 2004). The numerous inscriptions describe a wealthy society where religion and royal authority play a fundamental role. The local royal administration was probably as complex as the Arsacid one: many court officers are mentioned including a *rbyt' dy 'rb*, that is to say a "Steward of Arab," probably a royal officer in charge of maintaining a good relationship with the nomads living in the city territory (H 223, 224 and 364). Surprisingly, the inscriptions make no reference to the Arsacid royal authority even though we know from Roman sources that the later kings of Hatra were loyal servants of the Great King until his fall. This fact constitutes the most striking example of the territorial autonomy the Arsacid vassal king enjoyed (Gregoratti, 2013b).

In northern Mesopotamia the kingdom of Osrhoene existed on the Euphrates border, with its capital, Edessa. Its rulers, the Abgarids, established their lordship a few years before the Arsacid conquest. As already mentioned, their capital city was Edessa. They pledged allegiance to the new rulers and later obtained the title of kings. Osrhoene's geographical position, immediately east of Seleucia Zeugma, the most important crossing-point on the Euphrates on the main penetration route into Parthian land, rendered the Abgarid state one of the primary targets of any Roman military enterprise. Placed in the middle of two empires normally at odds, Edessa kings adopted an ambiguous policy, of which the role played by Abgar II in Crassus's affair is only the most resounding example. King Abgar II played a key role in delaying the military expedition of Crassus. Secretly a loyal servant to the Great King, he pretended to join Crassus's party in order to gain his confidence. He exploited the influence gained on the republican commander to draw him into the trap of Carrhae. In a plain land poor of water and suitable for Parthian war tactics, at the right moment he revealed his true face, openly taking the field at his lord's side (Cass. Dio, XXXVII, 5. 5; XL, 20-23; Plut., *Crass.*, 20-22). The Abgarids switched sides again in front of Trajan's legions. After L. Verus's campaign, they were included among the Roman client kings (Luther, 1999).

At Sumatar Harabesi, a site 50 kilometers southeast of Edessa on the Tektek mountains, a series of inscriptions makes explicit reference to the Edessene court and administration as well as to a commander of *'rb*, that is to say, the governor of "Arabia." He was probably a royal officer in charge of guarding the kingdom's eastern frontiers, endowed with an authority similar to that of the "Steward of Arab," later serving under the Hatreene kings (Healey, 2009, 228-234).

The small kingdom of Characene was founded on the northern shore of the Persian Gulf in the second century BC, following the disintegration of Seleucid rule. Its capital and most important city was Spasinou Charax, named after Hyspaosines, a Seleucid governor, self-proclaimed king, and founder of the local dynasty. Its harbor cities and capital played an important role in the long-distance trade connecting Mesopotamia with India (Schuol

2000, Gregoratti 2011).

When the Arsacids managed to subjugate Mesopotamia, Hyspaosines had already been able to exert effective control over the sea routes connecting Mesopotamia with the Gulf, as attested by a Greek inscription from Bahrein (Gathier, Lombard and Al-Sindi, 2002, 223-226). Later Characene rulers managed to establish control over the stations along the sea route, Bahrein Island, Kharg Island and Ed- Dur, influencing the rise of more complex societies on the northern coast of the Arabian peninsula. Such commercial traffic could represent a chance for huge income. This spoke against a direct occupation of Characene by the Parthians and Apodakos, Hyspaosines's son and successor, who was acknowledged as king of Characene. He maintained his father's throne as a vassal monarch of the Parthian Great King, bound to him by an oath of allegiance with the right to mint his own coins. Attambelos VII, king in Characene since AD 113/4, offered his submission to the Roman emperor Trajan, who with an army and a fleet was approaching Mesene (Cass. Dio, LXVIII, 28. 3 - 29. 1). The failure of the invasion and Trajan's death meant Attambelos's political ruin and the ruin of the Characene local dynasty as well. The Parthians solved the Characenian problem once and for all by putting on the throne a member of the Arsacid dynasty and putting an end to the Hyspaosinid line of succession. From Palmyrene inscriptions, we see the role played by the kingdom, and in particular by the Palmyrene trade colonies that its monarchs hosted in the commercial network of the Syrian city..

Remarkably a Palmyrene inscription reveals that Yarhai, son of Nebuzabad, a citizen of Palmyra, thus a subject of the Roman empire and certainly a pre-eminent figure within the circle of merchants operating in the Mesenian capital city (Spasinou Charax), managed to hold an office in the new king's administration as governor of the district of *Tylos*, that is to say, the present-day island of Bahrain (Starcky, 1949, X, 38).

The kingdom of Elymais, ruled by the local dynasty of the Kamnaskirids, is another subject that entered the political scene before the Arsacid conquest of western Asia. Originated by the settlement of the mountain populations of southwest Iran, the kingdom managed to gain control of Babylon for a while in the middle of the second century BC. Forced to submit to the Arsacids, the Elymaeans annexed the Greek city of Susa in the first century AD. A few decades later, the Great King put an end to the local dynasty, probably substituting it with an Arsacid one. The new dynasts remained loyal to the Parthians until the fall of the empire (Dąbrowa, 1998).

The role of the kings of Persis in southern Iran is much less clear. Located at the core territories of the Achaemenid empire, the kingdom of Persis always maintained a strong cultural and political identity under Greek and Parthian rule. The Arsacids surely exerted a certain influence on the local dynasty (the Frataraka); in fact the protagonists of the Sasanian rebellion did not come from among the highest rank of its ruling class, but from its lesser local lords (Wiesehöfer, 1998).

Some modern scholars also list the Indo-Parthian state among the Arsacid vassal kingdoms. This kingdom was established and ruled by Gondophares and his successors close to the Parthian eastern frontier during or slightly before the first century AD. It included parts of present-day Afghanistan, Pakistan and northwestern India and is considered somehow connected with the Parthian noble house of Surena (Boperachchi 1998).

Their high degree of autonomy allowed the vassal kings to develop an individual policy concerning both the international situation and the exploitation of territorial sources and the trade possibilities their lands offered. Throughout Arsacid history, these minor political entities tried to take advantage of the periodic weakness of the central authority to loosen the control the Great King was able to exert over their government activity and to increase their level of autonomy.

For the Parthian sovereign, a loyal vassal king constituted a valuable ally for resolving international and internal problems. The local proficiencies of such monarchs assured the exploitation of territorial resources and potential in areas where the often limited capacities of the central authority were not able to intervene or effectively respond to needs. The autonomy achieved by the vassal kings put them in a position where they could rule undisturbed in obedience to political and economic obligations towards their lord. The authority of the legitimate descendant of Arsaces was acknowledged as superior by the "client" kings. The history of the relations between the Parthian king and his royal servants can be explained as the attempt to strike a balance between autonomy, whose benefits for both the local courts and the central power were evident, and the dangerous centrifugal forces originating in the peripheral areas of the empire.

Figure. 1. The letter of Artabanus II/III to the city of Susa

Figure. 2. Khong-e Azhdar Relief

Figure. 3. Parthian soldier

Figure. 4. Funerary relief from Palmyra with Aramaic inscription

Figure. 5. Silver drachm of Arsaces I

Figure. 6. Silver tetradrachm of Mithridates I

Figure. 7. Silver drachms of Mithridates II

Figure. 8. Pharates IV/Queen Musa

Figure. 9. Aratabanus II

Figure. 10. Artabanus III

Figure. 13. The relief of Herakles near Kermanshah

Figure. 14. Aerial overview of Old Nisa

Figure. 15. Possible head-bust of Queen Musa

Figure. 16. Parthian silver rhyton

Bibliography

Aggoula B. 1991. *Inventaire des inscriptions hatréennes*, Paris

Alram M. 1998. *Stand und Aufgaben der arsakidischen Numismatik*, in J. Wiesehöfer, *Das Partherreich und seine Zeugnisse*, Stuttgart, pp. 365-387

Altaweel M.R. and Hauser S.R. 2004. *Trade routes to Hatra according to evidence from ancient sources and modern satellite imagery*, «BaM», 35, pp. 59-86

Arnaud P. 1986. *Doura-Europos, microcosme grec ou rouage de l'administration arsacide? Modes de maîtrise du territoire et intégration des notables locaux dans la pratique administrative des rois arsacides*, «Syria», 63, pp.135-155

Bernard P. 1990. *Vicissitudes au gré de l'histoire d'une statue en bronze d'Heraclès entre Séleucie du Tigre et la Mésène*, «JS», pp. 3-68

Bopearachchi O. 1998. *Indo-Parthians*, in J. Wiesehöfer, *Das Partherreich und seine Zeugnisse*, Stuttgart, pp. 389-406

Brizzi G. 1995. *Considerazioni di storia mesopotamica da un passo di Giuseppe Flavio (Ant. Jud. XVIII, 314-379)*, «CCG», VI, pp. 61-80

Chaumont M.-L. 1976. *L'Arménie entre Rome et l'Iran I. De l'avènement d'Auguste à l'avénement de Dioclétien*, in *Aufstieg und Niedergang der römischen Welt*, II, 9, 1, ed. H. Temporini und W. Haase, Berlin-New York, pp. 71-194

Dąbrowa, E. 1983. *La politique de l'état parthe à l'égard de Rome – d'Artaban II à Vologèse I (ca 11 – ca 79 de n. è.) et les facteurs qui la conditionnaient*, Kraków

Dąbrowa, E. 1998. *Zeugnisse zur Geschichte der parthischen Elymais und Susiane*, in J. Wiesehöfer, *Das Partherreich und seine Zeugnisse*, Stuttgart, pp. 417-424

Dąbrowa, E. 2011. *Studia Graeco-Parthica: Political and Cultural Relations between Greeks and Parthians*, Wiesbaden

A. De Jong. 2013. *Hatra and the Parthian Commonwealth*, in L. Dirven, *Hatra. Politics, Culture and Religion Between Parthia And Rome*, Stuttgart, pp. 143-160

Gatier P.-L., Lombard P. and Al-Sindi K. 2002. *Greek Inscriptions from Bahrain*, «Arabian Archaeology and Epigraphy», 13, pp. 223–233

Gregoratti L. 2011. *A Parthian port on the Persian Gulf: Characene and its Trade*, «Anabasis, Studia Classica et Orientalia», 2, 209-229

Gregoratti L. 2012a. *The Role of the mint of Seleucia on the Tigris in the Arsacid History*, «Mesopotamia», 47, 2012, pp. 129-136

Gregoratti L. 2012b. *The Parthians between Rome and China: Gan Ying's mission into the West*

(1st century AD); «Academic Quarter», 4, pp. 109-120

Gregoratti L. 2012c. *Parthian Women in Flavius Josephus* in M. Hirschberger, *Jüdisch-hellenistische Literatur in ihrem interkulturellen Kontext, Akten der Tagung, Düesseldorf, 10.–11. Februar 2011*, Frankfurt, pp. 183-192

Gregoratti L. 2013a. *The Journey east of the Great King, East and West in the Parthian Kingdom*, «Parthica», 15, 2013, pp. 43-52

Gregoratti L. 2013b. *Hatra: on the west of the East*, in L. Dirven, *Hatra. Politics, Culture and Religion Between Parthia And Rome*, Stuttgart, pp. 49-58

Gregoratti L. 2015. *A Tale of two Great Kings: Artabanus and Vologaeses* in A. Krasnowolska and R. Rusek-Kowalska, *Studies on the Iranian World I, Before Islam*, Cracow, pp. 203-210

Guey J. 1937. *Essai sur la guerre partique de Trajan (114-117)*, Bucarest

GregorattiL. 2016. *Dura Europos: a Greek Town of the Parthian Empire*, in T. Kaizer (ed.), *Religion, Society and Culture at Dura-Europos*, YCS, 38, Cambridge University Press, 2016 pp. 16-29

Hackl, U., Jacobs, B., Weber, D. 2010. *Quellen zur Geschichte des Partherreiches*, Göttingen

Hauser S. 2011. *Assur und sein Umland in der Arsakidenzeit*, in J. Renger, *Assur – Gott, Stadt und Land, 5, Internationales Colloquium der Deutschen Orient-Gesellschaft 18.-21. Februar 2004 in Berlin*, CDOG 5, Wiesbaden, pp. 115-148

Healey J.F. 2009, *Aramaic Inscriptions and Documents of the Roman Period, Textbook of Syrian Semitic Inscriptions, Volume IV*, Oxford

Invernizzi A. 1998. *Parthian Nisa. New Lines of Research*, in J. Wiesehöfer, *Das Partherreich und seine Zeugnisse*, Stuttgart, pp. 45-59

Kramer N. 2003. *Das Itinerar Σταθμοὶ Παρθικοί des Isidor von Charax – beschreibung eines Handelsweges?*, «Klio», 85, pp. 120-130

Keall E.J. 1975. *Parthian Nippur and Vologases' Southern Strategy: A Hypothesis*, «JAOS», 95, pp. 620-632

Kettenhofen E. 1998. *Die Arsakiden in den armenischen Quellen*, in J. Wiesehöfer, *Das Partherreich und seine Zeugnisse*, Stuttgart, pp. 325-355

Lepper F.A. 1948. *Trajan's Parthian War*, London

Lerouge Ch. 2007. *L'image des Parthes dans le monde greco-romain. Du debut du Ier siecle av. J.-C. jusqu'a la fin du Haut-Empire romain*, Stuttgart

Lerouge Ch. 2013. *Les banquets des Arsacides d'après les sources grecques*, in C. Grandjean, C. Hugoniot et B. Lion, *Le banquet du monarque dans le monde antique*, Rennes, 2013, pp. 1-13

Lukonin V.G. 1983. *Political, Social and Administrative Institutions: Taxes and Trade*, in E. Yarshater, *The Cambridge History of Iran, The Seleucid, Parthian and Sasanian Periods*, Cambridge, vol. III, 2, pp. 681-746

Luther A. 1999. *Elias von Nisibis und die Chronologie der edessenischen Könige*, «Klio», 81, pp. 180-198

Le Rider G. 1999. *Séleucie du Tigre, les monnaies séleucides et parthes*, Monografie di Mesopotamia, 6, Firenze

Marciak M. 2015. *Das Konigreich Adiabene in hellenistisch-parthischer Zeit*, «Gymnasium», 122, pp. 57-74

Milik J.T. 1961. *A propos d'un atelier monétaire d'Adiabene: Natounia,* «RN», VI ser., 3, pp. 51- 58

Millar F. 1998. *Dura Europos under Parthian Rule,* in J. Wiesehöfer, *Das Partherreich und seine Zeugnisse, Beiträge des internationalen Colloquiums. Eutin (27.-30. Juni 1996),* Stuttgart, pp. 473-492

Neusner J. 1984. *A History of the Jews in Babylonia I, The Parthian Period,* Chico, CA

Olbrycht, M.J. 1998. *Parthia et ulteriores gentes. Die politischen Beziehungen zwischen dem arsakidischen Iran und den Nomaden der eurasischen Steppen.* München

Posch W. 1998. *Chinesische Quellen zu den Parthern,* in J. Wiesehöfer, *Das Partherreich und seine Zeugnisse,* pp. 355-364

Reade J.E. 1998. *Greco-Parthian Nineveh,* «Iraq», 60, pp. 65-83

Sachs A.J. and Hunger H. 1996. *Astronomical Diaries and Related Texts from Babylonia, III, Diaries from 164 B.C. to 61 B.C.,* Wien

Schottky M. 1991. *Parther, Meder und Hyrkanier. Eine Untersuchung der dynastischen und geographischen Verflechtungen im Iran des 1. Jhs. n. Chr.,* «AMI N.F.», 24, pp. 61-134

Schuol M. 2000. *Die Charakene, Ein mesopotamisches Königreich in hellenistisch-parthischer Zeit,* Stuttgart

Sellwood D. 1980. *An Introduction to the Coinage of Parthia,* London

Slocum J.J. 1977. *Another Look at the Coins of Hatra,* «Museum Notes», 22, pp. 37-48

Starcky J. 1949. *Inventaire des inscriptions de Palmyre,* X, Damas

Vanden Berghe L. and Schippmann K. 1985. *Les reliefs rupestres d'Elymaide (Iran) d'epoque parthe* Iranica Antiqua, vol. Supp. 3

Walker J. 1958. *The Coins of Hatra,* «NC», 18, pp. 167-172

Wiesehöfer, J. 1998. *Zeugnisse zur Geschichte und Kultur der Persis unter den Parthern,* in J. Wlesehöfer, *Das Partherreich und seine Zeugnisse,* Stuttgart, pp. 425-434

Wolski, J. 1983. *Les relations de Justin et Plutarque sur les esclavages et la population dépendante dans l'empire parthe,* «Iranica Antiqua», 18, pp. 145-157

Wolski, J. 1993. *L'Empire des Arsacides,* Leuven

Zambelli M. 1963. *La lettera di Artabano III alla città di Susa,* «RFIC», 91, pp. 153-169

THE SASANIAN EMPIRE

Touraj Daryaee and Khodadad Rezakhani

The Sasanian Empire which ruled the Iranian Plateau and parts of Central Asia, the Caucasus, and Mesopotamia, and at times parts of Syria and Anatolia has been little studied. In comparison with its Mediterranean neighbor, the Roman Empire, the number of monographs and studies on this Iranian dynasty and its history is almost negligible. There are many reasons for such an unbalanced study of the Asiatic portion of the late antique world. The Sasanian Empire was a multilingual empire, whose official language, Pahlavi, and the sources related to it are few and far between. Most of these texts and historical narratives were either destroyed or were translated into Arabic and then into New Persian. There are Syriac, Armenian, and Jewish Aramaic sources from the Sasanian period that take on a communal and religious outlook, at times hostile against the Sasanian ruling elite. The later Arabic and Persian sources are written some two or three centuries after the Sasanian demise by Muslims, looking back at an earlier time when Zoroastrians were the elite. Hence, as important as the Arabic and Persian sources may be for historical inquiry, the Sasanian mentalité and worldview is lost and can only be understood from the early Sasanian inscriptions and some of the Pahlavi texts.

In the twentieth century only a handful of scholars have produced monographs on the Sasanian Empire. The outstanding work is that of Arthur Christensen, who has written the important tome *L'iran sous les Sassanides* (1944). It is a wonder why this work was never translated into any other language except that of Persian. Since then a few works in Russian, German, English, and Persian have appeared. Our knowledge of the empire has changed because of the many important discoveries and material culture finds, such as seals and sealings, along with archaeological excavations and new textual editions and a more rigorous historiography. Hence, a new tome is needed to take into consideration all of the recent scholarly activity on one of the great empires of late antiquity.

The Sasanian dynasty originated from the province of Fars/Persis in southwestern Iran. This is the home of some of the important ancient Iranian dynasties, such as those of the Elamites and the Achaemenids. During the Seleucid and Arsacid rule, local rulers, the Fratarakas (Sarkhosh Curtis, 2010), Dārāyānids (Shayegan, 2005), and the Kings of Persis

(Wiesehöfer, 1994) ruled over the area. The Sasanian connection to the past was through the idea of kingship developed by these local dynasties and the ideological underpinnings of the sacred Zoroastrian hymns, the *Avesta*. The early Sasanian remains at Persepolis and their association with the Achaemenid tombs at Naqš-e Rostam, suggest this attachment to the Persianate past.

The date for the beginning of the Sasanian Empire is 224 CE, when Ardashir I (224-41 CE) defeated the last Arsacid monarch, Artabanus/Ardawan IV (213-24 CE) at the Battle of Hormozdgān. Ardashir assumed the royal title of *Šāhān Šāh,* "king of kings," which was already used by the Arsacids, and proceeded to bring a territory roughly equivalent to modern Iran and Iraq under his control (Daryaee, 2009, 3-5). The Sasanian campaign to conquer *Ērānšahr,* "The Iranian Empire," had begun in 205/6 with Ardashir's father, Pabag, whose father, Sasan, the dynastic namesake, a priest of the goddess Anahid in the city of Istakhr, the capital of the province of Persis/Fars (Tabari/Bosworth, 4). The temple of Anahid seems to have become the rallying point for Persian warriors who united to dethrone the local the local ruler of Persis, seated in Istakhr. Thus the dynasty that claimed descent from a semi-legendary eponymous ancestor, Sasan, might have extended religious religious authority into secular power and remain on the throne from the third to the seventh century CE.

It appears that Pabag intended to make his eldest son, Shabuhr, the first Sasanian ruler (Tabari/Bosworth, 8), but that prince died under mysterious circumstances, and another son, Ardashir, was the one to complete the conquest of Persis/Fars and beyond. The emergence of this new power naturally alarmed the Arsacids, but they were unable to stop the Sasanian advances. Ardawan IV, and eventually his rival and temporary successor, Vologasses/ Walakhsh VI (d. 229 CE), soon fell victim to Ardashir. Conquests in the east, particularly the takeover of the important town of Marv in northeastern Khorasan, as well as the subjugation of the territory of the Indo-Parthians in Sistan were the final achievements of Ardashir I.

Ardashir has left us a number of rock reliefs and also minted many coin types which provide important clues to the intent and ideological framework of this late antique empire. The idea that the Sasanians were Mazda worshippers signaled their continuous interest in the old Persian religion. However, Ardashir and his clan claimed that he was more than simply human; he was perhaps closer to the gods and functioned as an intercessor between the gods and humans. This unprecedented image signaled a new and improved position of the king of kings among men and women of the Sasanian Empire (Harper, 2008). The interesting title -- he "whose seed is from the gods" (*kē čihr az yazdān*) -- provides us with an interesting ideological tradition which may suggest a sacral kingship of a mixed Irano-Hellenistic type (Daryaee 2008).

Initial conflicts with Rome and Alexander Severus ended in stalemate in Syria, and Ardashir appointed his son, Shabuhr I (241-70 CE), as co-regent and eventually retired to his home province. During the reign of Shabuhr I, the Sasanian Empire was consolidated. There also was a significant increase in the size of the administrative apparatus, consistent with imperial centralization. At this time Armenia became the major point of contention between the Sasanians and the Romans, and it remained so until it was partitioned between the two empires in the fifth century CE. The Ka'aba-i Zardosht of Shapur in Fars (Honigmann and Maricq, 1953 : Huyse 1999) is an important document in not only the organization of the empire, where the princes (*wāspūhrgān*) were given rule over the provinces, mixed with local kings, but also over the increasing number of offices and officers at the court. It seems that the power of the court and the attraction of the court, with its ritual and power brought ways to solidify Sasanian rule.

In his foreign policy, Shapur I was very successful, both in the east and the west. He famously defeated Gordianus III, captured Emperor Valerian, and forced Philip the Arab to a humiliating treaty, a set of events reflected in both his inscription at Ka'aba-i Zardosht, as well as on a major relief in the vicinity of the same inscription. Militarily, the reign of Shabuhr marked the return of the military back to form after a relatively long slump in the second and early third centuries that had allowed Roman incursions into the Near East and Mesopotamia in the terminal Arsacid period (Gyselen, 2010).

The next kings, Hormizd I (270-1) and Wahram I (271-4) had relatively short rules and very little is known about them. Homizd I, although younger, appears to have been chosen above the other brothers to rule because of his bravery in battle against the Romans. Thus, age does not appear to have been the deciding factor in electing the early Sasanian kings, but rather bravery, and the choice was specifically with the king of kings. Both Hormizd I and Wahram I were chosen over the heir apparent, Narseh (293-302 CE), the third son of Shabuhr I. Wahram I's eldest son, Wahram II (274-93 CE), also bypassed Narseh, probably with the backing of the Zoroastrian establishment and its powerful head, Kerdir. During his reign, Wahram II had to deal with hostile Romans and his own rebellious brother, Hormizd (Daryaee, 2008, 34-35). This Hormizd was to take refuge with the Roman ruler in Constantinople and is known in the Roman sources as Hormizdas. His palace was close to the court in Constantinople, which signaled a threat to the Sasanian king in power at Ctesiphon (Mosig-Walburg 2000). Then Wahram III, known as the *King of the Sakas* – a title showing his dominance over the former Indo-Parthian kingdom to the east of the Sasanian Empire - was brought to the throne through a conspiracy in the imperial administration. His grand-uncle Narseh, at the time functioning as the king of Armenia, managed to depose him through a major campaign which has been detailed in his inscription of Paikuli (Humbach/ Skjaervo, 1978, pt. 1).

The rule of Narseh (293-302 CE) coincided with the popularization of Christianity in Armenia, and its eventual adoption, and bitter wars over that kingdom with the Roman Empire. A defeat at the hands of the Roman general Galerius resulted in the treaty of Nisibis in 298, which allowed Tiridates III back on the Armenian throne and brought Iberia (the historical kingdom of Georgia) to the Roman sphere of influence (Daryaee 2009, 13). Narseh's death in 302 installed his son, Hormizd II on the throne (Daryaee 2008, 43-44). The new king also mainly presided over the conflict with Rome on the issue of Armenia, whose king Tiridates/Trdat III reputedly converted to Christianity in 301 (Agathangelos/Thomson, 243-244). Hormizd was initially succeeded by a son called Adur-Narseh who ruled only for a short while in 309 (Taffazoli, Ādur Narseh, *EIr*). There are, however, no notices of him from the numismatic evidence or in the later Islamic sources, while Byzantine sources only mention his existence as the elder son of Hormizd II.

The circumstances of the birth and reign of Shabuhr II (309-379), the longest reigning

Sasanian monarch, are quite legendary and include him being crowned while still in his mother's womb and forty days after the death of his father, Hormizd II *(Mojmal ol-Tavarikh, 34)*. When he came of age, he set off curbing Arab incursions in the south and punishing the perpetrators (Tabari/Bosworth, 50-56); he thus became known by the epithet "Lord of Shoulders" (Arabic *Dhu-l-Aktaf*). In the east, Shabuhr II was faced with a major invasion by the Huns (Chionites), who only agreed to form an alliance after fierce battles. This resulted in the termination of the rule of the Sasanian cadet branch, known as the Kushano-Sasanians, over Bactrian and the establishment of autonomous Hunnic rule in Transoxiana and Bactria (Amm. Marc., 17.5.1; Nikitin 1999). In the west, Shabuhr had to face the Romans under Julian the Apostate in 363, although that campaign was soon abandoned following the assassination of Julian by his own troops. The resulting peace treaty with Jovian put the important border town of Nisibis under Sasanian control and created a long-lasting point of contention between the two empires (Blockley, 1988). The long and relatively calm rule of Shabuhr helped bring stability to the Sasanian Empire, as well as establishing Sasanian control over both the eastern provinces, as well as the Persian Gulf region.

Ardashir II (379-83 CE) succeeded his brother Shabuhr II, probably as the result of an agreement with the latter. The relief at Taq-i Bostan (Tanabe, 1985; Kaim, 2009) shows the exchange of a diadem between the brothers, possibly a reward for Ardashir's bravery in the wars against Rome (Shahbazi 2011). Tabari associated Ardashir II with a great purge in the Sasanian nobility in order to control their increasing power, an act that resulted in his removal from the throne (Tabari/Boswoth, 67-68). The agreement between Shapur II and Ardashir II probably guaranteed the succession of Shapur III (383-388), the son of Shapur II (Shahbazi, "Ardašīr II," *EIr*). The reign of Shabuhr III can be called the beginning of a temporary weakening in the Sasanian royal power, as reported by the chroniclers. Like Ardashir II, his nobles were successful in removing him, this time through causing his death under the collapsing weight of his own tent (Tabari/Bosworth, 68; al-Yaghubi, I/183). Wahram IV (388-399), another son of Shabuhr II, seems to have had a similarly short reign. His most significant action was to be the replacement of his brother *Wahrām-Shabuhr* (Arm. *Vramšāpuh*) on the Armenian throne. Like his brother (or perhaps father?) Shabuhr III, Wahram IV also fell victim to the conspiracy of the court nobles and was removed in favor of his son (or perhaps brother?), Yazdgerd I (Klima, 1988).

The reign of Yazdgerd I (399-420) is the beginning of a restoration in Sasanian history. The king, occasionally called "the Sinful One" (Tabari/Bosworth, 70), was more strong-willed than his immediate predecessors. His less than complementary title in the Islamic sources, presumably based on the Iranian ones, has also been interpreted as a comment on his famous religious tolerance and accommodation of the Christians. Indeed, Christian sources from Rome (Procopius, 1.2, 8) consider him a noble soul and even a second Cyrus (McDonough, 2008; Shahbazi, "Yazdgerd I," *EIr*). His strong-handed treatment of the Sasanian nobility and priesthood made him many enemies among his courtiers (Socrates Scholasticus, 7.8), although he seems to have survived their wrath, finally being killed by a kick from his horse! (Shahbazi, 2003). On his coins, he calls himself Ram-Shahr "[bringer of] a calm realm," which might indeed be a reflection of his rule as a whole.

Wahram V (420-38 CE), a son of Yazdgerd I, who was sent to the Arab court at al-Hira, had to wrestle his crown from a usurper named Khosrow (Tabari/Bosworth, 90-93). Wahram's reign is highly romanticized in the Classical Persian literature, particularly in a great compendium of interrelated stories called *Haft Peykar* by the poet Nezami (twelfth century) whose fanciful stories might be drawing on actual Sasanian period romances. These stories include the coming of Indian minstrels known as *lur* (Gypsies?) and the pleasure the king took in drinking and hunting. Wahram is commonly known by the epithet *Gur/Gōr* (*Jur* in Arabic sources: Tabari/Bosworth, 82), meaning "onager," presumably because of his love of hunting. The story of his death is equally colorful, for it was said that while hunting in Mah (Media), Wahram fell into a marsh and disappeared (Daryaee 2008, 60-61). He was succeeded by Yazdgerd II (438-57 CE).

Yazdgerd II, unlike his namesake and grandfather, does not appear to have been very tolerant toward Christianity, at least in Armenia. The tale (attributed to Wahram V by al-Tabari: Tabari/Bosworth, 104-105) of the great rebellion of Vardan Mamikonian and its suppression at the battle of Avarayr by Mihr-Narse, Yazdgerd's vizier, is recorded in the work of Armenian historian Ełiše (Elishe/Thomson, 178ff). It seems that for Yazdgerd and Mihr-Narse the control of Armenia meant a re-conversion of Armenians from Christianity to Zoroastrianism, making them part of a Zoroastrian *oecumene* designed to create a centralized Sasanian state. Persarmenia, the majority of the Armenian territory under the Sasanian rule, was from this point on managed directly by the Sasanian court through a *Marzpan* (margrave) and was effectively incorporated into the Sasanian realm (Blockley, 1987). Yazdgerd is also significant because he is the first Sasanian monarch who uses the title of *Kay* (Phl. *Kdy*) on his coins, a reference to the shifting Sasanian ideology and incorporation of a Kayanid political identity (Daryaee, 1995).

According to al-Tabari, the two sons of Yazdgerd II, Hormizd III (457-9 CE) and Peroz (459-84 CE), ruled consecutively, although the latter deposed the former in a power struggle (Tabari/Bosworth, 107-109). During this confusion, Georgia gained independence, and the eastern borders of the Sasanian Empire were laid open to attacks from the Hephthalites. Peroz pacified Caucasian Albania and made an agreement with the Eastern Roman Empire to cooperate in defending the Caucasus from invaders (Pseudo-Joshua, 9-10). He was, however, captured by the Hephthalites in 469 CE, and the Sasanians were forced to cede territory in the east and pay tribute to the invaders. In an attempt to avenge his losses, Peroz was killed and his army destroyed in 484 CE; his rule is remembered as a low point for the Sasanian dynasty (Daryaee 2009, 25). Peroz was followed briefly by his son Walakhsh (484-8 CE), who was deposed in favor of Kawad I (488-97, 499-531 CE), the second son of Peroz.

Kawad I was faced with the economic and political problems of a Sasanian Empire in flux. It seems that as part of the weakness of the previous rulers and/or their engagement in extraterritorial wars, the nobility and the Zoroastrian priests attained new levels of influence. In this atmosphere, a radical cleric named Mazdak was able to form an alliance with Kawad I and instigate extreme religious reforms (for a different assessment, see Crone, 1991). It is likely that Kawad I was using Mazdak's movement in an attempt to weaken the more orthodox factions of the government and the priestly establishment. The latter, in turn, removed and imprisoned the king and set up his brother Zamasp (497-9 CE) in his place (Tabari/Bosworth, 136).

Kawad was able to escape, however, and later regained the Sasanian throne with Hephthalite assistance (Litvinsky, 1996: 140). His second reign, characterized by a prolonged war with the eastern Roman Empire, mostly under Anastasius and Justin, was also marked by a series of reforms, this time implemented more carefully (Schindel 2013). Upon his death, his eldest son Kawus, supported by the Mazdakites, made a bid for the throne, but was defeated and removed in favor of his younger brother, Khosrow I Anusheruwan (531-79), who then had Mazdak and many of his followers killed (Wiesehöfer 2010: 391-409).

Khosrow's reign was a high point in Sasanian history. He is remembered as a wise and just ruler in both Persian and Arabic histories (Tabari/Bosworth, 146ff). Kawad I and Khosrow I together reorganized the Sasanian Empire and made it one of the strongest in the world in the sixth century CE. The reforms initiated by Kawad were continued and strengthened by Khosrow, and in fact are mostly credited to the latter (Rubin, 1995). Khosrow is also known for continuing the war with the Eastern Roman Empire of Justinian I, the details of which can be found in the famous work of Procopius (Dignas and Winter, 2001: 100-109).

Hormizd IV (579-90 CE), however, did not live up to the example set by his father and grandfather, and managed to earn the enmity of the nobility and priesthood, who deposed him in favor of his own son Khosrow II Aparvez (590-628 CE) (Tabari/Bosworth, 298-103). The plot to remove Hormizd IV and to set Khosrow II in his place, however, ran into trouble when Wahram Chobin, the hero of the war with the Hephthalites, rose in rebellion, under the pretext of avenging Hormizd against Khosrow and the conspirators (Tabari/Bosworth, 303-314).

Forced to flee from the rebellious general Wahram, Khosrow went to the Eastern Roman Empire and sought the aid of Emperor Maurice (Tabari/Bosworth, 310-314). Wahram in turn declared himself as the new emperor, Wahram VI, marking the first time someone outside the Sasanian royal house had reached that position since the accession of Ardashir I. Emperor Maurice supplied mainly Armenian forces to Khosrow II, with whose help he managed to defeat Wahram and recapture his crown (Dignas and Winter, 236-240). Khosrow then took revenge on those who had contributed to the murder of his father, although it is possible that he himself had a hand in that crime. A second rebellion by Wistahm, a maternal uncle of Khosrow and a conspirator in the removal of Hormizd, was soon put down, allowing the new king to establish his role (Daryaee 2008, 85). Khosrow II consolidated his power around the Persian Gulf, and sent envoys to Arabia, as far as Mecca, to inquire about the situation there.

Starting in 602 CE, Khosrow II undertook a series of campaigns against the Eastern Roman Empire and managed to gain significant territorial gains. The campaigns started under the pretext of avenging the murder of Maurice, Khosrow's ally, at the hand of Phocas, a usurper who was now elevated to the position of the emperor (Dignas and Winter, 240-241). These campaigns resulted in the fall of Syria, Palestine, and Egypt, as well as significant portions of Anatolia into the hands of the Sasanians (Dignas and Winter, 115-115). The Sasanian general Shahin also managed to lay siege to Constantinople itself, which was ultimately unsuccessful. These gains in many senses marked the height of Sasanian power and the culmination of the dynasty's efforts at consolidating power and initiating socioeconomic reforms. A successful counteroffensive by Heraclius, who by this time had managed to remove Phocas and reorganize the defenses of the empire resulted in a quick reversal of fortunes in the mid 620s. By 628, not only were the territories in the Mediterranean realm restored to the Romans/Byzantines, but with the help of elements in the Sasanian court, the Roman emperor had routed the Sasanian armies inside their own territories (Howard-Johnston, 1999). Khosrow was removed in a palace coup and his eldest son, Shiroye, was installed as Kawad II (628) (Dignas and Winter, 148-151). The very short reign of Kawad II was marked by internal chaos as well as a major plague, which became known by his name, the Plague of Shireye, and which had devastating demographic effects (Morony, 2007).

The final phase of Sasanian rule was a period of factionalism and division within the empire, during which a number of kings came to power and were challenged by other distant members of the family of Sasan. Ardashir III (Sept. 628- April 629), the son of Kawad II, was a child who was soon removed from the throne by one of the commanders of the war with Byzantium, Shahrbaraz. He in turn was toppled by the nobility, who then installed Boran (628-630/31?), a daughter of Khosrow II (Emrani, 2009). Her rule was a period of consolidation of imperial power and rebuilding the empire. She was probably brought to the throne because she was the only legitimate heir. Another daughter of Khosrow II, Azarmigduxt (630-631?), replaced her sister. Boran and Azarmigduxt were deposed by another Sasanian general, and here we see that the military commanders were assuming more and more power in the face of the shaken monarchy, the competing nobility, and the Zoroastrian priests. Claimants such as Khosrow III or IV are also speculated mainly through numismatic evidence, before finally in 632, Yazdgerd III (632-651), grandson of Khosrow II, was installed on the throne (Shahbazi 2005).

Yazdgerd III's rule coincided with the conquest of the Sasanian Empire by the Muslims (Tyler-Smith, 2000). Starting in 637, the Muslim armies quickly managed to defeat the Sasanians in Qadisiyya, in southwestern Iraq, and soon in their capital at Ctesiphon. The last Sasanian king was forced to retreat to the east, from province to province, demanding loyalty and support from local populations. Finally, his dwindling forces were defeated by a coalition of local Persian and Hephthalite governors of Bactria. Tradition has it that Yazdgerd III was killed in 651 in Marv by a miller who did not recognize the king of kings.

The reasons for the fall of the Sasanians are debated (Pourshariati 2009; contra Wiesehöfer 2010: 139). However, the long war between the Eastern Roman Empire and the Sasanians stretched their resources and manpower to the brink of collapse. The chaos that ensued (and coincided with the unification of the Arab Muslims) caused a rapid blitzkrieg conquest of Mesopotamia and the heart of the empire, i.e., Ctesiphon. Once Mesopotamia and the western regions were taken, the Iranian Plateau lay open to the conquerors. The local lords, governors, or Zoroastrian priests dealt with the Muslims on their own terms, and as the conquest went on, the number of Iranians joining the conquerors increased (Zakeri 1995).

The sons of Yazdgerd III fled further east, asking the Chinese Emperor Gaozong to aid them in their battle against the Muslims. For a time Sasanian descendants continued to be recognized by the Chinese as legitimate holders of the Persian throne-in-exile and governors of a "Persian Area Command" (*Bosi dudufu*) in Sistan. In the early eighth century CE, a Sasanian named Khosw or made a final, failed attempt to retake Iran from the Muslims, and this is the last time we hear of the family of Sasan (Compareti, 2009). The world of ancient Persia had come to an end and a new chapter in the history of the nation had begun. The grandeur of the kings, along with their wisdom and opulence, was emulated by the Muslim caliphs and the name Khosrow, given as *Kisra*, became the general designation for a great ruler. The Sasanians also passed on the idea of *Eran*, "Iran," which held as a form of idealized territorial designation by dynasties from the Buyids to the Mongols, and was utilized effectively in the pre-Modern and Modern periods in order to form the modern nation-state.

Sasanians and the East

Sasanian state strategy is commonly summarized in the concept of centralization. Since the beginning, historiography has put the Sasanian monarchy in stark contrast to the Arsacid one, coloring the former as a centralizing force as opposed to the decentralized structure of the latter (Shahbazi, 2005). The Arsacids, with their multilayered system of power, are seen as the kings of many king(let)s, something that in the eyes of many -- including early Islamic historians, who called them *Moluk ut-Tawayif*, "kings of clans" - made them weak and ineffective. Instead, the Sasanian founder, Ardashir, and his immediate successors are seen as forces of unity who coerced their different Arsacid/Hellenistic princedoms to submit to a centralized Sasanian power (Tabari/Bosworth, 8-16).

However, there are reasons to believe in the continuation of the Arsacid system, at least into the first century of Sasanian rule, and perhaps beyond. Specifically, there appears to have been a continuation of the rule of minor princedoms, as well as perhaps a major kingdom, to the east of the Sasanian realm. The inscription of Shabuhr I at Ka'ba-i Zardosht (Honigman & Maricq, 1953) in Fars/Persis, mentions several "kings," including the sons of Shabuhr I himself, who are counted as part of the court of the king of kings. An Arman Shah, "king of Armenia," a Sakan Shah, "king of Sakas," and a Meshan Shah, "king of Mesene" (in southern Iraq), are quite prominent.

However, we possess, through numismatics, evidence of the existence of a "dynasty" of Kushan Shahs, "kings of Kushan," in the region of Bactria and perhaps Gandhara in the east of the Sasanian territories and northern India. This dynasty, which can legitimately be considered a cadet branch of the Sasanians, appears to rule the territories of the great Kushan Empire. Minting coins from the Kushan capital of Bactra/Balkh, this dynasty mainly copied the style of Kushan gold coins, while the silver coin types were borrowed from the Sasanians (Brunner, 1974). The relationship between the kings of the dynasty and the Sasanians is not ascertained and established, and the history of the dynasty is known only in a fragmentary manner and in almost absolute absence of written sources.

While the Kushan Shah dynasty, or the Kushano-Sasanians as they are sometimes called, is a direct manifestation of Sasanian interests in the eastern side of their empire, the involvement both predates them and also continues after the disappearance of this cadet branch. Indeed, from the beginning the Sasanians display a strong interest, and possibly even roots, in the territories in the east. Ardashir's conquest of Merv is in fact a watershed moment in his career, as demonstrated by his coin types, while his conquest and destruction of the Indo-Parthian kingdom in Sistan appears to have been the moment of his precise claim to the title of the emperor/king of kings (Alram, 2007).

Shabuhr I might have been the king elevating the Kushano-Sasanians to their position, while Wahram III is called the King of Sakas by Narseh in his Paikuli inscriptions. During the reign of Shapur II, the "Huns," moving south and west from the Inner Asian steppe, threatened the Sasanian borders in the east, and possibly put an end to the Kushano-Sasanian rule (Göbl, 1967). However, a confrontation leading to peace brought a Hunnic contingent, headed by King Grumbates, to the Sasanian army in the wars with the Roman Empire (Amm. Marc. 16.9).

The relief of Shabuhr II and his brother Ardashir II at *Taq-e Bostan* too might betray the existence of an eastern connection in the Sasanian court (Tanabe, 1985). The god under whose auspices the treaty between the two brothers is being concluded is Mithra, the god of contracts and treaties (Kaim, 2009). Both the god, as well as the lotus over which he stands, have been iconographically connected to eastern Iran, particularly the territory of the Kushans, leading to the suggestion that Ardashir II might have acted as a Kushan Shah prior to his accession.

Bactria and Transoxiana at this time, however, were being controlled by the aforementioned Hunnic forces, particularly a clan best known under the name of their ruler, Kidara. The coins of Kidarite rulers are a direct copy of Kushano-Sasanian (and by extension Sasanians) silver issues, using the Pahlavi script, in a clear case of connection to the Sasanian court and administration (Zeimal, 1996).

Kidarites and their immediate successors, known as the Alkhons, were pushed over the Hindu-Kush towards Gandhara by a new tribal group called the Hephthalites (Sunderman, 1996; Rahman et. al., 2006). It is with the Hephthalites that we start a period of intense Sasanian engagement with eastern Iran and Central Asia. The Hephthalites, known sometimes by the contemporary Byzantine sources as the White Huns, were probably a new tribal confederacy made up of several already settled "Hunnic" tribes. They appear to have enjoyed a relatively centralized administrative system headed by a king, and surely a very organized army. During the second half of the fifth century, Hephthalites formed the largest threat to the Sasanian dominance, controlling not only Bactria, but apparently parts of southern Transoxiana and borders of the Sasanian realm in the northeast. The Sasanian emperor Peroz indeed undertook several campaigns against the Hephthalites, having to pay heavy tributes to them after his defeats, before being killed in a war against the Hephthalite king Akhshunwar (sometimes Khushnawaz in Classical Persian accounts) in AD 484. Kawad I, Peroz's son, was left as a hostage with the Hephthalites, and later, when removed from the throne in the Mazdakite revolt, again took refuge with the Hephthalites.

It appears that from the second half of the fifth century onwards, the Sasanians lost effective control of Bactria, the core-territory of the Kushans and Kushano-Sasanians. This might be the reason for an increasing attention to the west of their empire and the prolonged wars with the Romans in the sixth century. It also will clearly explain the need for deep socioeconomic reforms in the Sasanian realm, since the royal treasury must have been fully bankrupted after the payment of hefty ransoms and tributes to the Hephthalites following the death of Peroz (Sarkhosh-Curtis, 1999). As the result, we hear little of eastern Iran in the sixth century from a Sasanian point of view. Bactria and Zawulistan appear to have been consolidated into the Hephthalite state, while Transoxiana, namely Sogdiana, was left on its own to thrive. The Sogdian trade network, quite important in the economy of sixth-eighth century China and the Middle Eastern world, was best developed during this period (de la Vaissiere, 2005).

The Sasanians, however, started acting to regain their dominance in the east around 558. Their actions were in concert with the advances of the Gok-Türk/Western Turk empire (Harmatta, 1996). In fact, we know from Byzantine sources that a Turk Khaqan named *Silzaboulos* advanced his armies against Transoxiana and Bactria at this time, while the Sasanian Khosrow I also attacked the Hephthalites from the south and the west. The Byzantine accounts of campaigns of Silzaboulos are corroborated by the report of Gok-Türk advances under Khaqan *Sinjibu* in Chinese sources, as well as the Orkhon inscription (Sinor, 1990).

The Sasanians appear to have regained the important city of Marv, as well as de facto control of Bactria and Zawulistan, while the Gok- Türk became masters of Sogdiana and Khwarazmia. This campaign indeed might be the same one in which Wahram Chobin, the future rebel, made his name, and his friendship with the Gok-Türk Khaqan is evident through the tale of his refuge at the court of the Khaqan following his defeat by Khosrow II and his Byzantine army supporters (Tabari/Bosworth, 315-316).

The last glaring episode of Sasanian involvement with east Iran is the terminal period of their rule, when Yazdgerd III flees towards Transoxiana, hoping to gather support in the area. While the local rulers appear to have been uninterested, it is in fact Transoxiana and Bactria that appear to have provided shelter for refugee Persians in the end. In the accounts of Mt. Mugh, the mountain fortress of Dewashtich, the last king of Sogdiana, one comes across the mention of a Persian general. Dewashtich, protecting himself from the Muslim armies in 724 CE, was seeking support from anywhere he could, including the Chinese. While his agent the Afshun/Afshin was busy betraying him, a Persian general, presumably with an army, was at a reasonable distance, trying to reach Mt. Mugh and Dewashtich. Resistance, however, proved futile for Dewashtich, but Sogdiana might have represented the last viable refuge for the remaining Sasanian armies resisting the Islamic conquests (Grenet & de la Vaissiere, 2002).

Ideology, Empire and Glory

The most important aspect of the Sasanians was in fact the realization of an imperial ideology that was implemented through the imposition of the old Iranian worldview contained in the Zoroastrian sacred text, the *Avesta*. Without this, there would be simply no reason for establishing an empire by Ardashir I (224-240 CE), or its Afro-Asiatic over-expansion during the reign of Khusro II (590-628 CE), which caused its eventual collapse. Many scholars believe that the Achaemenid Empire was the ideological tool which the Sasanians used against their Roman foes. However, it seems that there is little or no evidence to this end (Shayegan 2011: 29), but rather a more complicated and religious ideology that was based on epic and the mythic past.

In a sense, ideology was the driving force for the Sasanians and the *rasion d'être* for what came to be called *Eranshahr* or the "Empire of the Iranians." This vision of *Eranshahr* or its truncated form, *Eran*, was an invention of the Sasanians that did not exist in the preceding Arsacid or Achaemenid Empires. This invention or construct of an empire named *Eranshahr* is manifest from the fact that neither before the Sasanians, nor after its collapse at the hands of the Muslims, did their neighbors call this territory as such and instead used the traditional designation of *Persia, Fars* or *Persis*. The idea of *Eranshahr* came with all its religious and ideological trappings, which necessitated the unification of the locations where once it was associated with Iranian habitation. This complex construction of an imperial ideology, with the notion of kingship, religion, and a territory, was based on the Hellenistic, Mesopotamian, and Iranian worldviews, combined with the local tradition of the Persian lords in the province of Fars (Daryaee 2014, 12).

By the fifth and the sixth centuries CE the Sasanian family, namely the sons of the king of kings, kept the empire together through a sophisticated bureaucracy, as evidenced by the sigilographic and numismatic evidence (Gyselen, 1989). Beyond the Iranian Plateau, the Sasanian Empire, the self-designated "Empire of the Iranians" (*Eranshahr*), was centered at Ctesiphon in Mesopotamia. In a sense, the "Heart of *Eranshahr*," as the medieval Muslim geographers called it, was Mesopotamia – the Sasanian province of *Surestan* – a fact that served to demonstrate the influence of the old Near Eastern tradition on the newly found Sasanian Empire. The new empire was cognizant of the history and heritage of the lands it had come to rule.

This new empire, however, was maintained and controlled through the institution of kingship, which was not static in the four centuries of its existence but, based on internal constraints and requirements, continually attempted to redefine the role of ruler, ranging from a divine king to a *cosmokrator* (Panaino, 2009). Among the most important ideas were the Zoroastrian notions of Iranian kingship, which served in the takeover of the land and the territorial battles, later added to by much innovation to fit the realities of the late antique world. Consequently, this Iranian king with his/her attributes was inextricably tied to the concept of *Eranshahr*; one could not survive without the other.

Xwarrah, "Glory" (Lubotsky, 1998), is central to the ancient Iranian royal ideology as demonstrated in the *Avesta*, and is a prerequisite of rightful rule in the *Avesta*. In the Avestan Yašts, one encounters the Kayanid kings battling the enemies of the Iranians and those who seek to gain sovereignty over the Iranian lands. To gain this rule, every one of the rightful Kayanid rulers and those before them and the seekers of power make sacrifices to deities to be granted the *xwarrah*. The *xwarrah* is granted or withheld from the Iranian rulers and the false non-Iranian evil characters according to the judgment of the gods. In Iranian art the *xwarrah* or glory was shown usually by a halo around the king's head, which also appeared in Sasanian art (Soudavar 2003). In later Persian literature and starting with Ferdowsi, the composer of the *Book of Kings* (*Shahnameh*) based on the Sasanian *Khoday-namag* (*Book of Lords*), the concept was further elaborated and came to be used by the medieval Muslim dynasties on the Iranian Plateau and Central Asia to legitimize their rule. As in the *Avesta* and with the Kayanids, the Sasanian family claimed the royal "Glory" (*xwarrah*). The symbol at times appeared with the king as a ram or specific insignias associated with the family of Sasan. Of course *xwarrah* was bestowed by Ohrmazd and other deities such as Lady Anahita on the king of kings in the form of a diadem in the royal rock reliefs (Daryaee, 2014, 18)

Through fire-temples and instructions to the Zoroastrians throughout the empire, this idea was made current and accepted. For others the idea was understood, through silver gilded dishes, which depicted the awesome king in banquet, hunting, or battle scenes. For those who were able to come to the court, such as foreign ambassadors, the immense crown suspended from a vault that mimicked the cosmos suggested the importance of the king of kings in the universe. The image of Khusro on his coinage also placed the king with four stars and crescents on the four sides, suggesting that the king of kings of *Eranshahr* was the king of the four corners of the world. Indeed in such royal imagery, *Eranshahr* was the center of the world.

The sacredness of the king of kings and his importance for the well-being of the empire were paramount for the imperial ideology. Islamic sources mention that when an audience was given to see the king, he was usually hidden behind a veil, as he was not to be seen by all. He was like the sun and the moon, which held the same importance. Only during specific times of the year did the king make a public appearance. For example, during the *Nowruz* (New Year) and *Mihregan* (autumn) celebrations, gifts were exchanged and the king made speeches to the public. These biannual ceremonies were held so that the cosmic order and the order of the universe and empire could be maintained through the appearance of the king of kings, which ensured abundance, peace, and the well-being of the empire (Daryaee, 2014, 19-20). From the sixth century the well-being of the king of kings was so important that he did not participate in wars, as his loss would have symbolically meant the loss of the glory and hence the well-being of *Eranshahr* (Whitby 1994).

Economy and Trade

Like most ancient and mediaeval civilizations, Sasanian economy was greatly dependent on agriculture, both sowing and animal husbandry. The Sasanian realm, however, was not greatly fertile and, more important still, suffered from a lack of water, except in Mesopotamia. While Sasanian Mesopotamia *(Surestan)* enjoyed an ancient agricultural tradition and relatively reliable sources of water, the Iranian Plateau was made up of hilly ground and suffered from an acute lack of rain (P. Christensen, 1996, Ch. 6). As such, agriculture appears to have been highly localized and concentrated in certain areas. Surestan and Khuzestan possessed fertile land and semi-reliable water. Traditionally, these areas had been used for grain production, as well as limited horticulture (mostly dates).

Recent research shows that the Sasanian state invested heavily in these areas, creating hydraulic systems for irrigation, possibly with the aim of utilizing marginal land (Wenke, 1975; Neely, 1974). It has additionally been suggested that with the introduction of new crops, mostly cotton and sugar cane, these areas were made commercially important (Bulliet, 2011). Our information for agriculture on the Iranian Plateau is patchy, due to limited textual evidence and the paucity of archaeological surveys. It seems that whenever it has been possible to create irrigation systems such as Karez/Qanats (underground aqueducts), agriculture was heavily practiced. An example of this is on the Damghan plain in north-central Iran, where the irrigation resulted in intensive settlements around the central plain, before retreating to mountain valleys and switching production to horticulture (Trinkaus, 1985). The rest of the plateau, judging from its terrain and later sources, was heavily involved in transhumant cattle raising and animal husbandry.

In trade, the Sasanians were competing with the Romans over silk and disputing trade as far away as Sri Lanka. There was a Sasanian colony in Malaysia which was composed of merchants. Persian horses were shipped to Ceylon, and a Persian colony was established on that island, where ships came from Persia to its port. By the sixth century it appears that the Persians were bent not only on controlling the Persian Gulf and the Arabian Sea but were also looking farther east, which brought them into conflict with Rome. Silk appears to have been an important commodity, which the Romans wanted and therefore sought to circumvent Persian traders to get lower prices. Consequently, the Byzantines had to seek the aid of the Christian Ethiopians, who were expelled by the Yemenis with the backing of the Sasanians in that region.

We also have information on Sasanian trade with China. Imported objects, such as Tang dynasty export wares, and other items from Rome, were found at the port of Siraf. Trade with China was conducted through two avenues, namely, the famous Silk Road and the sea route. Because of the political situation, maritime trade became more important, and ports in Persis/Fars became increasingly central (Whitehouse and Williamson, 1973).

Off the coast of China there have been finds of Sasanian coins, which again suggest the importance of maritime trade between this region and Persia. At least three sites where Sasanian coins have been found along the southeast coast of China make it probable that ships from the Persian Gulf came there. These are the sites of Kukogng, Yngdak, Suikai, which had connections with trade in the Persian Gulf. Many of the coins belong to the late fifth through seventh centuries CE, which again attest to the importance of the Persian Gulf in the late Sasanian period.

As for domestic commerce, we rely on the seals and sealings which give some insight into the Sasanian administrative institutions. In terms of commercial activity, we can tell that there was a vibrant domestic exchange based on the placement of bullae and seal finds in the empire bearing the name of one of the cities or districts of the province of Persis/Fars. The bullae were used to seal packages destined for maritime or caravan trade, which is supported by later historical evidence. It is also important to note that bullae finds in east Asia, especially in Mantai in Sri Lanka, attest to Persian economic activity there as well.

Trade was conducted by companies and religious communities who combined their resources and formed partnerships. The term used for joint partnership in the Middle Persian legal texts is *hambayih* which really meant holder of a common share whose joint investment would have brought a better return and a larger purchasing power. These joint partnerships were probably based on religious association as well, where Zoroastrians created their own *hambayih* but may have dealt with other religious groups outside their regional reach.

We are well informed with regard to the legal aspects of trade and business agreements. Drafts of agreements were drawn up, signed, and sealed, and a copy was kept at the local office of registry, *diwan*. These agreements were legally binding and, if violated, the accused was brought before a lesser or higher magistrate who was also a high-ranking priest.

The principle commercial activity in the city was performed by the merchants (*wazarganan*) who were from the hutukhshašan estate. Commerce (*wazarganih*) was conducted in the bazaar (*wazar*), which today remains the economic center of small and large cities in Iran. As with today's markets, it appears that each group of artisans occupied a specific section (Persian *raste*) of the bazaar. A list of the various professions that occupied special places in the bazaar includes blacksmith, iron-molder, silversmith, silver-molder, roof-maker, string-maker, "iron smith," tailor, dressmaker, porcelain pot-maker, carpenter, washerman, general shoemaker (as well as a specialized type of shoemaker whose footware was made of strings), potter, baker, book-painter, painter, cup-maker, tanner, ironsmith, dyer, various types of builder, barber, tentmaker, cooks who prepared sweets and finger foods, tablecloth-maker, goldsmith, and saddler.

There were other professions, but we are not sure if they were in the bazaar. Each artisan (*kirrog*) guild was headed by a head of the guild (*kirrogbed*). The activity and the prices of the bazaar were overseen by a head of the bazaar (*wazarbed*), who probably represented the artisan class. It was in these centers where local products were produced, whereas commodities from other provinces as well as some foreign products entered the cities via caravan. These caravans (*karwan*) were led by a caravan leader (*sartwa*), who was either hired by the merchant or in partnership with him.

While the barter system was in use locally in villages and the like, the Sasanians brought about a standardization of weights and the minting of coinage which was directed from above and under the control of the imperial administration. The most common type of Sasanian coins were silver *drahm*, one-sixth silver *dang,* and copper coins, *pashiz,* made of copper and used for local daily transactions. Gold was only minted ceremonially and does not appear to have been in circulation for trade and exchange. While the increase in the use of copper and bronze coinage in certain parts of the empire attests to the increase in trade and governmental control, silver coinage was much more prevalent. On the obverse of these, we find the portrait of the King of Kings along with a name and title, such as "Ardashir, King of Kings of Eran, who is from the race of gods." On the reverse of the coinage is a fire-alter, sometimes alone and sometimes with two attendants flanking the fire. Until the late fifth century CE the coins did not indicate their mints, which makes it difficult to determine the number of mints and amount of production at each location. While there are more than one hundred mint-marks known, no more than twenty mints were producing the majority of the coins in the empire.

Religion

The Sasanian rule is most associated with Zoroastrianism, the ancient Iranian religion with close connections to the religion reflected in the Indian *Rig Veda*. Although our sources tell us about Zoroastrianism from the late Sasanian period, it is generally understood that the religion enjoyed wide observance in Iran from the ancient period, and certainly from the Arsacid times. Ardashir, the founder of the Sasanian dynasty, is given strong religious connections in historiography, and his grandfather and eponymous ancestor of the dynasty, Sasan, is said to be a priest of the goddess Anahid/Anahita in Istakhr. The coins of Ardashir and his descendants up to the fifth century bear the phrase "who is descended from the gods" on their obverse, while the reverse displays a fire altar, most closely associated with Zoroastrianism (Alram/Gyselen, 2003).

The famous inscriptions of Kerdir, the chief priest of Wahram II, are our best evidence of the state of religion in the early Sasanian period. In them, Kerdid chronicles his own rise to the position of the chief Mobed of Zoroastrianism and, at the same time, mentions his own persecution along with the purging of adherents of other religions, including Buddhists, Jews, Christians, and Manichaeans (McKenzie, 1989). Despite this harsh depiction, early Sasanian kings appear to be rather tolerant toward other religions and even positively accommodating toward them. Shabuhr I in fact allows Mani, the prophet of Manichaeism, to freely preach and convert; indeed, Mani writes a book in Middle Persian, named *Shabuhragan*, in Shabuhr's honor. Mani was similarly favored by Hormizd I and Wahram I, but the ascendance of Kerdir under Wahram II finally caused Mani's downfall along with a general extradition and execution of his followers.

Christianity also was accommodated in the Sasanian territories, although it was occasionally persecuted under various kings. The reason, particularly after Constantine and Theodosius I, had to do with the Sasanian administration's fear of the Christian community and its partiality toward the Christian empire of Rome. The efforts of Yazdgerd II and his chancellor Mihr-Narseh in the fifth century in converting Armenians to Zoroastrianism should also be treated in the same vein (Thomson, 1982). This fear, however, decreased after the Council of Chalcedon in 451, when internal disagreements caused the flight of many "Eastern" Christians to the Sasanian territories and the formation of a native, independent Christian community in the Sasanian territories. Eventually, under Khosrow I, Hormizd IV, and Khosrow II, this community established itself in the Sasanian realm and created a central patriarchal seat in Ctesiphon, as well as local bishoprics as far east as Darab in Fars/Persis (McCullough, 1982: 157-162). Members of this church were also responsible for the spread of Christianity in Central Asia and its transportation to Turko-Mongolian tribes of Inner Asia via the Sogdian trade network.

Jews had lived in the Sasanian territories, particularly in southern Mesopotamia, since the Achaemenid period. Headed by a Resh Galota, "leader of the exiles," these Jews were engaged in agricultural activities, artisanal production, and commerce, as is recorded in the Talmud. The greater part of this document, in fact, was composed and compiled during the Sasanian period, forming the larger of the two Talmuds known as the Babylonian Talmud or the Bavli. Based on its testimony, the Jewish community enjoyed autonomy in legal and judicial terms, possibly providing a glimpse of Sasanian official policies toward minorities (Secunda, 2013).

Starting in the fifth century, the Zoroastrian establishment gained more power in the Sasanian court. This is evident from Yazdgerd II's campaigns against Armenians, which were provoked by the proliferation of devotional literature addressed towards creating "orthodoxy" and resulted finally in the successful purge of the Mazdakites following the death of Kawad I in 531 CE. The Zoroastrian church, in unity with the Sasanian nobility, became the official religious institution of the government. During the course of the sixth and seventh centuries, judging from the proliferation of seals and bullae attesting to this, more and more governmental positions were bestowed on low- to high-ranking Zoroastrian clergy. In particular, the administration of legal contracts, from the sale and shipping of goods to land purchase, was witnessed by various *Dastwars* and *Hirbeds*. The role of social justice and provisions for the good was given to a particular cleric entrusted with the title "Judge and Protector of the Needy" (Daryaee, 2001), and indeed, the *Mowbedān Mowbed* (the Great Priest) enjoyed high prestige and influence. This is, evidently, the status quo which left a lasting impression on the minds of early Islamic historians, both Muslim and Zoroastrian, and by extension modern historians, imagining the whole of the Sasanian period as a period of "theocracy" and the dominance of a rigid Zoroastrian church.

Probably as a way of rebelling against this slowly developing status quo, Mazdak, himself a Zoroastrian priest, instigated a rebellion in the late fifth century. Mazdakism is described exclusively through hostile accounts, from contemporary Byzantine sources (Procopius or Joshua the Stylite) or from latter Muslim (Shahristani, Dinawari) and Zoroastrian (*Dēnkard*) accounts. Their universal condemnation springs from a charge of "communal sharing," mostly framed as "sharing of wives," in other words, sexual promiscuity, but also connotes the sharing of property and wealth. Modern historians, often influenced by twentieth-century Marxist idealism, have imagined Mazdakism as an ideal "proto-Communism" and recast the Sasanian efforts at eliminating the cult as a classic class-struggle (Rezakhani, 2014). Whatever the truth might be, it seems certain that Mazdakism was only one reflection of a wider socioeconomic and cultural movement in Sasanian society which was translated through a religious prism. The ideas and ideals which had been reflected in Mazdakism at one time did not cease to exist and appeared in different shapes and forms and under various rubrics in the early Islamic period.

Language and Literature

The official, or at least the most widespread, language of the Sasanian realm was Middle Persian, a language native to the province of Fars/Persis in the southern Iranian Plateau (Sundermann, 1989). The earliest major written source available from inside the empire itself is Shapur I's *Ka'ba-i Zardosht* inscription (ŠKZ). The inscription is carved in Middle Persian, Parthian, and Greek, reflecting the three linguistic traditions of the time: contemporary reality, the immediate past, and the classical Hellenistic period (Rubin, 2002). Soon after, we have an inscription from Shabuhr, son of Hormizd, a grandson of Shabuhr I, who was styled the king of Sakas (Daryaee, 1380/2001). His lapidary inscription, on a column in Persepolis, is in Middle Persian only, something that perhaps is justifiable by its unofficial tone and setting, carved over the course of a short campaign. Narseh, the son of Shabuhr I who claimed the crown for himself in 293, however, left us a major inscription, however damaged, in Paikuli, south of modern Sulaimaniya in the Iraqi Kurdistan. Here, Narseh uses only Middle Persian and Parthian, having abandoned Greek. Both ŠKZ and Paikuli are in the genre of official proclamations and victory literature and are quite formulaic. But both do betray a well-developed literary style, reflecting that Middle Persian was not a completely new language for the composition of literature and official declarations.

We have very few inscriptions after this point. Most of our written sources from the Sasanian period appear to have been composed in the fifth-seventh centuries and consigned to writing in the late Sasanian and early Islamic periods. However, it is fair to assume that many of these were simply compilations of earlier compositions whose latest manuscripts are simply those that have reached us. Here, the evidence of the creation of the Avestan script, based on the Middle Persian Pahlavi script (Weber, 2007), in the late Sasanian period itself is proof for the proliferation of the use of the latter. Surely, the widespread use of written Pahlavi caused the well-known realization that it is highly inefficient for the accurate transmission of complicated Avestan phonology and, more importantly yet, the sacred contents of the Avesta, the Zoroastrian holy book (Stausberg, 1998: 258-263).

Interest in literature and a need for recording the past also gave incentives in the fifth and sixth centuries for a movement to compose both new pieces and translations from other languages. It is often posited that the rule of Khosrow I saw the beginning of the compilation of the historical genre known as *Khuday-namag,* "the Book of the Lords," which in various texts, reflected the mythical and historical tales of the history of kings. This essentially acted as source material for the history of pre-Islamic Iran, as evidenced in the writings of Muslim historians like al-Tabari as well as in the great Persian epic, the *Shahnameh* of Ferdowsi. Alongside the Khuday-namag texts, other epics, romances, and pieces of devotional poetry were also composed, some of which, including *Ayadgar-i Zareran,* have reached us in their original form, while others like *Vis o Ramin* are known only through New Persian translations. At the same time, serious works such as *Mādayān ī Hazār Dādestān,* "the Book of a Thousand Judgments," a compilation of legal rulings and commentary, were composed and probably finalized in the seventh century (Macuch, 1993). However, the largest body of Sasanian works of literature can be found in the commentaries on the Avestan, the Zoroastrian holy scripture, which were composed in Middle Persian. Written either in the Pahlavi or the Avestan script, these texts (called Zand and Pazand respectively, based on script) formed a large body of works that continued well into the Islamic period and essentially comprise the vast majority of what we have in Middle Persian (Boyce, 1968). Last but not least were the translations from other languages, most importantly Indic languages (either Sanskrit or Prakrit), such as *Panchatantra* (de Blois, 1990). Although the original translations have not survived, we know from Islamic sources such as *Al-Fihrist* of Ibn Nadim that these works were brought into the Sasanian world by travelers like Borzoe the Physician, who is also credited with translating the work to Middle Persian. These Middle Persian translations were then used in the early Abbasid period for translations into Arabic, resulting, in the case of Panchatantra, in the great collection of fables known as *Kalila wa Dimna.*

Middle Persian and Avestan, however, were not the only languages used for literature. Aramaic, in both Iraqi and Syriac forms, was the vehicle for widespread composition in the Sasanian period. The Babylonian Talmud was in fact composed mostly during the Sasanian period in southern Iraq/Surestan and represents a major work of late antique literature and legal composition (Secunda, 2009). Syriac was the language of the Church of the East, centered in Ctesiphon, and the language in which church histories, local monastic histories, and even chronicles were composed by Syriac Christians (Brock, 1997). In the east, Bactrian was the official language, a remnant of Kushan dominance, and was used widely for the composition of legal documents, and presumably for literature as well, although little of the latter remains beyond fragmentary Buddhist texts (Sims-Williams, 2008). Sogdian, the great language of trade in Central Asia as far east as China, came from Sogdiana, the regions of Bukhara and Samarqand in Transoxiana. It was used as a major vehicle for the transmission of religious beliefs of the Manichaean and Christian communities of Central

Asia, resulting in a rich religious literature which includes many fables and anecdotes, as well as translations of texts such as the Psalms. Incidentally, the oldest Avestan manuscript we have in our possession is a copy of the well-known Zoroastrian prayer Ashem Vohu written in the Sogdian script (Rose, 2011: 151-152)!

Conclusion

The Sasanian Empire was one of the major forces of the late antique world. Often represented as the "adversary" of the Roman Empire in the east, and thus on its "periphery," the Sasanian Empire was in fact the center of a prolific sociocultural, political, and economic sphere that became widespread following its conquest by the Muslims. Its political centralization, robust and expanding economy, socio-religious innovations and changes, and growing cultural activities made the Sasanians the blueprint for subsequent polities in the region. Often underresearched, many aspects of Sasanian culture and society remain unknown, or thin connections are made via shallow indications of its influence. The emerging evidence and the development of more sophisticated studies of the period would no doubt show the centrality of the Sasanians in the late antique world, and assess their lasting legacy in the history of West and Central Asia until modern times.

Figure. 1. Ardashir I

Figure. 2. Ardashir I in combat with the last Arsacid king

Figure. 3. Palace of Ardashir I in Firuzabad/Gur

Figure. 4. Darabgerd

Figure. 5. Investiture scene of Ardashir I by Ohrmazd

Figure. 6. Shabuhr I's victory relief over the Romans

Figure. 7. Gold coin of Shabuhr I

Figure. 8. Sasanian stucco of a ram symbolizing Xwarrah

Figure. 9. Shabuhr I and his retinue from a relief at Naqsh-e Rajab

Figure. 10. Silver coin of Wahram II with his wife

Figure. 11. Barm-e Delak relief, possibly Wahram II and his wife

Figure. 12. Middle Persian version of the Hajjiabad Inscription

Figure. 13. Relief of Kerdir from Naqsh-e Rostam

Figure. 14. Investiture scene of Narseh and Lady Anahid at Naqsh-e Rostam

Figure. 15. Image of courtly life on a silver bowl from the National Museum of Iran

Figure. 16. Paikuli reflief

Figure. 17. Investiture scene: Shabuhr II & Ardashir II along with Mihr

Figure. 18. Wahram Gur on the hunt (Pushkin Museum)

Figure. 19. Bandiyan: Fallen enemies from the East

Figure. 20. Bandiyan stucco

Figure. 21. Khusrow I: from the National Museum of Iran

Figure. 22. Gold coin of Khusrow II

Figure. 23. Persian manuscript showing Mazdakites hung upside down

Figure. 24. Bandiyan: Fire-alter

Figure. 25. Relief of a hunting party showing Khosrow II, Taq-e Bostan, Kermanshah

Figure. 26. The investiture scene of Khusrow II by Lady Anahid and Ohrmazd, standing above the statue of Khusrow II in full armor

Figure. 27. Silver drachm of Queen Boran

Figure. 28. Bulla of a Sasanian Spahbed

Figure. 29. The Shiz fire-temple in Takht-e Soleiman, Azerbaijan

Figure. 30. Delijan fire-temple in central Iran

Figure. 31. Middle Persian ostracon from Hamedan

Figure. 32. A Christian seal impression

Figure. 33. The so-called Ka'aba-I Zardosht, at Naqsh-e Rostam

Figure. 34. Middle Persian version of the Psalms

Bibliography

Alram, M. and Rika G. 2003. *Sylloge Nummorum Sasanidarum, 1: Ardashir I-Shapur I.* Vienna. OeAW.

Alram, M. 2007. "Ardashir's Eastern Campaign and the Numismatic Evidence" in: J. Cribb and G. Herrmann (eds.) *After Alexander. Central Asia before Islam.* Oxford, Oxford University Press. pp. 227-242.

Bahar, M. T. 1939. *Majmal ol-Tavarikh wal-Qesas,* Tehran, Khavar. 1318.

Bivar, A.D.H. 1969. *Catalogue of the Western Asiatic Seals in the British Museum, The Sasanian Dynasty,* London.

Blockley, R. C. 1988. "Ammianus Marcellinus on the Persian invasion of AD 359."The *Phoenix*: 244-260.

Blockley, R. C. (1987) "The Division of Armenia between the Romans and the Persians at the End of the Fourth Century A.D." *Historia: Zeitschrift für Alte Geschichte,* Bd. 36, H. 2. pp. 222-234.

Boyce, M. 1968. "Middle Persian Literature." *Handbuch der Orientalistik* 4, no. 1: pp. 31-79.

Brock, S. P. A. 1997. *Brief Outline of Syriac Literature.* Kottayam. St. Ephrem Ecumenical Research Institute.

Brunner, C. J. 1974. "The Chronology of the Sasanian Kushanshahs," *American Numismatic Society Notes*: pp. 145-65.

Bulliet, R. W. 2011. *Cotton, Climate, and Camels in Early Islamic Iran: A Moment in World History.* New York. Columbia University Press.

Christensen, A. 1944. *L'Iran sous les Sassanides,* Copenhague: E. Munksgaard.

Christensen, P. 1993. The Decline of Iranshahr: Irrigation and Environments in the History of the Middle East, 500 bc to ad 1500. Copenhagen: Museum Tusculanum Press.

Compareti, M. 2009. "Chinese-Iranian Relations xv. the Last Sasanians in China," *Encyclopaedia Iranica.*Crone, Patricia. "Kavād's Heresy and Mazdak's Revolt." *Iran* (1991): 21-42.

Curtis, V. S. 2010. *"The Frataraka Coins of Persis; Bridging the Gap between Achaemenid and Sasanian Persia,"* in J. Curtis and S.J. Simpson, *The World of Achaemenid Persia.* London and New York, I.B. Tauris. pp. 379-394.

Curtis, V. S. 1999. "Some Observations on Coins of Peroz and Kavad I," in Michael Alram and Deborah E. Klimburg-Salter (eds), *Coins, Art, and Archaeology,* Vienn: Verlag der OeAW, 303-313.

Darayee, T. 2001. "The Judge and Protector of the Needy during the Sasanian Period"

Tafazzolī Memorial Volume, Tehran. pp. 171-187.

Darayee, T. 2001. "Katibe-ye Shapur Sakkanshah dar Takht-e Jamshid," *Farhang*, 37/38 (1380): pp. 107-114.

Daryaee, T. 2002. *Šahrestānīhā ī Ērānšahr, A Middle Persian Text on Late Antique Geography, Epic and History*, Costa Mesa: Mazda Publishers.

Daryaee, T. 2008. *Sasanian Iran (224-651 CE): Portrait of a Late Antique Empire*. Costa Mesa: Mazda Publishers .

Daryaee, T. 2008. "Kingship in Early Sasanian Iran." In V. Sarkhosh Curtis / S. Stewart (eds) *The Idea of Iran: The Sasanian Era*, London: pp. 60-70.

Daryaee, T. 2009. *Sasanian Persia: The Rise and Fall of an Empire*. London: IB Tauris .

Daryaee, T. "Sasanian Kingship, Empire and Glory: Aspects of Iranian Imperium," *Ranj o Ganj*. 2014. *Papers in Honour of Professor Z. Zarshenas*, eds. V. Naddaf, F. Goshtasb, M. Shorki-Foumeshi, Tehran: pp. 11-22.

De Blois, F. 1990. *Burzōy's Voyage to India and the Origin of the Book of Kalīlah wa Dimnah*. London: Royal Asiatic Society.

Dingas, B, and Engelbert W. 2007. *Rome and Persia in Late Antiquity*. Cambridge: Cambridge University Press.

Elishe, 1982. *History of Vardan and the Armenian War*, Translated and Commentary by Robert W. Thomson, Cambridge, Mass: Harvard University Press.

Emrani, H. 2009. "Like Father, Like Daughter: Late Sasanian Imperial Ideology & the Rise of Bōrān to Power." e-*Sasanika* 9: pp. 1-20.

Frye, R. N. 1973. *Sasanian Remains from Qasr-ī Abu Nasr*, Cambridge.

Frye, R. N. 1983. *The History of Ancient Iran*, Munich: C.H. Beck.

Frye, R.N. 1983. "The Political History of Iran Under the Sasanians," *The Cambridge History of Iran* 3(1), ed. E. Yarshater, Cambridge: CUP: pp. 116-180.

Göbl, R. 1971. *Sasanian Numismatics*, Braunschweig.

Göbl, R. 1967. *Dokumente zur Geschichte der iranischen Hunnen in Baktrien und Indien*. Wiesbaden: Otto Harrassowitz Verlag.

Grenet, F. and De La Vaissiere. E. 2002. "The Last Days of Panjikent." *Silk Road Art and Archaeology* 8.

Gyeslen, R. 1989. *La Geographie Administrative de L'Empire Sassanide – Les Temoignages Sigillographiques*, ResOrientales I, Paris.

Gyselen, R. 2010. "Romans and Sasanians in the Third Century. Propaganda warfare and ambiguous imagery." In H. Börm/J. Wiesehöfer (eds) *Commutatio Et Contentio: Studies in the Late Roman, Sasanian, and Early Islamic Near East: in Memory of Zeev Rubin* Düsseldorf: Wellem: pp. 71-87.

Harper, P. O. 2008. "Image and Identity: Art of the Early Sasanian Dyanasty." In V. Sarkhosh Curtis / S. Stewart (eds) *The Idea of Iran: The Sasanian Era*, London: pp. 70-87.

Harmatta, J. 1996. "Annexation of the Hephthalite vassal kingdoms by the Western Türks." *History of Humanity* 3, Paris: UNESCO: pp. 475-476.

Harper, P. O. 1981. *Silver Vessels of the Sasanian Period*, New York.

Honigmann, E. and Maricq, André. 1953. *Recherches sur les "Res gestae divi Saporis"*. Brussels: Palais des académies.

Howard-Johnston, J. 1999, "Heraclius' Persian Campaigns and the Revival of the East Roman Empire, 622-630." *War in History* 6, no. 1: pp. 1-44.

Humbach, H., and Skjærvø, P. O. 1978-1983. *The Sasanian Inscription of Paikuli*. Wiesbaden: Dr. Ludwig Reichert.

Kaim, B. 2009. "Investiture or Mithra: Towards a New Interpretation of So Called Investiture Scenes in Parthian and Sasanian Art," *Iranica Antiqua*, 403-415.

Klima, O. 1988. "Bahram V," *Encyclopaedia Iranica*.

Litvinsky, B. A. 1996. "The Hephthalite Empire." *History of civilizations of Central Asia* 3, Paris: UNESCO: pp. 135-62.

Lubotsky, A. 1998. "Avestan xvarənah-: etymology and concept," *Sprache und Kultur. Akten der X. Fachtagung der Indogermanischen Gesellschaft Innsbruck, 22.-28. September 1996*, edited by W. Meid, Innsbruck, pp. 479-488.

MacKenzie, D. N. 1989. "Kerdir's inscription." *Iranische Denkmäler*, fasc 13: 35-72.

Macuch, M. 1993. *Rechtskasuistik und Gerichtspraxis zu Beginn des siebenten ahrhunderts in Iran: die Rechtssamlung des Farroḫmard i Wahrāmān*. Wiesbaden: Otto Harrassowitz Verlag.

McCullough. W. S. 1982. *A Short History of Syriac Christianity to the Rise of Islam*. Chico, CA.

McDonough, S. 2000. "A Second Constantine?: The Sasanian King Yazdgard in Christian History and Historiography." *Journal of Late Antiquity* 1, no. 1 (2008): pp. 127-140.

Mosig-Walburg K. Die Flucht des persischen Prinzen Hormizd und sein Exil im Römischen Reich," In *Iranica Antiqua*, XXXV: pp. 69-109.

Morony, M. G. 1998. "Sāsānids," *the Encycleopaedia of Islam*, 2nd Ed.

Morony, M. G. 2007. "For whom does the writer write? the First Bubonic Plague Pandemic according to Syriac sources." In Lester K. Little (ed.) *Plague and the End of Antiquity*, Cambridge: CUP: pp. 59-86.

Neely, James A. 1974. "Sassanian and early Islamic water-control and irrigation systems on the Deh Luran plain, Iran." *Irrigation's impact on society*. University of Arizona Press, Tucson: pp. 21-42.

Nikitin, A. 1999. "Notes on the Chronology of the Kushano-Sasanian kingdom." *Coins, Art, and Chronology. Essays on the pre-Islamic History of the Indo-Iranian Borderlands*, Vienna: OeAW: pp. 259-263.

Panaino, A. 2009. "The King and the Gods in the Sasanian Royal Ideology," *Sources pour l'histoire et la géographie du monde iranien (224-710)*, ed. R. Gyselen, Res Orientales XVIII, Bure-sur Yvette: pp. 209-256.

Paul, Ludwig. ed. 2003. *Persian Origins: Early Judaeo-Persian and the Emergence of New Persian: Collected Papers of the Symposium, Göttingen 1999*. Wiesbaden: Otto Harrassowitz Verlag.

Pourshariati, P. 2008. *Decline and Fall of the Sasanian Empire: The Sasanian-Parthian Confederacy and the Arab Conquest of Iran*, I.B. Tauris.

Rahman, A. U, and Grenet F. and Sims-Williams N. 2006. "A Hunnish Kushan-shah." *Journal of Inner Asian Art and Archaeology* 1, no. 1: pp. 125-131.

Rezakhani, K. 2014. "Mazdakism, Manichaeism, and Zoroastrianism: in Search of Orthodoxy and Heterodoxy in Late Antique Iran," *Special Volume on Late Antique Iranian Religions*,

Jason S. Mokhtarian and David Bennett (eds.) *Iranian Studies*.

Jenny R. 2011. *Zoroastrianism: An Introduction*. London: IB Tauris.

Rubin, Z. 1995. "The Reforms of Khusro Anushirwan." *The Byzantine and Early Islamic Near East* 3, Princeton: Darwin Press: pp. 227-97.

Rubin, Z. 2002. "Res Gestae Divi Saporis: Greek and Middle Iranian in a Document of Sasanian Anti-Roman Propaganda." *Bilingualism in Ancient Society. Language Contact and the Written Text*. Oxford: OUP: pp. 267-97.

Schindel, N. 2013. "Kawād I i.reign" *Encyclopaedia Iranica*. (http://www.iranicaonline.org/ articles/kawad-i-reign)

Schippmann, Kl. *Grundzüge der Geschichte des sasanidischen Reiches*, Darmstadt, 1990.

Secunda, S. 2009. "Talmudic Text and Iranian Context: On the Development of Two Talmudic Narratives." *AJS Review* 33/01: pp. 45-69.

Secunda, S. 2013. *the Iranian Talmud: Reading the Bavli in its Sasanian Context*, Philadelphia: Upenn Press.

Shahbazi, A. S. 2005. "Sasanian Dynasty," *Encyclopaedia Iranica*.

Shahbazi, A. S. 2003. "The Horse that killed Yazdegerd," in K. Eslami and D. Daryaee eds., *Festschrift Hans Peter Schmidt*, Costa Mesa: Mazda.

Shayegan, M. R. 2011. *Arsacids and Sasanians: Political Ideology in Post-Hellenistic and Late Antique Persia*, Cambridge, Cambridge University Press.

Shayegan, M.R. "Nugae Epigraphicae." In Festschrift for Prods Oktor Skjærvø. Edited by Nicholas and Ursula Sims-Williams. 2005 [2009]. Bulletin of the Asia Institute 19. Bloomfield Hills, MI: Bulletin of the Asia Institute: pp. 169–179.

Sims-Williams, N. 2008. "The Sasanians in the East. A Bactrian archive from northern Afghanistan," In: Curtis, Vesta Sarkhosh and Stewart, Sarah, (eds.), *The Sasanian Era*. London: I.B.Tauris: pp. 88-102.

Sinor, D. 1990. "The establishment and dissolution of the Türk Empire." *The Cambridge History of Early Inner Asia,* Cambridge: CUP: pp. 285-316.

Soudavar, A. 2003. *The Aura of the Kings: Legitimacy and Divine Sanction in Iranian Kingship*, Mazda Publishers, Costa Mesa.

Stausberg, M. 1998. "The Invention of a Canon: The Case of Zoroastrianism." in *Canonization & Decanonization. Papers presented to the International Conference of the Leiden Institute for the Study of Religions (LISOR) held at Leiden 9-10 January 1997,* eds. Arie van der Kooij & Karel van der Toorn, Leiden, Boston, Köln: Brill, pp. 257-277.

Sundermann, W. 1989. "Mittelpersisch" in *Compendium Linguarum Iranicarum*, ed. Rüdiger Schmitt, Wiesbaden: Reichert.

Sundermann, W. 1996. "The Rise of the Hephthalite Empire." *History of Humanity: From the Seventh Century BC to the Seventh Century AD* 3, Paris: UNESCO: pp. 474-477.

Tabari, M. m. J. 1999. *The Sāsānids, the Byzantines, the Lakmids, and Yemen*, (History of al-Tabari, Vol. V), trans. C. E. Bosworth. Albany: State University of New York Press.

Tanabe, K. 1985. "Date and Significance of the so-called Investiture of Ardashir II and the images of Shahpur II and III at Taq-i Bustan." *Orient* 21: pp. 102-121.

Thomson, RW. 1976. Trans. Agathangelos *History of the Armenians*, Albany. SUNY Press.

Trinkaus, K. M. 1985. "Settlement of Highlands and Lowlands in Early Islamic Dāmghān."

Iran: pp. 129-141.

Tyler-Smith, S. 2000. "Coinage in the Name of Yazdgerd III (AD 632-651) and the Arab Conquest of Iran." *Numismatic Chronicle* 160: pp. 135-170.

Vaissière, É. De La. 2005. *Sogdian Traders*: a History. Leiden: Brill.

Sarkhosh Curtis, V. "Some Observations on Coins of Peroz and Kavad I." in Michael Alram and Deborah E. Klimburg-Salter. eds. 1999. *Coins, Art, and Archaeology*, Vienna: Austrian Academy of Sciences. pp. 303-13.

Watt, J. W., and Frank R. Trombley, eds. 2000. *The Chronicle of pseudo-Joshua the Stylite.* Liverpool University Press.

Weber, D. 2007. "Remarks on the development of the Pahlavi Script in Sasanian Times." In *Religious Texts in Iranian Languages: Symposium Held in Copenhagen May 2002*, vol. 98, pp. 185-195. Copennhagen: Det Kongelige Danske Videnskabernes Selskab.

Wenke, R. J. 1975. "Imperial investments and agricultural developments in Parthian and Sasanian Khuzestan: 150 BC to AD 640." *Mesopotamia* 10. pp. 31-221.

Whitby, M. 1994. "The Persian king at war," *The Roman Byzantine Army in the East*, ed. E. Dabrowa, Cracow. pp. 227-263.

Whitehouse, D. and Williamson, A. 1973. "Sasanian maritime trade," *Iran*. pp. 29-49.

Wiesehöfer, Josef. 2010. "King and Kingship in the Sasanian Empire," in *Concepts of Kingship in Antiquity: Proceedings of the European Science Foundation Exploratory Workshop Held in Padova, Novemeber 28th-December 1st, 2007*, eds. G.B. Lanfranchi & R. Rollinger, Padova. pp. 135-152.

Wiesehöfer, J. 2009. "Kawad, Khusro I and the Mazdakites: A New Proposal," in *Trésors d'Orient. Mélanges offerts à Rika Gyselen*, eds. Ph. Gignoux – C. Jullien – F. Jullien,Studia Iranica Cahier 42, Paris: pp. 391-409.

Wiesehöfer, J. 1996. *Ancient Persia From 550 BC to 650 AD*, I.B. Tauris Publishers, London & New York.

Wiesehöfer, J. 1994. *Die „dunklen Jahrhunderte" der Persis. Untersuchungen zu Geschichte und Kultur von Fārs in frühhellenistischer Zeit (330–140 v. Chr.)*, C. H. Beck, München.

Zaehner, R. C. 1961. *Dawn and Twilight of Zoroastrianism*, Oxford.

Zaehner, R.C. 1956. *The Teachings of the Magi*, London.

Zakeri, M. 1995. *Sāsānid Soldiers in Early Muslim Society: The Origins of Ayyārān and Futuwwa*, Wiesbaden: Harrassowitz.

Zeimal, E. V. 1996. "The Kidarite Kingdom of Central Asia." *History of civilizations of Central Asia* 3, Paris: UNESCO.

FROM THE KUSHANS TO THE WESTERN TURKS
Khodadad Rezakhani

The history of pre-Islamic East Iran – the region comprising Transoxiana, Tokharestan, Sistan, Kabulistan and the surrounding regions – is relatively unknown in the historiography of the greater region. Commonly, this region is dismissed as peripheral to the history of Iran and its political, social, and cultural events are not considered pivotal in the greater context of Iranian history. As a result, most of the political entitites of the region are rather studied in the context of their interactions with Chinese powers, where they are similarly considered marginal. Culturally too the area is better known within the context of the spread of Buddhism out of India. Even the Sogdians – the only actors in the history of East Iran who are studied within the context of Iranian history – are considered within the limited context of "exchange" (of commodities and ideas) along the Silk Road. This is perhaps due to their position outside the political controls of Iranian powers, something that despite conscious objections seems to be in fact the determining factor for many.

On the other hand, with the advent of Islam, the political, cultural, and social impact of East Iran (mainly presented as "the Greater Khurasan") becomes undeniable. Any study of Islamic history, from the Abbasid Revolution of AD 750 to the Timurid conquests of the fourteenth-fifteenth centuries, would indeed be inconceivable without considering the role of East Iran/Greater Khurasan. This rise to centrality, thus, begs the question of background and historical context. What, in fact, were the conditions in which the area of East Iran transformed itself from the marginal lands of the central Eurasian steppe and the mountains of Hindu-Kush to a centre of political, military, and cultural events that we know from the later periods? In order to try to provide an answer for this question, presenting a basic sketch of the history of the region in the period preceding the rise of Islam, that of late antiquity, seems useful and necessary. The following then is an attempt to provide such a basic outline and historical narrative based on the latest evidence that has become available through textual, epigraphic, numismatic, and material research.

The Kushan Empire in East Iran

The *Kushans* is the name given by historians to a dynasty that ruled Bactria, Gandhara, and large parts of northwestern India in the early centuries of the Common Era. The name is in fact what appears as part of the title of some of the earlier kings of the dynasty on their early coins (Cribb, 1993). Indian sources too call them the dynasty of the *Kuśana*, confirming the name. Their origin, however, is a matter of much controversy and debate. Historians therefore attempt to piece together Kushan history by matching textual – usually Chinese – sources with numismatic and scant archaeological evidence, with occasionally confusing results (Alram et al. 1999).

The early history of Kushans is normally given as part of a series of westward movements of a nomadic group named the *Yüeh-zhi*, presumably initiated through their defeat at the hands of the *Xiongnu*, a prominent tribal confederacy mentioned in the Chinese sources, and usually equated with the *Huns* cited in the Western ones (Yü 1990). Chinese sources mention that the *Yüeh-zhi* confederacy, living somewhere around the area of the Tarim basin in modern day Western China (Chinese Turkistan or Xinjiang) consisted of five tribes, one of whom, named *Guishuang* in Chinese, is alleged to be the Kushans (Liu 2001). The *Shiji* ("Records of the Grand Historian") and the *Han Shu* ("Records of the Han Dynasty") tell us that the Yüeh-zhi, allies of the Han Dynasty in their fight against the Xiungnu tribes, were defeated sometime between 209 and 177 BCE by Maodun, the founder of the Xiongnu Empire. Maodun, in a letter to the Han emperor claims:

> By the good fortune of Heaven, by the good quality of our officers and soldiers and by the strength of our horses, he [general Yu-Qienwang] has destroyed and exterminated the Yüeh-zhi. He has completely beheaded and killed, subdued and vanquished them. (*Shiji* 110.10b)

By the beginning of the first century BC, the remainder of the Yüeh-zhi had settled in northern Bactria where the occupation levels of cities such as Termez and Balkh can be dated to the Kushan period (Posch 1995; Coloru 2009). It is during this period that coins with legends clearly identifying them as Kushan (κορανον) appear, possibly from the mint of Balkh (Göbl 1984; Errington and Curtis 2007: 67).

Kujula Kadphises was the first authority to call himself *Kushan*, and is thus considered the first Kushan king. In Kharoshti script he names himself *Kujula Kasasa/Kadphisa Kushana* "(of) Kujula Kadphises, the Kushan" (Jongeward and Cribb 2015: 30-31) and in Bactrian as ΚΟΖΟΥΛΟ ΚΑΔΦΙΖΥ ΚΟΡΣΝΟΥ (Humbach 1966: 41; Jongeward and Cribb 2015: 32, coins 73-75). Kujula Kadphises was also the energetic early conqueror of the Kushan Dynasty. Chinese sources attribute the entry of the Kushans into the southern Hindu-Kush to him, alleging that he was responsible for conquering Kapiśa (Bagram/Kabul region) and Gandhara.

The son of Kujula Kadphises, Wima Takto, whose personal name was for long unknown to scholars, succeeded him on the throne. Based on the Greek legends of his coins, the successor of Kujula Kadphises was previously known as *Soter Megas* ("the Great Saviour"). However, the translation of an inscription of Kanishka I in Rabatak led to the discovery that his name was in fact Wima Takto (Cribb and Sims-Williams 1995). Wima Takto's other inscriptions and statues are known from further south and east in India, certifying his control of Gandhara and northwest India.

Wima II Kadphises (Bact. Οοημο Καδφισο), the next Kushan king, succeeded his father Wima Takto sometime in the early second century AD, based on the most widely accepted date for the Kushans. His name is known both from the coins and the Rabatak inscription. Perhaps the most important and lasting contribution of Wima Kadphises in administrative and economic historical terms is the introduction of a gold coin currency to the Kushan realm, which carries, in addition to Bactrian names and titles, also Kharoshti inscriptions. These coins bear several interesting features that become prominent in the subsequent Kushan coinage, although some had been already in use since the time of Kujula Kadphises (Staviskij 1986: 195-230).

By this time, the Kushans had also fully adopted the local Bactrian language, and its cursive Greek script, as the language and script of their empire. While the original language of the *Yüeh-zhi* is unknown, Kushan inscriptions show their whole-hearted embrace of Bactrian, an eastern Iranian language, as their own and its status as the primary means of communication. The Kushan territories, however, encompassed many lands beyond Bactria and were, by necessity, quite multicultural and multilingual. This is a fact that is obvious from the Kushan architecture, showing Indian, Buddhist, Iranian, and local Bactrian influences (Ball 2008: 71-80).

Kanishka, known as the Great and undoubtedly the most famous of Kushan kings, succeeded his father Wima II as the Kushan king of kings (Bact. *þαονανο þαο*). The reign of Kanishka was the beginning of a golden age of the Kushans, in both literal and figurative ways. Upon his accession to the throne, he inherited the control of the territories in Central Asia and northwestern India. In his own inscriptions, Kanishka claims that he expanded his rule to all of northern India and even as far south as Pataliputra (παλαβοτρο in Bactrian). Chinese chronicles talk about his battles with the Chinese general Ban Ch'ao (Hou Hanshou LXXVII; Chavannes 1906: 237), and he seems to have controlled much of the traditional Yüeh-zhi territories in the Tarim region (Rosenfield 1967: 42), allowing him excellent access to the trade routes that passed both to Central Asia and India. He is also known through mentions of him in many Indian epic and religious sources, where he is associated with the spread of Buddhism in Central Asia (Bivar 1983: 190ff; Staviskij 1986: 201-215). Despite this concentration on his support of Buddhism, however, he appears to have been a ruler more akin to Constantine the Great than Theodosius the Great, in that he did not himself convert to Buddhism, rather rendering his support to the religion (Stavinskij 1986: 215-229; Grenet 2006). Perhaps his most lasting foundation was the establishment of his own era, the so-called *Era of Kanishka*, which matched the beginning of his reign. Unfortunately, this beginning is unknown to us and can only be speculated through minute research of historical sources and epigraphic and numismatic evidence. The scholarly debate on the issue is quite intense, but as of late seems to have settled on the date of AD 127 as the beginning of the reign of Kanishka (Falk 2001) although opposition still exists (Schindell 2014).

Apart from the old centre of power in Balkh, Kanishka's most prominent capital was at Purushapura (in Peshawar Valley, close to the earlier site of Pushkalavati, modern *Charsada*), to the east of Kapiśa. Judging from his own Rabatak Inscription, Kanishka was in comfortable control of north and northwestern India. If taken as a genuine statement, this would suggest that Kanishka's empire extended from the Oxus to the eastern reaches of the Ganges. In his new capital of Purushapura, Kanishka built his famous *stupa* (Bivar 1983: 204), which was visited by the Chinese traveller Faxian (Loeschner 2012: 2-3). It was reputed to be the largest and most adorned of all Buddhist stupas (Loeschner 2012) and it contained a casket adorned with some of the earliest statues of the Buddha and containing possibly his relics, with a Kharoshti inscription describing the casket as being a donation of *Maharaja Kaniśka* (Rosenfield 1967: 34-36). The period of Kanishka is also associated with the proliferation of the so-called *Gandharan Art* whose greatest remains are Buddhist devotional statues, friezes and reliefs. It was probably under Kanishka's rule as well that Buddhism first spread to the region of Paropamisdae and eventually to the north of the Hindu Kush, leaving remains in the area of Bactria and beyond.

Huvishka, either a son or a brother of Kanishka, succeeded him in the twenty-fourth year of the Era of Kanishka (ca. AD 151). Huvishka continued to issue gold coins after his predecessor, expanding the variety of coin designs greatly and producing more gold coins than all other Kushan authorities combined. These were mainly produced in Balkh, north of the Hindu-Kush, and Purushapura/Peshawar to the south of the Hindu-Kush in Gandhara, as well as smaller centres in Kashmir and Mathura (Bracey 2012: 120). The reign of Huvishka in general appears to have been largely peaceful, spent on consolidating Kushan control over northern India and largely moving the centre of power to the southern capital of Mathura.

The successor of Huvishka was Vasudeva I, whose name might connect him to the cult of Krishna and the city of Mathura in particular (Jongward and Cribb 2015: 135), although the Bactrian rendition βαζυδευο might point to an Iranian root as well. Vasudeva can in fact be considered the last of the great Kushans, and he is also the last Kushan emperor to be mentioned in the Chinese sources, since his reign coincided with internal troubles in China and the withdrawal of the Chinese from Central Asia (Pulleyblank 1968: 258). Politically, Vasudeva's rule was centered more in northern India, although he continued to use one of the two primary mints of Huvishka in Balkh, while he probably had to contend with northern incursions into his territories. His coin issues follow the same style as Kanishka, almost canonically featuring Oēšo, with Shiva and the bull, on the reverse (Jongeward and Cribb 2015: 135-137). The relatively peaceful period of Vasudeva's rule is also indicated by increasing artistic production, including his monumental foundations and statues (Staviskij 1986: 242-246).

The reign of Vasudeva I (ca. 191-225) likely coincided with the rise of the Sasanians in western and central Iran (ca. 224 CE) (Jongeward and Cribb 2015: 135). Vasudeva's successor, Kanishka II (ca. 225-245) was the Kushan emperor who lost the northern parts of the realm, namely Bactria/Tokharistan to Shapur I (240-272 CE). Some scholars, however, disagree with the succession of Kanishka II to Vasudeva, suggesting that the two were contemporaneous and ruled in different parts of the Kushan Empire as successors of Huvishka (Zeimal 1983: 225ff; Göbl 1984). In his famous inscription in Naqsh-e Rostam (*ŠKZ*), Shapur counts the realm of the Kushans (MP *Kūšān šahr*) "up to Purushapura" to be part of his empire, indicating the loss of Kushan control in Bactria and possibly even south of the Hindu-Kush. This, in addition to the rock relief at Rag-i Bibi might be indications that Shapur I had indeed established his rule over Bactria at this period (Grenet et. al. 2007). Kanishka II might have had some successes in establishing his rule back over parts of Gandhara and possibly Kapiśa, an event which justified his establishment of a second Era of Kanishka on the hundreth anniversary of the original one (Bivar 2009).

Kanishka II was succeeded by Vasishka, who is known through four inscriptions, including a Kharoshti inscription in the Indus region, which establishes the extent of his rule in that region (Lüders 1961: 125-126). His coinage, increasingly minted on small flans and devalued, continues the canonical system established under Huvishka and Vasudeva I. His successor, Kanishka III, is most famous for using the title *Kaisaro* (Caesar) on his coins, displaying an awareness of the Roman power and probably declaring some sort of alliance with that power (Jongeward and Cribb 2015: 169). The last Kushan rulers, known mainly through their coinage, are Vasudeva II, Mahi, Shaka, and Kipunandha (Jongeward and Cribb 2015: 174-178). These rulers acted mainly as local authorities in the Taxila region, under the overall suzerainty of the Gupta Emperors, while maintaining the coinage style of the Great Kushans in greatly reduced values. As far as East Iran is concerned, the Kushan rule essentially ceased to exist following the death of Kanishka II, the dynasty in effect reduced to local rulers dominated by the Gupta emperor, Samudragupta (Dani 1996: 169).

Kushano-Sasanians or the Kushanshahs

The beginning of the Sasanian presence in Bactria/Tokharistan and the early foundations of a Sasanian dynasty in the region are best observed through the famous inscription of Shapur I. In his inscription on Ka'aba-i Zardušt (ŠKZ), Shapur declares himself an authority over several lands, including the Kushan territories:

> I, the Mazda-worshipping lord, Shapur, king of kings of Iran and An-Iran... (I) am the Master of the Domain of Iran (Ērānšahr) and possess the territory of Persis, Parthian... Hindestan, the Domain of the Kushan up to the limits of Paškabur and up to Kash, Sughd, and Chachestan.

This statement, although perhaps indicating the military successes of the Sasanians in East Iran, is not a statement for the establishment of a firm rule in the region yet. The dynasty that eventually did come to dominate the region, known mainly through its coin issues and known as the Kushano-Sasanians or the Kushanshahs, appears to have been a cadet branch of the Sasanian imperial family. However, the Kushanshahs seem too powerful to have been simply Sasanian governors and might reflect an early Sasanian continuation of Arsacid imperial settings, acting as an allied, but autonomous, cadet branch of the Sasanian royal house.

We should point out that the names of the Kushano-Sasanian kings closely resembled those of the Sasanian imperial onomastic. The difference, perhaps, is that a name like Peroz (MP Pērōz "victorious") appears in the Kushano-Sasanian line earlier than its appearance among the imperial Sasanian kings, namely in the third and the fourth century—that is, over a hundred years before the reign of the Sasanian king of kings, Pērōz (AD 459-484).

Similarly, the title of *kdy/kay* also appears on the Kushano-Sasanian coins, predating its use by the imperial Sasanian line, where it appears only with Yazdgerd II (438-457) (Daryaee 2009: 24 & 34; Shayegan 2003). Instead, the Kushano-Sasanian king, Wahram, already issued coins with the legend *kdy wlhl'n kwš'n MLKA* "Kay Warahran the Kushan King" at the end of the fourth century (Vondrovec 2014: 30; Göbl 1967: type 5-10). There is in fact no reason to suggest (*contra* Vondrovec 2014: 45) that the direction of cultural borrowing should have always been from the "hegemonic" (i.e. imperial Sasanian) toward the "peripheral" (i.e. Kushanshahs) entities. It is, on the other hand, easily observable that the "imperial" Sasanian line was quite influenced by the cultural production of East Iran from the period of Shapur II onwards, and that the adoption of the title of kay can be counted among one of these borrowed markers from the east.

Their first coin issuing authority is a certain *Ardasharo Koshano,* who may be called Ardashir 1 (using Göbl's convention of using Arabic numbers for Kushanshah rulers) and was most likely a contemporary of Kanishka II. Both silver and copper issues of Ardashir 1 were minted in Marw and then transported to Tokharestan for circulation (Schindel 2012: 67).

Ardashir's coins show clear Kushan, or at least Bactrian, influence, since they carry Bactrian legends as well as Pahlavi ones. The obverse Bactrian legends read as APΔAPOPO KOÞANO ÞAO, "Ardashir, the Kushan Shah" (Jongeward and Cribb 2015: 203, coin 2142-2143), and the reverse depicts the god Mithra (Bactrian *Miiro,* also depicted on Kushan coins). The Pahlavi legend on the obverse of some coins (Jongeward and Cribb 2015: 203-204, coins 2144-2153) reads *mzdysn bgy arthštr RBA kwšan MLK',* "The Mazda-worshipping lord Ardashir the Great Kushan Shah" (see also Alram 1986: 318). The reverse in turn depicts the goddess Anahita holding a diadem and a staff. These coins, issued mainly to the north of the Hindu-Kush, have also been found to the south in the Begram/Kapiśa area alongside the issues of the Kushan king Vasishka, suggesting a period of competition between the Kushano-Sasanians and the Kushans in this region. With the next Kushanshah, Pēroz I, the Kushano-Sasanians started to displace the late Kushans from Gandhara, confining them to Mathura in north India, where they were reduced to local princes.

A great shift in Kushano-Sasanian authority occured under the rule of Hormizd 1 (ca. 275-300?). While his early gold issues from Balkh similarly call him "Hormizd, the Great Kushan King," later issues of gold denars from the same mint switch the king's title to ΩYPOMOZΔO OOZOPKO KOÞANO ÞAONONO ÞAO, "Hormizd, the Great Kushan King of Kings" (Jongeward and Cribb 2015: 211, coin 2211). This is similarly reflected in the Pahlavi legend of his copper issues from Balkh, which read *'whrmzdy kwš'n MLK'n MLK',* "Hormizd the Kushan King of Kings" (Jongeward and Cribb 2015: 213 coin 2236). This change in the titlature of the Kushan King, claiming the title King of Kings, is a significant change in Kushano-Sasanian political ideology, and perhaps a direct affront to the "imperial" Sasanian line. It is safe to assume that during the time of Hormizd 1, the Kushano-Sasanians reached a new level of independence from the main Sasanian line.

The short reigning Hormizd 2 (300-303) might have signified a connection between the Kushano-Sasanian and imperial Sasanian lines, and possibly be the same person succeeding the imperial Sasanian throne as Hormizd II. During the reign of Pēroz 2 (ca. 303-330), copper drachms were issued in the region of Gandhara in the name of the local governors Kavad and Mēzē (Jongeward and Cribb 2015: 220). Perhaps, with the succession of Hormizd 2 to the Sasanian throne as Hormizd II, who might have indeed himself been the initiator of the claim to *king of king*ship, the need for competition with the imperial line ceased, and the Kushan kings were reverted to their original positions as the Kushanshahs.

Warahran (330-365) was the last Kushanshah in Tokharestan and a contemporary of Shapur II. It is easy to see that Warahran's grip over the Kushano-Sasanian territories on both sides of the Hindu-Kush was greatly threatened, and it was not long before his realm and power fell to the incoming Kidarites and the expanding reach of the Sasanian central power. The control of Gandhara by Shapur II, known through the issue of his copper denomination there, appears to be a side effect of the increased Sasanian interest in the east. Al-Tabari reports that Shapur made many cities in Sajistan (Sakistan) and Sind (Sindh) and brought to his capital a doctor from India whose knowledge was later spread throughout the Sasanian realm (al-Tabari 845). The Kushano-Sasanians simply disappear from history, perhaps due to their absorption, or seamless continuation, into imperial Sasanian and Kidarite powers.

Iran Huns and the Kidarites

The general invasion of nomadic tribes that came to overwhelm East Iran starting in the fourth century is attributed to the tribal confederations originating from the Central Asian steppe. The name most associated with this group, and one that has created the speculation that they are related to the Huns of Europe, is *Chionites* (*Chionitae*; Ammianus Marcellinus XVI.ix.4). The term might be related to the Iranian term *Xyōn*, and parallels Sogdian *xwn*, which in the Avestan terms was used to describe the archenemies of the king, Kay Wishtaspa, who supported Zarathushtra and spread his religion (Cereti 2010). Chinese sources refer to tribal groupings of Yüeh-zhi, themselves divided between Da Yüeh-zhi (Great Yüeh-zhi) and the Xiao (or Lesser) Yüeh-zhi, as well as the Xiongnu, identified often as the aggressors who set the Yüeh-zhi to flight (Maenchen-Helfen 1973; Atwood 2012). *Wei Shu*, the source which first talks about these invading tribes, names the *Ruanruan* (Juanjuan) as the aggressors who forced the Da Yüeh-zhi to moved westwards and set up their capital in *Po-lo Si* (city of Boluo) (Enoki, 1998: 60).

The troubles caused by a general nomadic invasion of East Iran are known already from the middle of the rule of Shapur II (AD 306-372). This is close to AD 357, when Ammianus Marcellinus reports about the troubles faced by the Sasanian Emperor Shapur II:

> Sapor, on the remotest frontiers of his realm, was with difficulty and with great bloodshed of his troops driving back hostile tribesmen... Constantius, being involved in very serious wars, entreated and begged for peace, but while these communications were being sent to the Chionitae and Euseni, in whose territories Sapor was passing the winter, a long time elapsed (Amm. Marc. *Re. Gest.* XVI.ix. 3-4)

Shapur, however, eventually made a peace treaty with at least some clans of these invaders. It appears that the treaty between the Sasanian king and the eastern invaders, as well as other allied eastern forces, was quite successful. Shapur, having secured his eastern border, turned his attention to the west. Less than two years after the above-mentioned treaty, Shapur put the frontier city of Amida under siege, this time with the help of his eastern allies. The involvement of the Chionites with the siege of Amida, however, goes beyond simple extras in Shapur's war against Rome. In fact, one character, identified as the "King of the Chionitae" and called Grumbates, became the focus of a rather dramatic episode during the siege:

> And so, at the first dawn of day, Grumbates, king of the Chionitae, wishing to render courageous service to his lord, boldly advanced to the walls with a band of active attendants; but a skilful observer caught sight of him as soon as he chanced to come within range of his weapon, and discharging a ballista, pierced both cuirass and breast of Grumbates' son, a youth just come to manhood, who was riding at his father's side and was conspicuous among his companions for his height and his handsome person. (Amm. Marc. XIX.i.7)

So, at least in some capacity, the peace treaty had allowed for cooperation between the newcomers and the Sasanian crown. At the same time, classical sources from the Roman world tell us of the existence of a particular group of the Huns/Chionites, known under the name Kidarites. Chinese sources mention a specific name that is assigned to the ruler of this dynasty, namely *Jiduoluo*, and interpreted as the Chinese transcription of Ki-da-ra (Kuwayama 2002: 128). This particular Hunnic grouping is said to have been located in Gandhara, with its capital at *Fu-lou-sha*, or Purushapura (Zeimal 1999: 126).

The Bactrian legends in the Kidarite coins declare them to represent the *King of the Kushan* (κοþανο þαο) (Vondrovec 2014: 29). This means that in their ideology, the Kidarites considered themselves a continuation of the Kushan, and Kushano-Sasanian, rule. A type which shows the king in frontal view and wearing a crown with ram's horn has a legend in Brahmi declaring the authority to be *Sa Piroysa*, "King Peroz," reminiscent of the Kushano-Sasanian kings (Vondrovec 2014: 28-29). We can date the Kidarite period, based on different evidence, to the period AD 370-457 for the rule of the Kidarites in Bactria, Kabul, and Gandhara, and possibly AD 468 for their ultimate defeat by the Sasanian King of Kings, Peroz (Errington and Curtis 2010: 82).

In the fifth century, a war between Wahram V and the Kidarites resulted in the victory of the Sasanians and the establishment of a boundary tower (al-Tabari I. 863-864). However, in 468 Peroz (AD 457-484) decided on an offensive against the Kidarites, possibly motivated by the help rendered to him by the Hephthalites when fighting for his crown against his brother Hormuzd III (al-Tabari I. 872). Priscus reports that the name of the Kidarite king at this point was Kunkhas (κουνχας). Following his defeat by Peroz in 467, Kunkhas fled from his capital of Balaam (Balkh?) (Priscus *frg 41*, Blockley 347-349), possibly taking refuge in Gandhara. The Kidarites thus lost their position in Tokharesran to the Hephthalites, or perhaps first to the Sasanians (al-Tabari I. 863-864), and only retained control of Gandhara, possibly in Swat (Göbl 1967, II, p. 224, issue 15).

The Alkhans

The Alkhan, alternatively written as *Alkhon* and *Alchon*, are a relatively new introduction into the historiography of East Iran. The name is known through the Bactrian legend αλχαν(ν)ο, "Alkhano," on their coins (Sims-Williams 2010: 33. no. 17). Compared with numismatic sources, textual sources about the Alkhans are quite scarce, a fact that has contributed to the tendency to associate them with better-known "Hunnic" entities such as the Hephthalites and to consider them a branch of the Hephthalites in older historiography (Errington and Curtis 2007: 90 & 98).

More recent research, however, allows us to put together the history of the Alkhans in a more coherent fashion and independent of the Hephthalites. Among Alkhan kings, Khingila is the most famous ruler in modern historiography. He was the leader of the Alkhan campaigns in Gandhara, which took over control of the region from the Kidarites. (Vondrovec 2014: 184). In the Shahnameh of Ferdowsi, he is mentioned as *Shengil*, where he is considered the king of India (*Shahnameh*, VI.1879ff). References to other kings called *Khingila* are made in various sources, such as a garnet seal with the inscription εþκιγγιλο ρωκανο χοηο, "Eshkingil the Lord of Rōkan" (Callieri 2002). The coins of Khingila, with the characteristic elongated skull, perhaps an Alkhan tribal custom, are among the best known coins of East Iran and a model for many later issues. It was previously thought that Khingila's son was Toramana, who then continued his father's campaigns to conquer India and succeeded him in Gandhara (Göbl 1967 II. 59). However, there is in fact no evidence to suggest that Toramana was a son of Khingila, numismatic or otherwise (Vondrovec 2014: 184).

Toramana's name indeed appears more than any other Alkhan ruler on the inscriptions from northern and central India. A famous inscription known commonly as the *Eran Stone Boar Inscription* is dated to the fifteenth year of the "...*Maharajadhiraja* Shri Toramana who is governing the earth with great fame and lustre..." (Biswas 1973: 56). Toramana is also mentioned in the inscription of Gwalior, where he is identified as Mihirakula's father (*CII* Vol III: 161-164). In book one of *Rajatarangini*, this Mihirakula is mentioned as a cruel king:

> "Then his son Mihirakula, a man of violent acts and resembling Kāla (Death) ruled in the land which was overrun by hordes of Mlecchas." (Stein 1900: I.289)... "the people knew his approach by noticing the vultures, crows, and other [birds], which were flying ahead to feed on those who were being slain within his army's [reach]" (op. cit I. 291)

In Indian sources, the defeat of Mihirakula in Malwa is the end of the "Huna" involvement in Indian affairs. However, there is no clear indication that the rule of the Alkhans in Gandhara and further to the west actually stopped with this event. It is presumably following this latest setback that the Alkhans retreat back to Gandhara, and possibly even further west to Kabul (Göbl 1967 I: 155ff).

Alkhan "Kings of the East": the Birth of Khorasan?

A class of Alkhan coin authorities must be classified as a separate entitiy, distinguished by the area of their influence outside northwest India. Among these, two kings named

Zabokho and Adomano include a legend on their coins that reads μιρασανο þαο or "the King of the East" (Vondrovec 2014: 202-206). This is particularly interesting since this legend connects these Alkhan kings to both later Turkic rulers of the region, including the "Tegin of Khorasan" (Vondrovec 2014: 203) as well as the later division of the Sasanian Empire into four distinctive (military) administrative divisions (Gyselen: 2001). One of these divisions indeed received the Middle Persian name of *Xwarāsān* "Khorasan," an exact parallel of Bactrian μιρασανο with the same meaning of "the East."

Two more Alkhan kings also issued coins that show their connection to the "east." The first one is *Rāja Lakhāna Udayāditiya,* some of whose coins also bear Bactrian *Alkhano* (Humbach 1966: 28-31; Vondrovec 2014: 191). Like Pūrvāditiya, another authority who minted coins in the "Eastern Style" (Vondrovec 2014: 207), the title of *Udayāditiya* means "east," or specifically, "the rising/place of the sun" (Errington and Curtis 2007: 97). Linguistically, this also corresponds to Bactrian μιρασανο, "the place of the sun," and the Middle Persian *khwarāsān,* "the place of the sun." The occurrence of references to the East on coins of these authorities, and their later Sasanian and Turkic reflections might hint at the start of the idea of Khurasan as a region and its relation to post-Kidarite politics of East Iran.

The Hephthalites
The fame with which the Hephthalites are known in the historiography of Central Asia is quite disproportionate to what we actually know about them from historical records. The debate on whether they are to be considered a separate entity from the Alkhans, as promoted by numismatists, is among the most important issues surrounding the identity of the Hephthalites (Göbl 1967: 89ff and Vondrovec 2014: 405-406, *contra* Grenet 2002). On the other hand, their reputation as the mighty enemies of the Sasanian King of Kings Pērōz and the benefactors of his son Kavad is already quite notorious – and indeed forms the basis of our familiarity with them. The period of their ascendance in Tokharestan and Transoxiana between AD 470-560 – when we hear of them in the context of their interactions with the Sasanians – has been dubbed the period of *Imperial* Hephthalites (Grenet 2002: 209). Following their defeat at the hands of the joint Sasanian-Western Turk confederacy around AD 560, their remaining "principalities" formed autonomous small authorities that survived under the Sasanian and Western Turk rule (Grenet 2002: 209-220).

In textual sources, the Hephthalites are first mentioned in the context of their interaction with the Sasanians. Following the defeat of the Kidarites in 466, the Hephthalite confederacy appears to have set about expanding its power over the rest of Tokharestan from an eastern base, possibly in the Badakhshan region. The Hephthalite control of Tokharestan must have been complete by 260 of the *Bactrian* Era (AD 483) (de Blois 2006).

The most well-known king of the Hephthalites is one *Akhshunwar* about whom we have no evidence from the coinage (Al-Tabari I-874). He is called *Khushnawaz* in the *Shahnameh* of Ferdowsi, where he is anachronistically called "the King of the Turks." Their capital probably was located around the present city of Kunduz in eastern Tokharestan, known to Al-Biruni as *War-Walīz,* a name that might be connected to the Chinese designation of the Hephthalites as *Hua* (K. Czegledy 1984: 216).

Their expansion put Hephahlites into contact with the Sasanians, perhaps triggered by the help they offered Peroz, the son of Yazdgerd II, in his fight against his brother Hormizd III over the Sasanian throne. Peroz, however, eventually launched a campaign to check the expanding Hephthalite power in Tokharestan in the process of disregarding the boundaries set by his grandfather, Wahram V. However, his early attempts at controlling the Hephtalites were disastrous and initially forced him to agree to a treaty and give up Talaqan to the west of Balkh to the Hephthalites (Pseudo-Joshua 9; this is different from the Taloqan in Panj-Āb as mistaken by Noeldeke/Tabari, p. 116 n. 1). A second campaign ended up in the capture of Peroz and his agreement to the payment of thirty mule packs of silver drachm in ransom, parts of which he paid through imposing a poll tax, and for the rest, left his son Kavad as a hostage with the Hephthalites (Pseudo-Joshua, 10-11) (Blockley 1983 II: 344). On his last campaign against the Hephthalites, Peroz approached the Hephthalites with a large army. Dinawari relates that Peroz destroyed the tower built by Wahram V as the boundary between the Sasanian territories and the land of the "Turks," here standing as an anachronistic term for the Chionites. Akhshunwar, not wanting to be directly engaged with Peroz, dug a large trench across the battlefield while still within his own country (Procopius *Wars*, I.iv.7) and covered it with shrubbery and loose wood to conceal it. When Peroz and his men, including "thirty of his sons" (Procopius *Wars*, I.iv.2) attacked the retreating Hephthalite army, they fell into the trench and perished in the trap, their bodies never recovered (al-Tabari I.879). The Hephthalites, marking a period of control over the Sasanian crown, eventually installed Kavad, the son of Peroz who was a hostage at the Hephthalite court, on the Sasanian throne.

Outside the narrative of Sasanian history, the Hephthalites are known through ambiguous notices in Chinese and Byzantine sources, as well as numismatic evidence.

The name Hephthalite is mentioned in the work of the Byzantine historian Procopius, who calls them Ἐφταλῖται, while pseudo-Joshua the Stylite who lived close to the period of Sasanian engagement with them always calls them Huns or the Chionites. A seal bearing the legend ηβοδαλο ββγο, "Yabghu/governor of the Hephthal," shows the local, Bactrian form of their name, ēbodāl, which is commonly abbreviated to ηβ on their coins (Vondrovec 2014: 404). In Armenian sources, they are known as Hep't'al, and in Middle Persian sources as ēftāl (Litvinsky 1996, 138). In Arabic and Classical Persian histories, they are often mentioned as *Hayātila* (sg. Hytāl), most likely a spelling mistake for *hbtāl/hptāl* (al-Tabari I.872-873; Bal'ami, 835). In Chinese sources, they are called *I-ta* or *Yida* (Kuwayama 2002: 130; Enoki 1959: 7).

Without a doubt, the significant setbacks experienced by the Sasanians in the last quarter of the fifth century – directly caused by the Hephthalite power – were a prime mover for the reforms undertaken by Kavad and his son Khosrow I (Howard-Johnston 1995 and Rubin 1995). Most significantly, the creation of four major defensive, and presumably administrative, zones in the Sasanian administration was a direct response to the inefficiency of centralised defence. The northeast and east of the Sasanian realm were entrusted to an *Ispahbed of Khwarasan* (Gyselen 2001), in fact the first time we hear of this term.

The presence of the Hephthalo-Alkhan king Meyam/Mehama is probably a good indication of the progress of Hephthalite power after their defeat of Peroz and their prominent role in installing his son on the Sasanian throne. Initially acting as a local administrator of Peroz, "the king of the people of Kadag, governor of the famous (and) prosperous king of kings Peroz" (BD *ea 1-2* and *ed 1-2*, dated 239 and 252 in the Bactrian Era respectively),

Meyam eventually was raised to the position of *Mahāṣāhi Mehama* (Melzer 2006). This rise to power parallels the defeat of Peroz at the hands of the Hephthalites and the political vacuum left in the region, allowing local authorities to claim independence. The situation stayed the same in Tokharestan, and further south and east in Kabulistan and Gandhara, until the destruction of the Hephthalite power.

A joint Sasanian and Western Turk expedition in 560-561 eventualy resulted in the destruction of the *Imperial* Hephthalites and the end of their hegemony in Tokharestan (Grenet 2002: 213-214). Ferdowsi, in his Shahnameh, treats this episode most comprehensively. In Ferdowsi's narrative, the Haytal (i.e. Heptal/Hephthal) first enter the war with the "Faghfur of China" (from Bactrian βαγοποορο "son of god") when they kill an envoy of the latter who was on his way to the Sasanian court with many presents to offer an alliance. The Faghfur of China, seeking revenge for the ambush, sends his *ispahbid* (general) who is called Sinjibu and holds the title of Khaghan of China, later claiming to be a son-in-law of the Chinese *Faghfur*. We know Sinjibu from other sources to be the same as Sizibulous and Sinjibu Khan, the leader of the Western Turks. Sinjibu Khan in turn is the same as Ištämi, the brother of Bumin Khan, the founder of the Turk Empire, who indeed was the son-in-law of the Wei Emperor (Sinor 1990). The defeat of the Hephthalites, thus brought about by the expanding power of the Western Turk Empire and supported by the Sasanians, effectively divided East Iran between the two allies, with the Western Turks receiving the lion's share of the spoils and territories.

Not much known is about the remnants of the Hephthalites, although their survival in the region seems to be indisputable as well as the basis of the theory that their origins were in fact local (Enoki 1959: 34-36). Al-Khawarazmi (Bosworth & Clauson 1965: 6, 8) remarks that the Khalaj Turks are the descendants of the Hephthalites. An immediate aftermath of the battle was to bring the Sasanians into direct contact and control of the regions to the south of the Oxus, most importantly the region of Tokharestan. At the same time, the Sasanians themselves became more involved with the East Iranian world. Some of the cultural influences of Sasanian interactions with both Tokharestan and the southern Hindukush can be seen in the early Islamic and Classical New Persian texts. Burzōy-ī Tabīb (Burzōy the Physician) is a prominent composite character known from early Islamic histories, whose travels to "India" allowed him to bring copies of Indian books to Sasanian Iran and translate them. Among these was a copy of Pancha Tantra, translated into Middle Persian by Burzōy and later into Arabic by the famous translator of the Abbasid court, Ibn Muqaffa. To the same period should be assigned the increasing interest of the Sasanians in East Iranian epic, including the tales of the hero Rostam, who displays clear East Iranian characteristics (Grenet 2002: 218-220). Frescoes depicting episodes of the Rostam cycle and related cycles can be found in Sogdian mural paintings (Marshak 2002; Shenkar 2014) and show common East Iranian artistic influences.

The Nezak and the Turk Periods

The sixth century proved to be transformative for all the political and social groups involved in the history of East Iran. The Hephthalite defeat of Sasanian Iran in the late fifth century and the loss of the eastern territories forced the Sasanians to undergo a major restructuring of their empire. This was reflected in historical sources as the reforms of Khosrow I and the rebellion of Mazdak, in fact exposing political, social, and religious contexts. This successful restructuring, including the creation of autonomous military zones, rejuvenated the Sasanians, and in AD 560, allowed them to crush the Hephthalites with the help of the Western Türk Empire. However, the power vaccum already left in the southern Hindu-Kush after the deafeat of Peroz in AD 484 had allowed for the rise of an independent dynasty in Kabulistan and Zabulistan known as the Nezak (Vondrovec 2014: 453-457). The Nezak Shahs, despite never being as hegemonic as the Kidarites, Alkhans, or the Hephthalites, and in fact at one point dividing their territories between the two branches of Kabul and Zabul, did manage to create local cohesion and establish an influential coin style. This local cohesion was highly useful in checking the Muslim expansion of the middle of the seventh century, with widespread political and cultural repercussions, including a pivotal role in forming the early Islamic Persianate culture.

The local rulers of the region of Kabul and the neighbouring western region of Zabul (alt. *Zawul*; *Zawulestan*, the area around modern day Qandahar) emerged as autonomous powers already in the second half of the fifth century (Vondrovec 2010). The dynasty dominated the region of Kabul and beyond until the seventh century when their waning power was replaced by a Turkic dynasty of Kabul Shahs and the expanding power of Muslims based further west in Sistan.

The Nēzak dynasty is known mainly through its coin issues and few textual references (Vondrovec 2014: 450; Göbl 1967, I). In textual sources, little reference is made to the Nēzak Shahs of Kabul, except in Chinese sources where the word *Nisai* and sometimes *Nishu* is used to refer to them, despite the possible "Hephthalite" origins of the terms (Inaba 2010a: 199). Their coins, long known as the most elaborately designed of the "Iranian Huns" emissions, carry a legend that reads *nycky MLK* "nēzak šāh" in Pahlavi script (Frye 1974, Harmatta 1968). The most famous Chinese reference to the Nēzak Shahs is the account of of *Suishu*, which says that the king of Kabul wore a crown topped by a bull's head (Kuwayama 1999: 36-37 & 45-52), a detail that has been interpreted as referring to the buffalo skull appearing on top of the crown of the Nezak Shahs on their coinage (Göbl 1967: 135). The Nēzak Shahs survived independently until at least 661 when a king called Hejiezhi (Kuwayama 1999: 41), claiming to be the twelfth king of a dynasty to rule over Jibin or Kabul, ruled in the region according to Tangshu (Kuwayama 1999: 41). The Nēzak branch ruling over Zabulistan probably also survived into the same period as the Late Nēzak before succumbing to the Turkic rule (Vondrovec 2014: 516). The local nature of the Nezak and their connection to the Alkhans, however, meant that they survived as local administrators under Turkic suzerainty, and even after the fall of the Turkic power.

Following the establishment of their power in Tokharestan, with their capital north of the Oxus, the Turks established the position of the Yabghu of Turkistan. This position appears to have been the supreme governor of Turkic domains south of the Oxus, as his authority was acknowledged south of the Hindu-Kush in Kabul and Zabul as well (Kuwayama 1989: 139). In this region, we probably first hear of them through a mention of the *Ser* of the Turks in the Bactrian Documents (BD **S**) which were written in BE 470 (AD 693). A series of coins, with the title of *Sero*, appearing alongside the Pahlavi *nycky MLKA*, further strengthens this identification, which we assigned to the Kabul region (Vondrovec 2014: 521).

At the same time, we known of the existence of a Zabulistan branch, based on Chinese sources which assert that the king of Zabulistan is a nephew of the King of Kabul (Kuwayama 1999: 56). The Chinese envoy Xuanzang who visited the region in AD 640 also reports that the new ruler of Kabul was a Khalaj Turk and that the family had a branch in Zabul (Inaba 2010b: 445) while Bamiyan has an independent ruler (Kuwayama 2005). Huichao, a Korean monk, also reports that the area of Uddyana (modern Swat) was under the control of the king of Jibin or Kabul (Inaba 2010b: 416), supposedly belonging to the new incoming Turkic ruling family or still in the hands of the Nezak Shahs.

The king of Zabul (*Caojuzha*; Kuwayama 1999: 29-32) in turn is called *Rtbyl* in the Islamic sources (Tabari I.2706). Kuwayama, who also correctly speculated that there was more than one person called *Rtbyl* in Zabulestan (Kuwayama 1999: 64), previously interpreted this as a personal name. *Tarikh-e Sistan*, a Persian local history of Sistan written in the eleventh century, confirms this and provides an extensive account of the wars of the *Rutbil* of Sistan and Zabulistan with the Muslim conquerors of the region, including Salm b. Ziyad (Bahar 1387: 121ff). These wars, starting with the confrontation of Rabi' al-Hārithī in AD 666, continued well into the ninth century when the Rutbil at the time is only defeated by Yaghub b. Laith, the founder of the Saffarid Dynasty.

At the same time that the early Muslim conquerors of Sistan and Zabulistan were struggling against the Rutbil, a struggle lasting over 150 years, the Rutbil himself was using the kingdom of Kabul for refuge. Indeed, whenever the Rutbil is pressured or forced into an alliance, he leaves for farther north and east to upper Zabulistan and Kabulistan, and he seems to have a huge reserve of money and soldiers to either buy off or fend off the Muslims, and the source of this lies in Kabul. As early as the middle of the AD 650s, a king of Kabul is said to have faced off Muhallab b. Abi-Sifra in a heroic battle and the agreed to peaceful coexistence (Bahar 1387: 117-118).

This fares quite well with the numismatic evidence of this period. An authority identified on his coins as the Tegin (Sims-Williams 2010: no. 457) issued coins, dated to post-679, which bear the inscription σρι τογινο þα(υ)o, "His perfection, Tegin, King." This Tegin is most likely the same king as Burha Tegin, named as the founder of the Turki-shahi dynasty of Kabul by Al-Biruni. He is claimed to have expelled the Arabs from Kabul in 666 and according to Gyselen, is succeeded by Rutbil in the 680s (Gyselen 2010: 237). This coin is related to a later type, issued after 687, with a Pahlavi inscription of *tkyn' bg hwt'p hwl's'n MLKA*, "Tegin, His Majesty, Lord, King of Khorasan," but bearing a mint signature of *z'wlst'n* "Zabulistan."

Tegin's son and successor was From Kesar (Humbach 1966: 21-22), who, according to scholars, must have ascended the throne of Kabul shortly before 738, although he was possibly a powerful viceroy based in the eastern capital of Wayhind in Uddiyana (Inaba 2010b: 448-449). The coins carrying his name and titles in Bactrian, and sometimes Brahmi, read φορομο κησαρο ζηορο βα(γo) χοδηο, "Phromo Kesaro the Mighty (?) the King, the Lord" (Vondrovec 2014: 553). This, transcribed *zēoro*, has been translated tentatively by Sims-Williams as *Zāwariya*, "mighty." Additionally, the legend ζηβαρο *Zēwaro* on the type 327 of Phromo Kēsaro is considered a mistake for κησαρο, *Kēsaro*, alleging a mistake in the writing of k that is z-shaped, a suggestion I cannot quite understand (Vondrovec 2014: 554

and note 777). I would like to posit the possibility that this is the well-known name Zawāra, known from the Shahnameh as the brother of the hero Rostam, and thus well placed in the cultural vicinity of Zabulistan. On the obverse of one type of his coins, Phromo Kesaro calls himself "From Kesar, His Majesty, the Lord, who smote the Arabs," in a countermark, thus showing his successes in fights against the Arabs. Considering the mint mark of *z'wl* (Zabul) on at least one type (247), we could speculate that *Phromo Kēsaro* is either the same as the Rutbil of the Islamic sources, or is the Kabulshah on whom the Rutbil, possibly a series of local rulers of Zabulistan, are relying for their continued fight against the Muslim governors of Sistan.

The Western Turk period was of particular importance in Sogdiana and for the Sogdians. The Turks destroyed local dynasties such as the dynasty of Paikand, but the integration of the Sogdians into the Türk state allowed for an expansion of Sogdian culture and commercial activities. The Sogdians started to colonise the regions further to the east, including Semirech'e, thus setting up their expansion into China (Marshak 1999: 242). The rise of the Turco-Sogdian "milieu" was an important part of the formation of the Sogdian trade network, and the main sustenance of the Turk Empire (de la Vaissiere 2005: 1999: 215). The western extension of the network allowed trade with Sasanian Iran, where silk, received as tribute from the Tang due to Turk military successes, was traded with the Sasanians who much valued the textile. This also allowed for the opening of the Khurasan Road, creating an integration of the Sogdian network into a Sasanian one (de la Vaissiere 2005: 226ff). While Sogdians became the high administrators of the Turk state, the Sogdian language became the *lingua franca* of the Turk empire and expanded well eastwards to China, and lent its script to the Old Turkic and many subsequent Turkic and Mongolian languages (de la Vaissiere 2005: 202). In turn, the Turkic nobility became part of the Sogdian society, with marriages between the families of the kings of Samarkand and that of the Turk Khaghan. Penjikent indeed had a Turkic ruler at the beginning of the seventh century (Marshak 1999: 242-243).

The Western Turk Empire, however, started to disintegrate rather quickly after gaining its initial quick successes, losing power in the middle of the seventh century, and by AD 682, it had ceased to exist (Stark 2008; Sinor 1990). Even before that, the Tang Empire of China had started to establish a protectorate in Central Asia, known as the protectorate of *Anxi* (Kuwayama 1989: 134). Despite a restoration of the Turk power at the beginning of the eighth century (Klyashtorni, 1999), the Tang held nominal power in the region until AD 751. In the 710s, Qutaiba, the governor of Khorasan, confirmed the Sogdo-Turkic ruler of Samarqand, Ghurak/Ughrak, in his position (Naymark 2013). Family feuds, however, drove his sons to the court of Dewashtich, the ruler of Panjikent. The latter had a famous "last stance" against the Muslims in 722 in his mountain fortress of Mugh, whose details are known from the very vivid accounts given in the Documents of Mugh Mountain (Livshits 2015). The defeat of Dewashtich marked the beginning of the formal accession of Transoxiana to the Islamic Empire, and soon resulted in the increasing Muslim control of the eastern regions as well (Grenet and de la Vaissiere, 2002). This caused, among other things, the break up of the Sogdian commercial network, and ultimately an integration of Sogdiana into the Islamic empire (de la Vaissiere 2005: 264-276).

Conclusion

East Iran, stretching from the time of the Kushans to the arrival of Islam, was a self-contained region with its own particular political and socioeconomic characteristics. Influenced both by the steppe zone in the north and the subtle realities of Transoxiana, Tokharestan, the Hindu-Kush, and the fertile Gandhara, it was the scene of activities for powerful empires and effective local dynasties. The admistrative structure set by larger empires such as the Kushans continued to influence the region. Cultural traditions and religions, from the Bactrian language to Buddhism, shaped the East Iranian World throughout late antiquity. The influence of newcomers from the steppe and their interactions with the local sedentary culture of the region also determined the socioeconomic fate of the region. All these forces created a particular form of regional identity observable through historical sources and cultural representations such as art, literature, and other material culture. The forces that created the region's identity were then the predecessors of the entities that came to dominate the region in the early Islamic period and eventually determined the mediaeval history of the Islamic world.

Figure. 1. Early Kushan "Heraios" with the word KOIIANOY (*sic., "of Koushan"*) on the reverse. CNG Triton XVIII, Lot: 265

Figure. 2. Gold issue of Wima II Kadphises, showing the Kushan *tamgha* behind the king's head on the obverse and the image of Oēšo/Śiva on the reverse. CNG 152, Lot 159

Figure. 3. Gold issue of Kanishka, showing Nana on the reverse. CNG 362 Lot 24

Figure. 4. a copper drachm of Ardashir 1, Kushanshah, minted in Marv. CNG 319, Lot 177

Figure. 5. Gold *scyphate* denar of Hormizd 1, Kushan King of Kings. CNG Triton XVIII, Lot 867

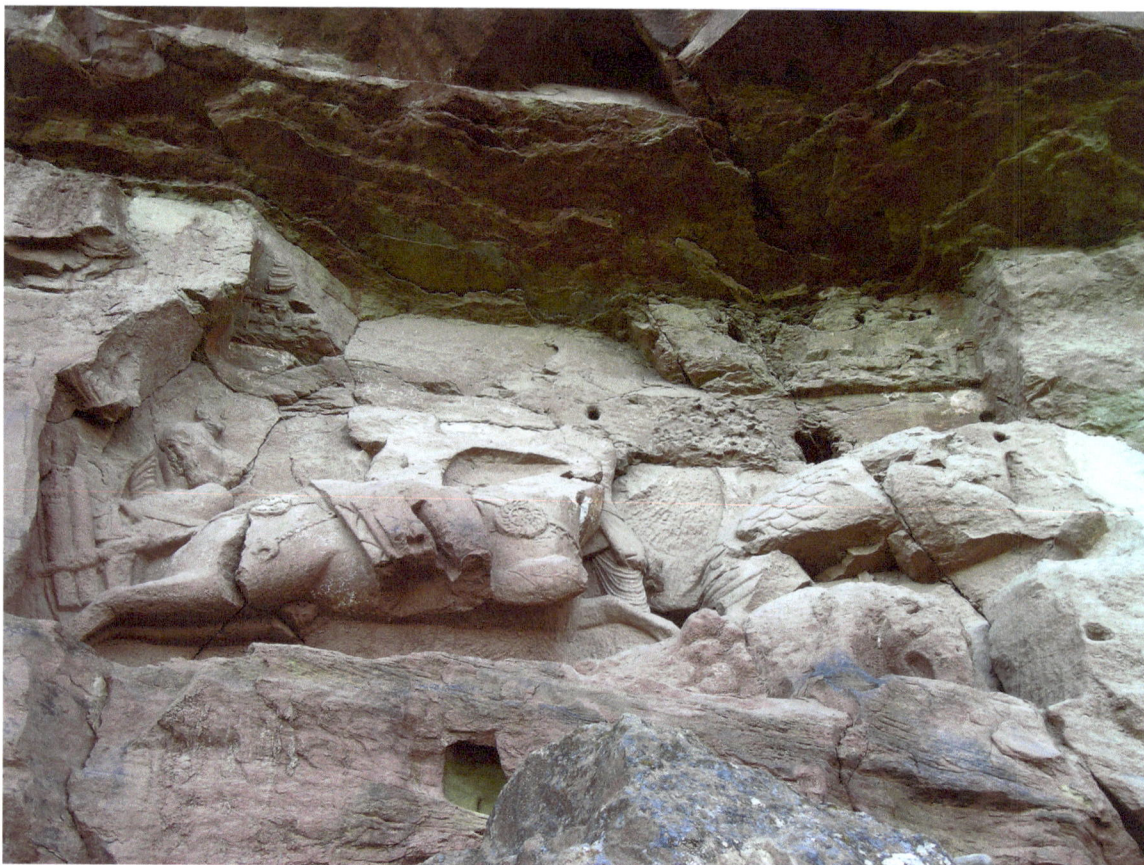

Figure. 6. A Sasanian relief in Rag-e Bibi, northern Afghanistan

Figure. 7. Silver drachm of Kidara. CNG 227, Lot 95

Figure. 8. Silver drachm of Khingila. CNG 323, Lot 193

Figure. 9. Silver drachm of the Hephthalites, imitating coins of Peroz. CNG 375, Lot 490

Figure. 10. Copper drachm of Nezak Shah. CNG 339, Lot 234

Figure. 11. Billon drachm of Tigin, King of Khurasan. CNG 264, Lot 282

Bibliography

Primary Sources

Ammianus Marcellinus. 1956. *Ammianus Marcellinus*. Translated by John C. Rolfe. Loeb Classical Library. Harvard: Harvard University Press.

Bal'ami, Abu Ali. 1386. *Tarikh-E Bal'ami (History of Bal'ami)*. Edited by Mohammad-Taqi Bahar and Mohammad Parvin Gonabadi. Tehran: Hermes.

Ferdowsi, Abolghasem . 1987. *Shahnameh*. Edited by Djalal Khaleghi-Motlagh. Winona Lake: Eisenbrauns.

Pseudo-Joshua the Stylite. 2000. *The Chronicle of Pseudo-Joshua the Stylite*. Translated by Frank Trombley and John W. Watt. Liverpool: Liverpool University Press.

Procopius of Caesaria. 1914. *History of the Wars I-II: The Persian War*. Translated by H. B. Dewing. Loeb Classical Library. Cambridge, MA: Harvard University Press.

Ṭabarī, Muhammad b. Jarir. 1999. *The Sāsānids, the Byzantines, the Lakhmids, and Yemen*. Translated by C. E. Bosworth. Albany: SUNY Press.

Tabari, Muhammad b. Jarir al-. 2010. *Ta'rikh Al-Rusul W'al Muluk*. Edited by Michael J. de Goeje. Leiden: E. J. Brill.

Secondary Sources

Alram, M. 1986. *Nomina Propria Iranica in Nummis*. Vienna: Verlag der ÖAW.

Alram, M. and D. E. Klimburg-Salter. 1999. *Coins, Art, and Chronology: Essays on Pre-Islamic History of the Indo-Iranian Borderlands*. Vol. 33. Vienna: Verlag der ÖAW.

Atwood, C. P. 2012. "Huns and Xiongnu: New Thoughts on an Old Problem." In *Dubitando: Studies in History and Culture in Honor of Donald Ostrowski*, edited by Brian J. Boeck, Russel E. Martin, and Daniel Rowland, 27–52. Bloomington IN: Slavica.

Bahar, M-T., ed. 1387. *Tarikh-E Sistan (the History of Sistan, Written between 445-725 AH)*. 2nd. ed. Tehran: Moin.

Ball, W.. 2008. *The Monuments of Afghanistan : History, Archaeology and Architecture*. London; New York; New York: I.B. Tauris.

Biswas, A. K. 1973. *The Political History of the Hunas in India*. New Delhi: Munshiram Manoharlal Publisher.

Bivar, A. D. H. 1983. "The Political History of Iran under the Arsacids." In *The Cambridge History of Iran*, 3/1:21–99. Cqambridge: Cambridge University Press.

Bivar, A. D. H. 2009. "Kushan Dynasty, I. Dynastic History." *Encyclopaedia Iranica (Online)*.

Blockley, R. C. 1983. *The Fragmentary Classicising Historians of the Later Roman Empire.* Oxford: Francis Cairns.

Bosworth, C. E., and G. Clauson. 1965. "AL-Xwarazmi on the Peoples of Central Asia." *Journal of the Royal Asiatic Society,* 2–12.

Bracey, R. 2012. "The Mint Cities of the Kushan Empire." In *The City and the Coin in the Ancient and Early Medieval World,* 117–31. BAR International Series 2402. Oxford: Archaeopress.

Callieri, P. 2002. "The Bactrian Seal of Khingila." *Silk Road Art and Archaeology* 8: 121–41.

Cereti, C. G. 2010. "Xiiaona- and Xyôn in Zoroastrian Texts." In *Coins, Art, and Chronology II,* edited by Michael Alram and Deborah E. Klimburg-Salter, 412:59–72. Vienna: Verlag der Österreichischen Akademie der Wissenschaften.

Chavannes, E.. 1903. *Documents Sur Le Toukiue (Turcs) Occidentaux.* St. Petersburg: Commissionnaires de l'Académie Impériale des Sciences.

Chavannes, E. 1906. "Trois Généraux Chinois de La Dynastie Des Han Orientaux." *T'oung Pao* 7 (2): 210–69.

Coloru, O. 2009. *Da Alessandro a Menandro: Il Regno Greco Di Battriana.* Studi Ellenistici 21. Pisa/Rome: Fabrizio Serra editore.

Cribb, J. 1993. "The 'Heraus' Coins: Their Attribution to the Kushan King Kujula Kadphises, C. AD 30-80." In *Essays in Honour of Robert Carson and Kenneth Jenkins,* edited by M. Price, A. Burnett, and R. Bland, 107–34. London: Spink.

Cribb, J. and N. Sims-Williams. 1995. "A New Bactrian Inscription of Kanishka the Great." *Silk Road Art and Archaeology* 4: 75–142.

Czegledy, K. 1984. "Zur Geschichte Der Hephthaliten." In *From Hecataeus to Al-Ḥuwārizmī,* edited by János Harmatta, 213–17. Budapest: Akadémiai Kiadó.

Dani, A. H. 1996. "Eastern Kushans and Kidarites in Gandhara and Kashmir." In *History of Civilizations of Central Asia,* 3:166–80. Paris: UNESCO.

Daryaee, T. 2009. *Sasanian Persia: The Rise and Fall of an Empire.* London: I B Tauris.

De Blois, F. C. 2006. "Du Nouveau Sur La Chronologie Bactrienne Post-Hellénistique: L'ère de 223-224 Ap. J.-C." *Comptes Rendus Des Séances de l'Académie Des Inscriptions et Belles-Lettres* 150 (2): 991–97.

Enoki, K. 1959. "On the Nationality of the Ephthalites." *Memoirs of the Research Department of the Toyo Bunko* 18: 1–58.

Enoki, K. 1998. *Studia Asiatica: The Collected Papers in Western Languages of the Late Dr. Kazuo Enoki.* Tokyo: Kyuko-shoin.

Errington, E. 2010. "Differences in the Patterns of Kidarite and Alkhon Coin Distribution at Begram and Kashmir Smast." In *Coins, Art and Chronology II: The First Millennium C.E. in the Indo-Iranian Borderlands,* edited by Michael Alram, Deborah E. Klimburg-Salter, Minoru Inaba, and Matthias Pfisterer, 412:147–68. Verlag der Österreichischen Akademie der Wissenschaften.

Errington, E. and V. Sarkhosh Curtis. 2007. *From Persepolis to the Punjab: Exploring Ancient Iran, Afghanistan and Pakistan.* London: British Museum Publications Limited.

Falk, H. 2001. "The Yuga of Sphujiddhvaja and the Era of the Kusanas." *Silk Road Art and Archaeology* 7: 121–36.

Frye, R. N. 1974. "Napki Malka and the Kushano-Sasanians." In *Near Eastern Numismatics, Iconography, Epigraphy and History:Studies in Honor of George C. Miles*, edited by Dikran K. Kouymjian, 115–22. Beirut.

Göbl, R. 1967. *Dokumente Zur Geschichte Der Iranischen Hunnen in Baktrien Und Indien.* Wiesbaden: Otto Harrassowitz Verlag.

Göbl, R. 1984. *System Und Chronologie Der Münzprägung Des Kušānreiches.* Vienna: Verlag der Österreichischen Akademie der Wissenschaften.

Grenet, F. 2002. "Regional Interaction in Central Asia and Northwest India in the Kidarite and Hephthalite Periods." In *Indo-Iranian Languages and Peoples*, The British Academy, 203–24. Proceedings of the British Academy 116. Oxford: Oxford University Press.

Grenet, F. 2006. "Iranian Gods in Hindu Garb: The Zoroastrian Pantheon of the Bactrians and Sogdians, Second–Eighth Centuries." *Bulletin of the Asia Institute*, 87–99.

Grenet, F., P. Martinez, and F. Ory. 2007. "The Sasanian Relief at Rag-I Bibi (Northern Afghanistan)." In *After Alexander: Central Asia Before Islam*, edited by Joe Cribb and Georgina Herrmann. Oxford: Oxford University Press.

Grenet, F., and É. de la Vaissière. 2002. "The Last Days of Panjikent." *Silk Road Art and Archaeology* 8: 155–96.

Gyselen, R. 2001. *The Four Generals of the Sasanian Empire: Some Sigillographic Evidence.* Rome: Istituto italiano per l'Africa e l'Oriente.

Gyselen, R. 2010. "'Umayyad' Zavulistan and Arachosia : Copper Coinage and the Sasanian Monetary Heritage." In *Coins, Art and Chronology II: The First Millennium C.E. in the Indo-Iranian Borderlands*, edited by Michael Alram, Deborah Klimburg-Salter, Minoru Inaba, and Matthias Pfisterer, 219–41. Vienna: Verlag der ÖAW.

Harmatta, J. 1969. *Late Bactrian Inscriptions.* Vol. 17. Budapest: Akadémiai Kiadó.

Howard-Johnston, J. 1995. "The Two Great Powers in Late Antiquity: Comparison." In *States, Resources and Armies*, edited by Averil Cameron, 157–226. The Byzantine and Early Islamic Near East 3. Princeton: Darwin Press.

Humbach, H. 1966. *Baktrische Sprachdenkmäler.* Vol. 1. Wiesbaden: Otto Harrassowitz Verlag.

Huyse, Ph. 1999. *Die Dreisprachige Inschrift Šābuhrs I. an Der Ka 'ba-I Zardušt (ŠKZ).* Vol. 1. London: School of Oriental and African Studies.

Inaba, M. 2010a. "From Kesar the Kabulshah and Central Asia." In *Coins, Art and Chronology II: The First Millennium C.E. in the Indo-Iranian Borderlands*, 443–55. Vienna: Verlag der Österreichischen Akademie der Wissenschaften.

Inaba, M. 2010b. "Nezak in Chinese Sources." In *Coins, Art and Chronology II: The First Millennium C.E. in the Indo-Iranian Borderlands*, 191–202. Vienna: Verlag der Österreichischen Akademie der Wissenschaften.

Jongeward, D., and J. Cribb. 2015. *Kushan, Kushano-Sasanian, and Kidarite Coins.* New York: American Numismatic Society.

Klyashtorny, S. G. 1998. "Al-Biruni's Version of an Old Turkic Genealogical Legend. On the Semantic of Turkic" Baraq." *Turkic Languages* 2 (2): 247–52.

Kuwayama, S. 1989. "The Hephthalites in Tokhharistan and Northwest India." *Zinbun* 24: 89–134.

Kuwayama, S. 2002. *Across the Hindukush of the First Millennium.* Kyoto: Institute for

Research in Humanities.

Kuwayama, S. 2005. "Chinese Records on Bamiyan: Translation and Commentary." *East and West* 55 (1/4): 139–61.

Litvinsky, B. A. 1996. "The Hephthalite Empire." In *History of the Civilisations of Central Asia*, III:135–62. Paris: UNESCO.

Liu, X. 2001. "Migration and Settlement of the Yuezhi-Kushan: Interaction and Interdependence of Nomadic and Sedentary Societies." *Journal of World History* 12 (2): 261–92.

Livshits, V. A. 2015. *Sogdian Epigraphy of Central Asia and Semirech'e*. Edited by Nicholas Sims-Williams. Translated by Tom Stableford. Corpus Inscriptionum Iranicarum, Part II Inscriptions of the Seleucid and Parthian Periods and of Eastern Iran and Central Asia, Vol. III Sogdian. London: School of Oriental and African Studies.

Loeschner, H. 2012. "The Stūpa of the Kushan Emperor Kanishka the Great, with Comments on the Azes Era and Kushan Chronology." *Sino-Platonic Papers* 227: 1–24.

Lüders, H. 1961. *Mathurā Inscriptions*. Göttingen: Vandenhoeck & Ruprecht.

Maenchen-Helfen, O. 1973. *The World of the Huns: STudies in Their History and Culture*. Berkeley; Los Angeles: University of California Press.

Marshak, B. I. 2002. *Legends, Tales, and Fables in the Art of Sogdiana*. Ehsan Yarshater Lectures, SOAS 1. New York: Bibliotheca Persica.

Marshak, B. I. 1999. "Sogdiana." In *History of Civilizations of Central Asia, Volume III*, 237–81. Paris: UNESCO.

Melzer, G. 2006. "A Copper Scroll Inscription from the Time of the Alchon Huns. In Collaboration with Lore Sander." In *Manuscripts in the Schøyen Collection: Buddhist Manuscripts*, edited by J. Braarvig, 3:251–314. Oslo: Hermes Publishing.

Naymark, A. 2013. "One More About the Coinage of Samarqand Ikhshid Ughrak." In *Commentationes Iranicae, Vladimiro Aaron Livschits Nonagenario Donum Natalicium*, edited by Sergei P. Tokhtasev and Pavel Lurye, 343–67. St. Petersburg: Nestor-Historia.

Nöldeke, T. 1879. *Geschichte Der Perser Und Araber Zur Zeit Der Sasaniden*. Leiden: Brill.

Posch, W. 1995. *Baktrien Zwischen Griechen Und Kuschan: Untersuchungen Zu Kulturellen Und Historischen Problemen Einer Übergangsphase: Mit Einem Textritischen Exkurs Zum Shiji 123*. Wiesbaden: Otto Harrassowitz Verlag.

Pulleyblank, E. G. 1968. "Chinese Evidence for the Date of Kaniṣka." In *Papers on the Date of Kanishka*, edited by Arthur L. Basham. Leiden: Brill.

Rosenfield, J. M. 1967. *The Dynastic Arts of the Kushans*. Berkeley; Los Angeles: University of California Press.

Rubin, Z. 1995. "The Reforms of Khusro Anushirwan." In *States, Resources and Armies*, edited by Averil Cameron, 227–97. The Byzantine and Early Islamic Near East 3. Princeton: Darwin Press.

Schindel, N. 2012. "The Beginning of Kushano–Sasanian Coinage." In *Sylloge Nummorum Sasanidarum Paris-Berlin-Wien*, by Michael Alram and Rika Gyselen, II:65–73. Vienna: Verlag der ÖAW.

Schindel, N. 2014. "Ardashir 1 Kushanshah and Vasudeva the Kushan: Numismatic Evidence for the Date of the Kushan King Kanishka I." *Journal of the Oriental Numismatic Society*

220: 27–30.

Shayegan, R. 2003. "Approaches to the Study of Sasanian History." In *Paitimāna: Essays in Iranian, Indo-European, and Indian Studies in Honor of Hanns-Peter Schmidt.*, edited by Siamak Adhami, 363–84. Costa Mesa, CA: Mazda Publishers.

Shenkar, M. 2014. *Intangible Spirits and Graven Images: The Iconography of Deities in the Pre-Islamic Iranian World.* Leiden: Brill.

Sims-Williams, Nicholas.. 1998. "Further Notes on the Bactrian Inscription of Rabatak, with an Appendix on the Names of Kujula Kadphises and Vima Taktu in Chinese." In *Proceedings of the Third European Conference of Iranian Studies Part 1: Old and Middle Iranian Studies*, edited by Nicholas Sims-Williams, 79–93. Wiesbaden: Reichert Verlag.

Sims-Williams, Nicholas.. 2002. "Ancient Afghanistan and Its Invaders: Linguistic Evidence from the Bactrian Documents and Inscriptions." In *Indo-Iranian Languages and Peoples*, edited by Nicholas Sims-Williams, 225–42. Oxford: Oxford University Press.

Sims-Williams, Nicholas.. 2010. *Bactrian Personal Names.* Vol. Band II, Faszikel 7. Iranisches Personennamenbuch. Vienna: Verlag der ÖAW.

Sinor, D. 1990. "The Establishment and Dissolution of the Türk Empire." In *The Cambridge History of Early Inner Asia*, edited by Denis Sinor, I:285–316. Cambridge: Cambridge University Press.

Stark, S. 2008. "Approaching the Periphery: Highland Ustrūshana in the Pre-Mongol Period." In *Islamisation de l'Asie Centrale: Processus Locaux D'acculturation Du VIIe Au XIe Siècle*, edited by Étienne de la Vaissière, 215–35. Studia Iranica Cahier 39. Leuven: Peeters.

Staviskij, B. Ja. 1986. *La Bactriane Sous Les Kushans(problèmes D'histoire et de Culture).* Translated by Paul Bernard, M. Burda, F. Grenet, and P. Leriche. Paris: Librarie Jean Maissonneuve.

Stein, M. A. 1900. *Kalhana's Rajatarangini: A Chronicle of the Kings of Kasmir.* Vol. 2. London: Archibald Constable and Co.

Vaissière, É. de la. 2005. *Sogdian Traders : A History.* Leiden; Boston: Brill.

Vondrovec, Klaus. 2010. "Coinage of the Nezak." In *Coins, Art and Chronology II: The First Millennium C.E. in the Indo-Iranian Borderlands*, edited by Michael Alram, Deborah E. Klimburg-Salter, Minoru Inaba, and Matthias Pfisterer, 412:169–90. Vienna: Verlag der Österreichischen Akademie der Wissenschaften.

Vaissière, É. de la. 2014. *Coinage of the Iranian Huns and Their Successors from Bactria to Gandhara (4th to 8th Century CE).* Vienna: Verlag der Österreichischen Akademie der Wissenschaften.

Yü, W. 1990. "The Hsiung-Nu." In *The Cambridge History of Early Inner Asia*, edited by Denis Sinor, 118–49. Cambridge: Cambridge University Press.

Zeimal, E. V. 1983. *Drevnie Monety Tadzihkistana.* Dushanbe.

Zeimal, E. V. 1996. "Münzen von Der Seidenstrasse." In *Weihrauch Und Seide. Alte Kulturen an Der Seidenstrasse*, edited by Wilfried Seipel, 357–80. Vienna: Kunsthistorisches Museum.

Contributors
(in alphabetical order)

Kamyar Abdi   7
  Samuel M. Jordan Center for Persian Studies, UC Irvine, USA

Omar Coloru   105
  Archéologie et Sciences de l'Antiquité, Nanterre FRANCE

Touraj Daryaee   155
  Dr. Samuel M. Jordan Center for Persian Studies, UC Irvine, USA

Hilary Gopnik   39
  Department Middle Eastern & South Asian Studies, Emory University, USA

Leonardo Gregoratti   125
  Department of Classics & Ancient History, Durham University, UK

Lloyd Llewellyn-Jones   63
  Department of Ancient History, Cardiff University, Wales, U.K.

Khodadad Rezakhani   155, 199
  Sharmin and Bijan Mossavar-Rahmani Center for Iran and
  Persian Gulf Studies, Princeton University, USA

www.ingramcontent.com/pod-product-compliance
Lightning Source LLC
Chambersburg PA
CBHW042031090426
42811CB00016B/1804